Embracing the Legend

Jim Harrick revives the UCLA mystique

Jim Harrick

with John McGill and Tom Wallace

Bonus Books, Inc., Chicago

99   98   97   96   95   5   4   3   2   1

Library of Congress Cataloging-in-Publication Data

Harrick, Jim, 1938–
     Embracing the legend : Jim Harrick revives the UCLA mystique / Jim Harrick with John McGill and Tom Wallace. — 1st ed.
        p.   cm.
     ISBN 1-56625-054-4 (hardcover)
     1. Harrick, Jim, 1938–   . 2. Basketball coaches—United States—Biography. 3. University of California, Los Angeles—Basketball.
     I. McGill, John (John A.) II. Wallace, Tom (Tom F.) III. Title.
     GV884.H244A3   1995
796.323'07'7092—dc20
[B]   95-42229

Bonus Books, Inc.
160 East Illinois Street
Chicago, Illinois 60611

First Edition

Printed in the United States of America

*This book is dedicated with endless love and respect to
Sally, Monte, Jim Jr., Glenn, Melanie and Morgan.
Having them in my corner has made all the difference.*

— *Jim Harrick*

*For Denny Slinker,
friend, fellow road warrior and longtime partner in crime.*

— *T.W.*

*For Sara Levy, Thelma Case, Joan Reitz, Caroline Buckman, David
Medley, Barry Bronson, Beverly Glass, Annie Petersen,
Bill Garriott, Lonnie Tall Chief and Steve Goetzman
— friends whose support and encouragement will never be forgotten.
For my mother and father. For my brothers, Phil and Dave,
who still won't let me win a game of horse. And for Lynne, who
taught me much.*

— *J.M.*

CONTENTS

ACKNOWLEDGMENTS

A coach is only as good as the players in his huddle. No coach can win a national championship unless he surrounds himself with talent. The same holds true for writers trying to put together a book that encompasses the whole of a man's life and career. Without the help and encouragement of a strong support group, their project is likely to fall short. One of the great myths is that writing is a solitary occupation. In fact, it's anything but. The writing is only part of a total team effort.

The authors of *Embracing the Legend* have a number of people we wish to thank, all of whom went far beyond the call of duty to help us see this project through. It was truly a joint effort, and we were lucky to have championship-caliber teammates.

This book could not have become a reality without Larry and Bunny Holman, co-founders of WYNCOM, Inc. Their relationship with Coach Harrick dates to long before UCLA's championship run, and it was his high level of trust in them that allowed this project to get the green light. We are greatly indebted to Larry and Bunny for their help and support.

Our "general" was Jerry Miller, who entrusted us with such a worthy endeavor, and whose faith and insights provided us with the strength to forge ahead, even during some dark moments. Jerry was always there, putting this project together and always ready to get us what we needed. For that we owe him a great deal.

There is no way we could have completed this book without the advice, counsel and wisdom of our fellow WYNCOM Writers' Bloc gang of Robin Roth, Paul Sanders, Keith Elkins and Jeff Walter — and the brilliance of our "overseer," Ken Davis. They were quick to praise or to bring out the red pen. Above all, they were always honest. Their talent is on these pages.

Thanks to Ashley Begley, heretofore known as Ashley Liaison, for taking over the middle ground, connecting all the dots and juggling a hundred different tasks that otherwise would have fallen on our shoulders. Her willingness to get in the trenches and do much of the dirty work bailed us out on numerous occasions.

Joni Parrent and Patty Knapke at Word Pro had the thankless and difficult task of transcribing our interview sessions. The speed and accuracy in which they accomplished this were instrumental in our being able to meet an unyielding and fast-closing deadline.

Thanks to Bill Bennett, John Dolak and the rest of the UCLA sports information department for their help and research. Included in that group is photographer Scott Quintard, whose photos helped bring UCLA's championship season to life. Also, a special tip of the hat to Susan Tokuda and Doug Erickson for acting as traffic cops. They handled dozens of phone calls, correspondence, photos and faxes — always with unerring accuracy. We also want to acknowledge the sage advice of Ed Morris of Nashville, who helped us negotiate the publishing jungle.

A special thanks goes to Coach John Wooden for his keen insights and wonderful stories, and for giving two writers one of the most memorable afternoons of their lives. He is the genuine article, and is truly better than advertised. We are better men for having been in his presence.

However, the biggest thanks go to Sally and Jim Harrick. Without their full cooperation and willingness to share such a remarkable journey, this book couldn't have become a reality. Jim suffered through endless and torturous (for him) hours talking about himself, something he clearly would rather not have been doing. We appreciate his time and patience.

In the end, we feel that all readers, not just those with a love for sports or college basketball, will appreciate Jim Harrick and what he has accomplished. He is the classic example of a person with dreams who has the willingness and the perseverance to make those dreams come true. Through hard work, dedication and a genuine love for his job and for the young people he coaches, he has done what few of us ever do — reach the very top of his chosen profession.

It has been our honor to share his story with you.

> — John McGill
> Tom Wallace
> October 1, 1995

The views expressed in this book are my own personal views and not those of the University of California at Los Angeles or any of its officers or employees, and no endorsement by the University of the views expressed in the book is intended.

> — Jim Harrick

FOREWORD

It was very pleasing to me to see Jim Harrick's 1995 UCLA basketball team win the NCAA championship. Primarily, because he has paid his dues and, secondly, because of the unselfish team play and conduct of his players both on and off the court.

As a very successful junior high and high school teacher/coach, as an assistant coach of fine programs at Utah State and UCLA, as a head coach at Pepperdine University where he was selected "Coach of the Year" of his conference more than all other coaches combined during his tenure there, and following several fine years as head coach at UCLA, it was nice to see him reach what many consider to be the pinnacle of his profession.

My definition of true success was coined in 1934 and remains much the same in this changing society of today. Success, I firmly believe, comes to those who know they made the effort to do the best of which they are capable. Consequently, it is my opinion that only the individual involved can validly determine whether he or she has been successful.

In some ways success can be compared to character and reputation. Reputation is what others perceive you to be, but your character is what you really are. If you will be honest in your self-evaluation, you are the best judge of your character. Only you can truly know whether or not you made the effort to prepare yourself to the best of your ability.

Jim Harrick is a good friend and it was truly a joyful experience to see his repeated efforts culminate in a national title. However, I do not think this championship suddenly made him an outstanding coach. He has been for many years. It is regrettable that many fans and people of the media often tend to base success merely on the winning percentage or championships won.

I once heard Jim say that he felt he had never done a finer job of teaching than he did in his third or fourth year as a junior varsity coach at Morningside High School. He felt that he came closer to getting full potential out of the material he had than he has during any other season. I fully understand that feeling, as I have personally experienced it.

My greatest satisfaction from my years at UCLA comes from knowing that almost all of my players earned their degrees and have achieved success in many professions. It is also pleasing that our relationship has continued after their graduation and that they often express appreciation for the fact that I was interested in them in a much deeper sense than merely as basketball players. Does that mean I am not proud of our championships? Of course not. But just as Jim remembers that junior varsity team, I too can name some of my teams that did not win championships, but came closer, in my opinion, to reaching their full potential than some that might have gone undefeated.

I truly feel that — although the alumni, the student body and the media might not agree — you get more joy and satisfaction from that kind of team than from many others. Jim has received much criticism at UCLA, much of it based on unrealistic expectations, but he has learned to permit neither criticism nor praise to affect the job at hand. If you permit either praise or criticism, whether deserved or undeserved, to affect you, it will surely be in an adverse way.

It was very heartwarming to see the manner in which Coach Harrick and his staff brought the 1994-95 Bruins together as a team. They had "togetherness" at both ends of the court, and off the court as well.

I was fortunate to get to know most of these players rather well, and it would be very difficult to find a nicer young man than George Zidek, or Tyus Edney, or the O'Bannon brothers, or many of the others. They were very considerate of one another off the court. Their unselfish play and desire to help one another on both offense and defense could well be the most common denominator for their success. It is often easier to love a person than it is to like them, but it appeared to me that all the members of this team really liked each other.

While I am appreciative of the many things Jim has said about learning from me, we all know that we learn from others, even though, as my favorite American, Abraham Lincoln, said, "I never met a person from whom I did not learn something, even though many times it was something *not* to do." As long as we do not get lost in our own egos and stay open-minded, we should learn something every day that can be of help to us.

It was great to see how Jim and his assistants brought their team along. Every single player improved from the year before and during the season. Ed O'Bannon and Tyus Edney provided fine leadership, Charles O'Bannon got his game under better control, George Zidek was much improved, and the progress of freshmen Toby Bailey and J.R. Henderson was remarkable. Also, Cameron Dollar proved his progress by the way he took over for Edney in the championship game against Arkansas. Everyone contributed — coaches and players alike.

The situation may not seem comparable, but when thinking about Jim's tenure at UCLA, I am reminded of Socrates in the hours before he had to drink the hemlock. Although he was facing unjust and imminent death, his jailors could not understand his serenity and one asked him rather abruptly, "Why aren't you preparing for death?" Very quietly, Socrates replied, "I've been preparing for death all my life by the life I've led." So he was at peace with himself, and all who make the effort to do their best will always be at peace with themselves.

The doer will often make a mistake, but the greatest mistake is failure to act when action is necessary. We are all imperfect and will fail on occasion, but we must learn from our mistakes and not repeat them. The determination and persistence that Coach Harrick has shown should be a lesson to all. He came to UCLA with considerable skepticism surrounding him, but kept pushing on without fear of failure. This made him a winner long before he was holding the championship trophy.

When I talk about this UCLA team, I often find myself saying "we" or "us," and that is because I continue to feel a part of the family. I am glad to see Jim committed to keeping the family feeling at UCLA, encouraging his young men to get their degrees, teaching them worthy values, and understanding how true success is measured. When his ability was questioned, Jim never lost track of what was important and kept a steady course.

I hope you enjoy his story and the story of this very special group of young men. It is a lesson in perseverance from which we can all learn.

— John Wooden
August 31, 1995

WHY?

W^{hy?} The question keeps swirling in my mind. A whirlpool of whys. At its center is this awful sense of dread. I look at the door. Don't wanna go out there. Beyond that door is everything I've ever dreamed of, but here I sit, lost in the whirlpool. This just isn't like me. Gotta gather it up. Gotta make sense of all this. What? Five minutes now? Five minutes or so 'til showtime.

Out that door, my UCLA players are getting in their last shots in warmup. Billy Packer's probably adjusting his headset, the strobes above the court are heating up to full glare, and the bands are playing, no doubt, at full tilt. There's 47,000 people out there and somewhere there are 50 million more watching on TV. Right outside that door, the chance of a lifetime awaits. UCLA versus defending champion Arkansas for the NCAA title. In here, however, in a Seattle Kingdome locker room, I'm playing another game. It's a game of one-on-one. Jim Harrick versus Despair.

Why? Why would you bring me to this spot right here, take my best arm away from me and send me out there to get embarrassed? Against Arkansas! They've got the best talent in the country. Why? Why would you DO that?

It won't let up. I've got the right question, but I don't even know who I'm pleading with, and nobody seems ready with any answers. This must be what clinical depression is like. You think you should howl, but all you feel is hollow, like there's some deep and dark pit that's swallowed up all your sense of anger and fire and force of will. *Sleepless, and Hopeless, in Seattle.* Now there's a title.

I shake my head. Un-bee-leeeeeeeeee-vuh-bul. My favorite word when something intrigues me. But there's no passion to it now. My heart feels like it's on the floor. I almost feel physically sick. So quick, this change. From the grandest moment of my coaching life to the gloomiest, a change that came as quick as the flick of a wrist. Tyus Edney's wrist.

"Jim, c'mon! C'mon now . . . sports is an unbelievable thing. Anything can happen. Remember Willis Reed in '72 . . . went out there on the court with one leg against the Lakers, played a couple of minutes and hit a couple of shots and inspired everybody! Led the Knicks to a championship. Remember Willis Reed?"

"Hey fellas, get real! You've got to be kidding! That's crazy. That's Arkansas out there. ARRRR-kuhn-sah! Remember them? You can give me all that crap about inspiration . . . but this is the REAL DEAL!"

My assistants can see it, how down I am. So they try to pump some life into me. Can't really blame 'em. They're young. They still have the luxury of holding dreams in the face of disaster. Me? I keep thinking about the sign that used to hang over a different doorway, the one in the high school gymnasium where all this coaching business began so long ago. Back when I, Jim Harrick, former junior high teacher of music appreciation (though melodically challenged), former assembly-line maker of Mattel automatic water rifles (4,000 daily or the bosses would scream), former painter of primer on airplanes for Northrup Aviation (the fumes would follow me all the way to grad school classes) — way back then, when I'd advanced from those early jobs to assume the lofty position of high school JV coach.

Whew. How many unlikely roads, how many improbable twists and turns to get to this painful place I find myself in now? I remember hearing how Joe Hall, who succeeded the legendary coach Adolph Rupp at Kentucky, said he should have been the one to follow John Wooden at UCLA as well. "Why ruin two people's lives?" Joe Hall said. When I took over in Westwood, wasn't I the sixth sacrificial lamb — uh, coach — in 13 years to try the UCLA legend on for size? And hadn't most outsiders been telling me all along that it was a baggy fit? And yet I'd actually campaigned for this job — a little fish in a big ocean of big names who for one reason or another didn't take it. Me? I wanted it right down to my bones. And I've worked at it with all my strength ever since. But for what? For this miserable feeling? And so it is that right now, moments before the game I'd always strived to coach in — to win — that long-ago memory of the sign in the high school gym hits me in the gut.

GOD REWARDS THOSE
WHO PAY THE PRICE

I believe that with all my heart. But hadn't Tyus Edney paid the price? Hadn't he saved us all in the second round against Missouri with that incredible length-of-the-court dribble and that impossible float-through-the-lane shot at the buzzer? (We lose that one, and life's unbearable.) Wasn't he the nicest, most polite, well-mannered kid I'd ever coached? Wasn't he the hottest player of all the players of the 64 teams that made up this tournament? Didn't the little guy suffer more bumps and bruises than anyone and turn them into, well, so many baubles and bangles game in, game out?

Why?

Why keep this kid from the game of his life, in his senior year? Two years ago he'd have been a national hero if he'd shot the ball against Michigan, but because he's so unselfish he passed off. They pushed him on that play, but they didn't call it. That sent the game into overtime. Where we lose. Wasn't that enough? Why this? Why now? Why do you take the opportunity away from this guy?

Fact is, I don't know if I'm feeling more sorry for him or me. That's the honest truth, because while Tyus has spent four years, I've spent three and a half *decades* climbing this ladder — only to find myself in this black hole of a locker room, like I'm in the middle of some cosmic joke. But nobody's laughing. Least of all me.

I want a ball!

That was five minutes ago, when I'd asked for the ball. I'd looked over at Tyus. He hurt his wrist in the semifinal win over Oklahoma State on Saturday, and our trainer and orthopedic surgeon have been working on it ever since. On Sunday they told me the wrist was very, very swollen and very sore, that he couldn't play if we were playing that night. Had I been worried? Well, sure. A little. But all along I thought, "Yeah, he's going to play." Of course he'd play. I refused to believe he was hurt. When you're a coach and it's March Madness, you always put in your mind and in the player's mind this axiom: You just can't get sick or hurt during the tournament. That's against the rules. So you fool yourself. You spend all day Monday, title day, thinking Edney's going to play. And here you are, 10 minutes before the opening tip, asking for a ball. They've tried four or five different wraps on his hand, his right hand, his Damn the Torpedoes and Dribble to Daylight hand, until he found one that feels comfortable. Some comfort. I can see it in his face.

I want a ball!

They go out to the court and get me one. I take the ball and I sail a pass to Edney across the locker room. He catches it with his left hand. Uh oh. Then he starts to dribble it. On first bounce, the ball doesn't rise enough to make it back up to his hand. Trouble. Big trouble.

Seeing Edney so, I am absolutely devastated. But I can't let on to the players. All season long we've been talking attack, attack, attack. And against an aggressive, potentially intimidating team like Arkansas, we want to take our intensity to an even greater level. I learned a long time ago in this business that you always exude that to your kids. You stay in that high-gear mode or you can really get caught in a bad situation. I can't let the players see how I feel. I send them out with a little fireburst of emotion — thank God it takes only a few seconds, because that's all I can muster — and I watch them run through the doorway. Then the door closes. And despair closes in.

Why send me through all this?

It's 1983. I'm at Pepperdine, beautiful little campus in Malibu, soft by the Pacific, where you can walk out of your office and the waves look tall and the pressure feels small. And we're in the NCAA for the second straight year — Cinderella stuff — and we've got North Carolina State down six with a minute to go. Better still, we've got the ball.

But we miss a one-and-one at 0:29 and another at 0:20 and suddenly NC State's down only two. Then they miss a bonus at 0:09, but they get a long rebound and a guy who's 6-feet-11, a guy who hasn't scored in 44 minutes and 51 seconds, banks one in to get them into overtime. And we go a second overtime. And they beat us. And nobody knows Jim Valvano before then, but NC State goes on to win an NCAA championship and Jim is frozen forever in that happy dance of unexpected joy when his team wins the championship on a putback of an airball at the buzzer.

And what if it had been Pepperdine that had won that game instead, Pepperdine that had gone on to complete that impossible roll that ended in a national title? Instead, it's Jim Valvano who becomes a big-time name — one of the men, in fact, who turned down this job before I got it. Remember how he joked with me a few years later, saying he was the guy who got me the UCLA job? And now poor Jim is no longer with us. And I keep thinking about fate, how it's always seemed to play such a huge role in my life. In everybody's, I guess.

And now this. And why, why, why?

You just can't understand it, and all those thoughts are compressed into an emotion. I don't know what you call it other than gloom — brought on by so many shoulda's and woulda's and coulda's. Now there's this. That's what I'm feeling, the weight of all these overtimes and near-misses and dues paid. Hasn't it been enough?

It's 1990, my second year at UCLA, and it's Duke, on a roll, in the tournament, and for the bounce of a ball and an official's call we'd have beaten them. Didn't happen. It's 1993, and we go overtime against Michigan and do everything in the world to beat them — in every way, shape or form, except, natch, on the scoreboard. It's 1994, and it's going 14-0 to start the season and be ranked No. 1 early — and finally it's tournament time, but it's also Tulsa time, and we're dyin' on it. Down

46-17 in the first half — man, it still hurts just to think about that score — and eventually losing 112-102. Worst of all, it comes in the NCAA's first round. Sports Illustrated *noted that the loss to Tulsa was considered by many to be the nadir of UCLA basketball. All I know is that there was hell to pay back in L.A.*

So why? On this of all nights, why leave me without a fighting chance? Haven't I earned at least that much?

You take the job at UCLA, you go right into the aquarium. No, make that the tank. You know, that lobster tank at the restaurant where all the people come up and gawk and gaze and lick their lips and you're floating in there and you're thinking, "Naw, not me! Gimme a break!" But you know you're going to be dunked in the boiling water from time to time and you just hope you're as tough a crustacean as you think you are, lest why would you subject yourself to this fishbowl/fishfry existence in the first place?

But I'll tell you: All this talk about trying to escape the long shadow of Coach Wooden, all the hype about the Ghosts of Pauley Pavilion that are supposed to haunt any man who tries to take on the UCLA challenge in the post-Wooden era . . . well, I never paid it much mind. Truly. You just can't afford to worry about that. Do it, and you'd *really* be living in la-la land. No, what's gonna make or break you is coaching games and recruiting the right kids.

That doesn't mean, of course, that you're living some kind of hermetically sealed existence. You're still a lobster. I know coaches like to say they don't read newspapers and don't listen to Stalk Radio (talkin' while stalkin', that's what it usually sounds like) and how they don't pay attention to the barbs. Well, of course you do. There've been times, particularly after Tulsa, when I felt I'd been accused of everything in the world short of child molesting. I was the Can't Guy. Can't coach. Can't recruit. Can't win the big ones. Can't, can't, can't.

I've talked about that with Pat Riley a lot. Living in L.A. for 31 of the last 35 years, I know it's a lot like New York. Big sports town. Big pro influence. Big expectations and big criticism. So I know what to expect. Pat's been in both, coaching the

Lakers and the Knicks, so we've been able to reflect on that Big Apple/Big Avocado similarity. These are towns that test you. They wanna know if you're the real deal.

But the biggest irony to me is this long shadow business, this idea that John Wooden is someone to shy away from, if not downright escape. I love John Wooden. And long before I took over at UCLA, I was pleased to call him friend. Since I've been here, the friendship has grown. And it goes way, way beyond basketball. It goes to the heart of everything, just as John Wooden always does. You just don't understand how much this man means to me. I've got clippings on him that would stack two, three feet high. I want to write a book on him someday. And I've seen him get through the biggest challenge of his life.

My wife Sally and I got to know Coach Wooden and Nell. They were such a love story. For 37 years they went to the NCAA Tournament together, and when Nell was in intensive care for more than 100 days near the end of her life and Coach was there every day . . . well, I know what it did to him. I saw his spirit die. Everyone who knew him was very worried for him. Thank God he got through it. It took years, and it took the glow in his great grandchildren's faces to make him connect again. And tonight he is here. And it isn't a shadow sitting there near the court, it's a light. Run from the ghosts? No, with this man the thing to do is simple. You embrace the legend. But I don't have time for that kind of thinking now. Any perspective I might have has been squeezed and flattened under the weight of the moment. Tyus Edney flying on one wing, and me without a prayer.

Time's up! Don't just sit there moping. Move!

Suck-it-up time. From somewhere, another little pinpoint of rage shoots out of me. "The hell with it!" I yell to my assistants. "Let's just go play." We leave the locker room, and now there's a different swirl. Inside, you don't get a feel for the magnitude of what's about to go down. Outside, you're awash in it. Faces everywhere. A growing buzz. This is it.

Adrenaline. Maybe the adrenaline will kick in.

That's what I'm thinking. I've seen adrenaline do wonders for young men. Makes them jump higher, shoot straighter, play better than they ever imagined. Good for what ails ya, too. I've seen how adrenaline can block pain, particularly in one so young, particularly with a dynamo like Tyus Edney. So as I'm walking to my seat courtside, maybe I'm rationalizing and maybe I'm fantasizing but definitely I am feeling a slight sense of hope. I'll start him.

Game begins. Tyus with the ball, dribbling with his left, trying to attack the rim, but not able to shoot, trying to protect the ball and . . . BOOM-BOOM! Has it stripped. Writing's on the wall. Two and a half minutes in, I call for Cameron Dollar to go to the scorer's table. Maybe a few years ago I don't take Tyus out. Maybe back then I let desperation override everything else. I don't know. But I know now. You got a hunch, you bet a bunch. In this case, a Dollar.

Why even play this game?

I'm devastated. Just devastated. But nobody's gonna see it, least of all my players. You can fool a fool and you can con a con, but you can't kid a kid. That's what I've always said. But, nossir, this is gonna be the exception to that rule. We may be sinking fast, but it won't be because I put fear in my players. We didn't come all this way for that. We've been destroying demons all season long. This team was forged from adversity. This team dedicated itself for this night. Ever since that Tulsa loss, this team has put all its focus, all its heart, into being something special, something full of purpose. And can't I say the same for me? You don't drive out of the West Virginia hills for California 35 years ago for a $4,500 job, you don't sweat and struggle and build and plan ever since just to give in now.

Stay with it! Stay with that thought. Don't let 'em see.

Buzzer sounds and Cameron Dollar begins to jog onto the court and all I do with Tyus is throw him The Look. The "take a seat, son" look. I just let on like it was nothing. I don't ask him. I make it look like any other substitution. I don't give them an opportunity to show rejection or whatever. I just say it. "Go sit down, son."

Don't let on anything's wrong!

Plenty is. First time Dollar touches the ball, Clint Mc-

Daniel of Arkansas swipes it, goes down and hits a layup. I look at the scoreboard and it's 12-5 and I might as well see BYE-BYE spelled out in big, bright lights on that board.

Don't even dream about it now. No way we can win.

*   *   *

It's strange to look back on all this now. So much for listening to the demons inside, huh? From that last moment of doubt until the final buzzer, my team played with such ferocity, focus and finesse that, sitting there and watching the masterpiece unfold, I almost felt like pinching myself. From nightmare to dream: UCLA 89, Arkansas 78 and finally, after six coaches and 20 years, the last seven under my watch, there's an 11th NCAA CHAMPIONS banner to hang in Pauley Pavilion.

How did it happen? Well, I'll tell you this. It wasn't just that Edney's injury provided a spark that lit an emotional fuse in the rest of the guys, though that surely played a part. It wasn't just that Ed O'Bannon, who had become a true leader in the second half of that awful loss to Tulsa the previous season, showed what a year of determination and inspiration can do. Ed scored 30 points, grabbed 17 rebounds, had three steals and three assists — yet you look around him and you see that these take-over-the-game numbers only complemented, not dominated, our performance.

At the pre-game meal that day, I told the team that, if the little guy couldn't go, they were going to have to tie their shoelaces a little tighter, pull that rope a little harder and play the game of their lives. And so they did. And I'll let you in on a little secret. You can't turn on that kind of effort like you do a faucet. So much led to that moment, that incredible moment when we all clasped hands out there on the Kingdome court and thanked the Lord for what we had.

I began that night asking why. I've had time to think about it since, and I think I've got the answer. Given how we played, even had we lost to Arkansas, the answer would be the same. When the graying gentleman who set the standard for excellence rose from his seat with a minute to go and the title se-cured, I knew he'd done it in order not to steal my thunder. But when Coach Wooden walked out of the Kingdome, thunder wasn't on my mind. Character was. The lesson can wait. This is the story of what that improbable 1994-95 season was like for me and the UCLA Bruins, but I hope it's more. To appreciate what I learned, I need to tell you what it was like, not just during the season, but in a life where I'd always clung to the belief that the Lord doesn't put you in positions you're not ready to handle. Coaching UCLA can be a handful. And a crisis like the one fac-ing me and my team that night in Seattle can test you to the foundation. But I'll give you a hint of what I learned. It's not about escaping shadows, or slaying ghosts. It's about embracing a legend.

DYIN' ON
TULSA TIME

2

The headline in the Los Angeles *Daily News* on March 19, 1994, read:

FOLLOWING LATEST FIASCO,
HARRICK SHOULD BE FIRED

Welcome to my world. Of all the slings and arrows aimed my way, I guess the greatest barrage came following the fiasco in question: our 112-102 loss to Tulsa in the first round of the 1994 NCAA Tournament. The one *Sports Illustrated* called perhaps the nadir of UCLA basketball. Well, I don't know about that, but it was a low point, and a crucial period. As it turned out — though I had no way of knowing it in the controversial days of the game's immediate aftermath — the Tulsa loss was actually the beginning of our '94-95 championship run. It might have been the pivotal part for us setting the tone for the following season. From that defeat, good things grew — further evidence that manure makes for good fertilizer, I suppose you could say.

Make no mistake, it was a game where you wanted to hold your nose. We were down 10-0 before it even registered. We were down 46-17 before the first half even ended. And though we fought back in the second half and had a decent chance to get all the way back, we were in the hot seat hardly before the final horn even stopped blaring.

That's because right there at the scorer's table, just a couple of seats down from our team bench, a cellular phone was ringing at game's end. The phone belonged to one of our assistant athletics directors. The man calling was none other than the A.D. himself, Pete Dalis. I mention this because, next day in L.A., one newspaper quoted my assistant, Mark Gottfried, as saying: "I guess we'll have to go back and see if we still have jobs." On the phone, Pete said he wanted to meet with us the following Monday (the game was on a Friday). Well, I understood. He had a legitimate question. Of course your athletics director would want to know what had happened. Perfectly understandable. But the enormity of the defeat coupled with the dramatic timing of the call made some stomachs a bit nervous, to say the least.

I'll get to all that, but first it's important to recall some things that happened in the Tulsa game. Namely, Ed O'Bannon happened. For two years I'd tried to get him to take charge, telling him he was really the leader of our team. He had so much competitive spirit and talent, and you just sensed he was a natural-born leader, a guy who didn't want to lose. But it wasn't showing in terms of leadership. He has such a nice and kind personality that his tendency was to believe that if there were seniors around, he'd defer to them. But, in essence, he was the one others wanted to follow. Ed, though, figured the seniors were the leaders, that it wasn't his place. So he'd just play.

But when I stood outside our locker room during the five-minute cooldown period we give our players at halftime — with Tulsa ahead, 63-38 — the new Ed O'Bannon emerged. Through the door I could hear him. His voice just rattled around the room, spilling out into the hall. Ed lit into all of his teammates. Given Ed's previous demeanor, this outburst carried tremendous impact. So much so, in fact, that I changed what I'd been planning to say once I went inside. "It's embarrassing! You guys are killing us! Nobody's playing!" That's what Ed was screaming. I had my own volcano brewing, but Ed raked them out so royally, and effectively, that I knew it wasn't necessary. I went in there and just said: "Fellows, we've still got a chance. The way Tulsa plays, they're going to let you back in."

If you'll check, that's what happened. We actually came out strong in the second half, cutting 13 points off the deficit in the first eight minutes. We had a two-shot foul for a chance to get within 10 at about the 12-minute mark, but we missed both, Tulsa came back with a three-pointer and that put a needle in our balloon. Ed was absolutely magnificent, scoring 30 points and grabbing 18 rebounds, but he didn't have any help. What he did have, however, was a new identity. He'd established himself as the kind of player and leader he would be all the way to the national title the following year. After hearing Ed get on them, I don't think any of his teammates ever wanted to experience it again — not so much out of fear, but out of respect for Ed and out of pride in themselves. (I know. I felt the same way when I played alongside Jerry West years ago, during summer basketball leagues back in West Virginia.)

The significance of Ed's emergence was lost, of course, in the shock of the loss, the anger of the fans and the heat from the media. What followed the Tulsa defeat was a vivid example of how intense things can get at UCLA.

Some of the headlines: "HARRICK: SHOULD HE STAY OR SHOULD HE GO?" ... "JUDGE HIM FOR HIS COACHING? FINE: IT STINKS" ... "BELEAGUERED HARRICK HASN'T HEARD END OF SNIPING" ... "HEAT WAVE WILL HIT HARRICK" ... "HARRICK UNDER THE GUN" ... " 'POOR JIM?' C'MON, GIVE ME A BREAK!" ... "LET THE CRY BEGIN FOR HARRICK AX."

Warms the heart, doesn't it?

Some articles noted that when I was granted a contract extension the previous spring, the buyout clause was altered to make it cheaper, and thus easier, for UCLA to get rid of me before the contract expiration date (I'm not so sure if they were re-

porting it, or celebrating it). One columnist said UCLA's administration wouldn't fire me because they'd be admitting they
made a mistake in extending my contract. Bill Walton told Roy
Firestone on ESPN that I'd have to win the NCAA title and go
undefeated to win him over. Even Jay Leno got in on the act. In
one of his "Tonight Show" monologues, Jay said: "I'm sure you
know, another disaster struck Los Angeles — but enough about
UCLA basketball." Pretty funny, but not to me. Not then.

Jack Hirsch, who'd been an assistant coach at UCLA during the tenure of Walt Hazzard, the man I succeeded, didn't
mince many words. Hirsch had been a co-captain on UCLA's
first national championship team in 1964. He was also the only
man I know who would actually call Coach Wooden "J.W." Did
it during his playing days, making sure to always smile when he
said it. Anyway, one article quoted Hirsch as saying "you don't
want to get humiliated and this coach did . . . I feel there's an un-
derlying current on the team that's keeping them from playing
harder and I think it has a lot to do with coaching. Everyone
knows [Harrick] is not a great basketball coach. I watched them
play one day and I didn't know what they were trying to run on
offense."

Amazing stuff.

I have to say that not everything was negative. Many of
the larger newspapers, like the *Los Angeles Times*, were far more
restrained and fair — and some actually defended my record.
One reporter bothered to ask Tulsa coach Tubby Smith his assessment, and Tubby said: "Jim Harrick has done a tremendous
job. But anybody coaching at UCLA will be under a lot of pressure." And Coach Wooden came to my defense. "I definitely
think it's unjustified," Coach said when asked about the criticism. "How many coaches in the country have won 75 percent of
their games? Certainly, it seems to me he's proven himself pretty
well at this level. He's paid his dues . . . I think Jim has done a
fine job at UCLA." And it warmed me to hear what USC coach
George Raveling said. "When other coaches look at Harrick's
record and his accomplishments, it scares the hell out of them,"
George said. "They think, 'If Harrick is winning this many

games and he's nationally ranked and he's taking this kind of heat, what's going to happen to me?' "

Mike Waldner of the *South Bay Daily Breeze* had perhaps the most perceptive assessment of the kind of team I had on my hands by the time we played Tulsa — noting some injuries that affected us during the season. "Where does this leave UCLA basketball?" he wrote. "Possibly in better shape than anyone understands right now, when the hurt and anger are so acute." Given the climate at the time, that was a gutsy thing to do. He was opening himself to ridicule by making such an "outlandish" statement. But I felt he was closer to the truth than most people understood.

However, for every good thing being said, an abundance of flak obscured it. One columnist wrote this: "Harrick's supporters like to remind people he's won 20 games or more six straight seasons, but that's not an acceptable standard."

In my early years at UCLA, I remember asking Coach Wooden once to assess my team. And he said: "Jim, I can't help you with your team. I'm not there at practice every day. I don't know the idiosyncracies of each player. I don't know if one day one of them is sick and can't play or if one of your players has missed a practice because he's got a class or he has to go study. I can't know all the things that go on within the framework of your team."

Well, my job is really easy — because everyone else tells me how to do it. Following Tulsa, they not only seemed to know my team, they seemed certain that I didn't. Make no mistake, it was a time when we deserved to be criticized, but I think the criticism went beyond the pale. I had two or three writers calling for my job. Talk radio — true to its stalk-talk nature — was having a field day. In Los Angeles you're going to take your share of flak, and I was ready to. I could accept it. But when you start seeing stuff like this: "Fire the coach. Fire him for his role in the most embarrassing defeat UCLA's basketball team has suffered in many years . . . Fire him for one result? You bet. And fire him, too, for not understanding the magnitude of the disaster that one game represented." That's what one columnist wrote. (I'll leave it to you to consider whether a columnist should fire himself over one column — for not understanding the magnitude of harm it can cause a man and his family.)

Such was the climate when I joined my assistants for the meeting with Pete Dalis. I was not fearful of losing my job. But when you hear so many people calling for your head, you certainly consider what your attitude would be to such a thing happening. And what I thought to myself was this: *"If they're going to fire me over one game in the NCAA Tournament, then I'm at the wrong institution. I need to be somewhere else."* But I knew that wasn't the case. The game bothered me, but the possibility that UCLA would actually act on calls for my hide didn't.

In our meeting, I told Pete what had gone wrong. Much of it he knew to some extent, but I gave him an in-depth assessment. As a coach, you always evaluate everything. Was there any more you could have done personally? What could we have done as a staff? And you don't just do it at season's end, you do it after every game. So I'd already mulled everything over in my mind. I also knew that sometimes things happen to a basketball team that a coach can't control. This team had gone to hell in a handbasket, but much of the reason was beyond my control. That might sound like rationalizing, but *I knew*. I'm my biggest critic. Anybody can be blind to their own failings, certainly, but I'd pondered what had happened long and hard. What happened against Tulsa shouldn't have, but I also knew that by that stage of the season, we were not a very good team (after going 14-0, we'd played the last 14 games at 7-7).

There were many reasons why.

When we were 14-0 and ranked number one in the country, I thought we had a very fine team. We were defending people as well as any team I'd had. We had a nice combination going, seven or eight guys playing, and we were very productive. But we hadn't gotten into the meat of our schedule — and when we did, other things started to happen.

I knew that Rodney Zimmerman's back had been bothering him. We'd been getting great results in the middle by alternating Zimmerman with George Zidek. We called them the Z&Z

Boys. George wasn't the solid player he'd be by his senior year, but together with Rodney we were getting double figures in points and double figures in rebounds out of the center position. But Rodney's back problems grew worse. He came in one day and told me he'd had an MRI done, and they'd discovered a herniated disk. He'd been playing through it, but all of a sudden Zimmerman is basically gone from our team. He's one of our co-captains, a leader, and really contributing — but not so much after the disk problem.

Shon Tarver, our senior guard, was also in trouble. Back in mid-December, against LSU, Shon had sprained his ankle. At least that's what we thought. But I began to see Shon's effectiveness lessen, and it wasn't long before we discovered that the "sprain" was actually a ligament tear in his ankle. It cost him almost the whole season. It took the heart, guts and soul out of him. He was always hurting. Toward the end of the season, he could practice fully only one day a week, and really only perform well maybe one game out of the week. By now, as a team, we'd seriously started to lose our edge.

And then there was Tyus Edney. He'd been hurting much of the year — tendinitis in the left knee, back spasms, a problem with his right thigh and an injury to the right clavicle — and it got worse. It happened just before the last game of the regular season. We were at Oregon, where a win would give us a share of the Pac-10 Conference championship. In a shoot-around the day before the game, I hear this huge popping sound and then I hear Tyus screaming aaaah! I look, and he's falling down, with these tremendous back spasms. Thinking back, I still can't believe the sound when his back popped. It was like somebody had shot a rifle from the stands. For an instant there, I actually thought somebody'd shot him.

Next day I wound up playing Tyus virtually the entire game against Oregon — and I was probably a fool for doing it. I probably should have played Cameron Dollar more, but Cameron was a freshman and the conference title was on the line. Tyus goes 1-for-13 from the field and misses a last-second shot that would have won the game, and we lose, 80-79, and also lose a share of the conference title. The Tulsa game in the NCAAs was next. We just weren't a very good team by then. Ed O'Bannon would be superhuman against Tulsa, but even Ed had suffered in the second half of the season. For now, suffice it to say that through the last part of the year, I had three guys with physical injuries I couldn't control, and one guy with an emotional injury.

Sometimes you'd read a passing reference to injuries, but nobody seemed to fully realize their significance. Their effects are often something only a coach can fully appreciate. I think that some people see a player walk out on the floor and if he's not on crutches or his leg isn't in a cast, they think he's OK. They don't realize that even the slightest injury can take you off your game. And that's why I've often said I have 18- to 22-year-olds running up and down the court with my paycheck in their mouths. What happens to them — in ways I can't control — often can affect my future.

So that's the way it was. It didn't change the climate around L.A., but I knew in my own heart what the situation was. After our meeting, one headline read: "DALIS 'DISAPPOINTED,' BUT HARRICK WILL STAY — UCLA ATHLETIC DIRECTOR SAYS COACH TOLD HIM: 'IT'S MY FAULT.' " Pete was also quoted as saying the season "was reasonably good" and "I don't think we were very sound fundamentally."

So much for that. One week after the Tulsa debacle, I had a team meeting and we got out on the track for off-season running. We started talking Kingdome right then and there. We talked about having a bigger, stronger, faster philosophy in the weight room, on the track and in the gym. And the players got to work, hard, in the spring — with Ed leading the way. From that moment on, it was Ed O'Bannon's team.

By the time pre-season publications arrived for the 1994-95 season, most were making the standard remarks. A writer in *Basketball Times*, under the caption of "20 things guaranteed to happen" in the upcoming season, said: "UCLA will lose in the first round of the NCAA Tournament and Jim Harrick will get fired." Another publication made note of what they termed a "rather lukewarm endorsement" from my A.D., suggesting I'd be occupying a severely hot seat if we got eliminated early in the tournament again. Me? I preferred to recall what Pete once told me about the UCLA job. "The only way to make everyone happy is to go 30-0, win the national championship and fire the coach." That's the kind of wry understanding you need from an athletics director whose coach is always one step away from being plucked from that lobster tank and dropped into the boiling pot.

*   *   *

What's it like in the tank?

Well, first keep in mind that one way I deal with the demands is to develop, without any conscious intent, a sort of tunnel vision. You kind of divorce yourself from the boosters and the hype and the media crush, and you focus on the job at hand. But you can't completely. It's like you're on a train running down two tracks at the same time. On one track you see the sights (and sounds, and the wailing gets pretty loud) intruding on your journey; but on the other track, the one that really gets you where you want to go, you're up there throwing coal in the boiler and making sure the whole thing doesn't jump the rails. That's the one you quite naturally focus on. Still, the UCLA experience won't let you ignore the other track. So what's it like? Great, awful, challenging, frustrating, exhilarating, debilitating, funny, grim, rewarding, annoying, fulfilling, absurd. And then comes Tuesday.

It does sometimes feel like that, just a huge swirl of conflicting emotions and events. If there's an overall theme, I guess you'd have to say it's expectations. I have them, fans have them, the administration has them and the media most certainly have them. It's when expectations butt up against reality, when the yardstick for measuring success gets outrageous, that things get dicey. Of course, sometimes it's so foolish that it's just funny.

Like the time I got an envelope in the mail from a "fan." It was just my second year at UCLA, and we'd played a great game, giving Duke all it wanted before losing in the Sweet Six-

teen of the NCAA Tournament. Late in the game, we tried fouling to stop the clock in a last-gasp attempt to win, but Duke kept
hitting their free throws and it made the final margin bigger than
how closely we'd actually played them. Anyway, I open this letter and the only thing in it is a betting sheet, a real small card,
from the Stardust Hotel in Las Vegas. Seems this guy had bet on
us and taken the points, but lost thanks to those late free throws.
In green ink on the card, he'd written: "You got no f—ing clue!"
The funny thing was, the cheapskate had bet only $20. He'd lost
20 bucks and was mad as hell.

Then there was the time we were playing Cal at home and
we were having trouble hitting free throws. Well, our bench is
right in front of a walkway and some guy is walking past. He
just sticks his head in as I'm sitting there and says "Cal *made*
their foul shots!" You learn pretty quick that everybody's a fan
and emotions run high. And believe me, you never know from
what corner it's going to come next. My first year at UCLA in
particular, we struggled at the foul line. We had a guy who just
couldn't shoot free throws, and he'd get fouled all the time.
About 50 percent of the time he'd miss 'em. You know how many
points that is? I'm talking about missing a hundred foul shots
over a career. Anyway, my wife and I are sitting at home on the
couch and, as usual, I'm watching a tape when Sally looks over
at me. "Do you *ever* work on foul shooting?" she says. Those are
the times when you want to say "All right, now, enough!" Actually, you want to say something a lot stronger, but you don't.
Clearly, there are times when even my wife can become a dis-
gruntled fan. And a coach, too.

I understand all that. I understand the emotions of people, that there's a guy in the office who's worked all day, bustin'
his butt, and then he comes to the game and he likes to yell and
scream and get his frustrations out. But in college in particular, I
think there's a certain type of loyalty involved, too. Fans should
understand that. These players don't deserve any of those catcalls and griping. They're young and they have full-time jobs as
students. And as players, they have a lot of weight on their
shoulders. I remember what Ed O'Bannon once said to a reporter

as he pointed to a picture of the Kingdome: "I hope we get there, so the freshmen and sophomores in this room won't have to go through college with the stigma of being underachievers, because I can promise you, it's not pleasant."

These young men aren't professional players. And we've turned this thing into a kind of vicious circle. When you consider that the NCAA Tournament makes $215 million in three weeks and that athletic departments like ours need the money we bring in to help fund 21 men's and women's sports, and we've got pressure to recruit and to win . . . well, it can get crazy. We've got to fill our arena, we've got to make good money in the tournament and from television, but the players don't get any of it. They're getting a good education and that's enough, I agree, but they shouldn't have to put up with a lot of negative comments and pressure. When they get to the pro ranks, fine. But not as college players. I have feelings in the same direction about college coaches, but I have some leniency in that regard. I realize we're adults and sometimes we need to take criticism. But not the young players. And the sad fact is, in many cases the criticism of coaches isn't fair, either.

A lot of it is anything but funny. I've seen some great and decent men who were coaches, who did it the right way and still got chewed up by the system. I look at friends like Digger Phelps and Frank Arnold and I just cringe at how men of such character and talent could wind up getting fired. Take Digger. He's doing TV commentary now, and we talk on the phone a lot, and while he's really happy in what he's doing, in reality I know that nobody wants to go out the way he did at Notre Dame. Digger graduated all his players and did things right. Never, ever once got in trouble with the NCAA. And they end up firing him. To me, that just doesn't send the right message about college athletics. I tell you what it did to Digger, it just tore his heart out. He'll survive, because he's a survivor and a tough guy, but what happened to him was shameful. Frank Arnold? I think he got three firsts and two seconds in his league at Brigham Young in his last five years. And they called him into the office — just called him in and fired him on the spot. He had no idea. I swear, it's like taking a guy and cutting his heart out. I don't know what some people are thinking when they do people that way, just no idea. And yes, it seems to be a trend that's happening outside of athletics as well. I mean, you see people who've spent 20 or 30 years working for a company, and suddenly they're shown the door. When everything gets to be bottom line and there's no real value put on people, we are getting in deep trouble as a society.

Have I ever feared losing my job at UCLA? I've never felt that pressure. Never at all. Now maybe I'm naive, but that's how it's been. The examples of Digger and Frank make me know it can happen, but I've always just refused to believe it could happen to me. For one thing, I think the athletics department here really understands the mission of education. Our chancellor, Charles Young, has been at UCLA for 25 years and he's taken it from being a relatively small, growing school to one of the most valued institutions in the nation, maybe one of the top five academic schools in the country with a great legacy as a research institution. So he understands the role athletics should play. He's been on about every committee the NCAA has, I think, and on the President's Commission, so he has an enlightened perspective. And Pete has been at UCLA for more than 35 years, so he too appreciates the climate UCLA wants to create as an educational leader.

So I've never really had a fear of being fired. On the other hand, I'm sure there've been a lot of coaches fired who never saw it coming. You can get hit by a two-by-four out of the blue, and it can really hit you hard. When you talk about the pressures here, well . . . I'm probably too stupid to really understand all that's gone on in the media and with the fans, and maybe that's served me well. But I'll tell you this: If Tyus Edney had missed that shot against Missouri in the NCAA Tournament, things here really would have been unbearable. People don't understand that you've got a family and they listen to all that negativity. If Tyus had missed, I'd have known real quick who my true friends are. Still, I've never felt my job was in jeopardy. Then again — jumping over to that other track — I also know that as far as administration is concerned, their families can get caught up in things and they can get emotional and say "Get rid of that guy! He can't win the big game," and sometimes they listen. One of the things I learned from winning the championship is that you find a lot of people even in our athletics department and everywhere on campus who can become fans. They can get on that same emotional roller coaster. You just have to understand that in March, it's an unbelievably emotional time. But I've had a real strong chancellor. Chuck Young knows we're doing it the right way. He knows we're not cheating, that our players are graduating and socially they handle themselves just great. Ultimately, he has the final say. In the end, it's Chuck Young and Pete Dalis who matter. Not the media.

One of the good things about being in the public eye in L.A. is that it's a Cinemascope eye — wide and far-ranging, so even when the media focuses on you, it usually doesn't last very long. You're in the crosshairs one day, but generally the newspapers and TV are taking aim elsewhere the next. They'll come back, of course, but there's always another hot trail beckoning. You either have Darryl Strawberry in town or Al Davis leaving it, or O.J. on trial or Fernando Mania (and now it's Nomo Mania). Los Angeles is an ever-changing sports scene, and that usually means there are plenty of targets — you know, kind of like those ducks that keep swimming by at one of those carnival shoot 'em-ups.

It's also good on a personal basis. As big and as star-populated as L.A. is, a coach is low enough in the pecking order to go about his life pretty much on an anonymous basis. I think one of the reasons Lute Olson got away from Iowa was because he couldn't go out in public anymore without someone always recognizing him. Of course, then he turns around and does the same thing in Tucson, creates another monster down there by winning so much. So maybe you're just destined. Thankfully, I don't have that problem. A good example of that came right on campus. I went over for a question-and-answer session with UCLA students (this was just a couple of months after we won the championship) and there were about 200 or 300 people there. Next week, the theater arts department had Tom Hanks in for a

session. I went and, golly, there must have been 3,000 people —
standing room only. It just goes to show you the kind of town
this really is, a town of Magic Johnsons and Sylvester Stallones.
The UCLA coach might get recognized, but he won't get mobbed
when he walks down the sidewalk. A few people might come up
and talk, but that's usually enjoyable. It's not like I can't go to a
restaurant without people gawking or always interrupting me.

The atmosphere at UCLA helps keep you from developing a circle-the-wagons mentality. I'm told that my office is
rather small and unimposing compared to the ones many big-
time programs have for their coaches. No fortress here. And no
sense of being out of touch with the educational environment. I
look out my window and right there are students shuffling up
and down the Bruin Walk, the sidewalk that runs through a
good part of the campus and leads, just a couple hundred feet
from the athletics department building, to the student center. I'll
usually eat in the student cafeteria a couple of times a week. Students will come up every now and then to chat. I had one writer
tell me that you wouldn't find the college coach he covers doing
this — that the coach probably didn't know the names of any of
the buildings on campus. My reaction was: "Oh, you're kidding!" I just can't imagine that.

UCLA is not a flashy place. Gorgeous natural surround-
ings, but not flashy. We're a public school with public funds, so
there's not a lot of excess or ostentatious offices. Besides, I don't
know if an office has ever won a national championship for you.
Coach won his first two in the old men's gym. I've always believed I'd rather have stable, great recruits than a great office.
The one I've got is nice enough. I think they offered to build a
new place at Duke for Mike Krzyzewski, but he's cozy right
where he is, in that great old arena. They're getting ready to re-
model Pauley Pavilion and add some seats and whatnot, but I've
never been carried away by these places with flashy, big-time
locker rooms and facilities. We want our players to have nice,
comfortable things, but country club spa stuff doesn't matter. If
Pauley is remodeled, we'll have some more modern trappings.
But give me guys who are sound and solid and who work hard.

I know people say great facilities help attract them, and sometimes they do. But I don't think it's a must.

The UCLA environment helps ground you — and sometimes, when those media galestorms hit, you need all the grounding you can get. One thing you learn early on is how a small story can become a big one, how one comment can get scrutinized, repeated, expanded and enlarged beyond all proportion. It happens, I think, because of the sheer number of L.A. media outlets that jump on whatever story one of them originates. The trouble is, you've got so many papers and so much TV and radio that when one reports something, everybody's got to cover it. Things snowball. Nobody wants to get scooped, and if they do, they figure they have to find more to the story, whether "more" is there or not. It gives what might have been a fairly moderate story a heaviness beyond its true weight.

A lighter example, I remember, was when Larry Brown was here. He used to always have people around him. So one writer started calling this group "Larry Brown's toadying minions." Everybody picked up on the theme, and pretty soon that was the automatic label for Brown's entourage. The toadying minions. The point is, any time the media can find a thing to jump on, no matter how small, they will. Larry Farmer? Larry's a good friend, and I really don't know why they'd want to go after him. I remember one time Larry invited a writer to dinner, and one of his players belched at the table and, before you knew it, the media was getting on Farmer for not disciplining the player or something. I mean, it got to be a big deal. What I've found in this job is that you're always open to criticism, and that's why you wind up ultra-careful not to say things or do things that leave you vulnerable. You have to understand that a lot of times when they interview you, they're operating under the idea that negativism sells and makes the front page. And I don't want to get into arguments with a guy who buys ink by the barrel.

To me, there's a difference between criticism and downright meanness, between holding someone accountable and holding them up to ridicule, between putting thoughtful perspective into criticism and taking superficial, poorly thought-out

potshots. You want to criticize me? Fine. But bring something to
the table. If I can't coach, give me specific instances. Tell me why
you think what you think. If we're not fundamentally sound,
how aren't we? If we don't play good defense, tell me why. So
many things I've read about my coaching ability were so shallow
in their assessment as to be laughable. If I'd have brought as little preparation to the basketball court as some writers bring to
their comments, you'd really see a lousy team out there. But
there are thoughtful writers. Where you usually get the outrageous comments are on talk radio. Blatant and ignorant comments are the ones that get you going, and talk radio is a hotbed
for them. People on the radio make a blanket statement and then
are off the air. When's the last time you saw one of them held accountable?

Coach Wooden gave me a quote once that I've kept on
one of my sheets of favorite quotations. It says: "I react nega-
tively to things I know are dishonest and blatantly ignorant . . . A
well-considered criticism is always respected." But I guess my
favorite in this regard is the one made by Teddy Roosevelt. I
can't begin to tell you how many good people have sent this
quotation to me in the mail during my career at UCLA, with a
"hang in there" or a "don't give up" written on it. I must have
gotten 50 letters with this on it over the years. You might have
heard it before, but like most good things it bears repeating.
Roosevelt said:

> It is not the critic who counts; not the man who points out
> how the strong man stumbles, or where the doer of deeds
> could have done better. The credit belongs to the man who is
> actually in the arena, whose face is marred by dust and sweat
> and blood; who strives valiantly; who errs, and comes short
> again and again, because there is no effort without error and
> shortcoming; but who does actually strive to do the deeds;
> who knows the great enthusiasms, the great devotions; who
> spends himself in a worthy cause; who at the best knows in
> the end the triumph of high achievement, and who at the
> worst, if he fails, at least fails while daring greatly, so that his

place shall never be with those cold and timid souls who know neither victory nor defeat.

Roosevelt said that in a speech delivered in Paris on April 23, 1910. I suppose if he'd given it today, he might get a 10-second sound bite out of it. Meanwhile, a media poll would claim he had only a 37 percent approval rating on the speech. Commentators would say he was trying to cover all his bases because he sensed he might fail. And tabloid headlines would say: "SWEATY PREZ CLAIMS HE LIKES BLOODY, DUSTY FACES!" I might be exaggerating, but I think you get the point. It's a different world now, and the differences aren't always good.

There's just so much negativity that surrounds sportswriting today. I really believe a huge number of sportswriters don't understand what it's like to win and what it's like to get beat. I guess you could say that for a lot of people in general — or at least they conveniently forget it when they start tearing into a sports figure. I remember reading a young writer for the Santa Monica paper who I thought was always very critical. One time he came out with an article just ripping Steve Garvey up one side and down the other. Now, Steve Garvey was a great, great baseball player. And this guy, who I know has never thrown a ball or tried to hit one in his life . . . this guy is ridiculing Garvey. That was unfathomable to me. How can this guy, who probably never took P.E. (and if he did, probably had his skivvies showing below his gym shorts), how could he grow up to heap criticism on a guy like Garvey — a five-time All-Star and six-time World Series performer?

Because he wanted to.

And wasn't required to have any real justification for doing so.

It's not limited to professional media. That "microwave world" I complain about has created a climate where everybody has fast cars, fast food, instant coffee . . . and the majority of people want an instant winner in sports. That's one thing. There's also some angry people out there, people who are going to lash out at almost anything and everything they can get their hands, or vocal cords, on — and they have a knack for finding a bandwagon to jump on. I think there are some — and I do mean only some — who are very, very negative about everything. Some who want nothing but for you to fail. So, with that in mind, you come to realize that there's always going to be that kind of sentiment in some corners. And I really believe among those people a lot of it isn't even directed at you personally. It's just the way life is today. It's part of our society. And a coach is an easy target. Almost every town I go into, I'll see a coach getting ripped and wonder "Why is that, why is that?" But I don't wonder for long. It's just the nature of this business. The nature of the beast.

In dealing with all this, I again call on things Coach Wooden taught. He always said that if you listen to critics, it will affect your coaching. And if you listen to too much praise, it will hurt your coaching, too. So what I try to do is keep an even keel about everything. If you do that, everything will work out fine.

Not that it's always easy. I've always said that I don't listen to talk radio or read the newspapers, but that's not really true. You know, you're conscious of everything that's going on out there. You'd better be. But what I've learned is not to really worry about what "they" say. I don't even know who "they" are a lot of the time. And it's taught me one of my greatest lessons, one I'd never learned before coming to UCLA. Living through some of these experiences, I hope I've been able to pass along to my team how to meet with the media and get positive results out of it, or at least get them most of the time. I have a philosophy that most writers and talk-radio guys are just doing their job. They really have no feeling about it. They're just trying to do two things, get good ratings and make a buck. And what their shtick is . . . well, I don't think they really care much about me personally or our team personally. A lot of people ask me, "Why don't you tell some of these guys to put it where the sun doesn't shine?" Well, sometimes it would be easy to do. But, you know, I would rather walk by you, pat you on the shoulder and say, "Hey, howya doin'?" Because if you're the writer I'm greeting, now you'd know, or at least I hope you'd know, that I'm here for awhile and I can run this playground, and I'm *going* to run this playground. That's it. You let your coaching do your talking. I'm not going to say "I told you so" or "stick it up your rear" or things like that. That's not me. And I tell my players to shut their mouths and let their playing do their talking. That's the same advice I give myself: shut my mouth and just coach. You can't worry about what you can't control, and I have no control over what the media does.

Writers like Jim Murray and Mike Downey and Scott Ostler and Frank Burlison are all wonderful. I liked John Hall quite a bit, but he's retired now. Mark Whicker is another columnist who thinks things out. Not only are the best of them fair-minded, they're often funny. It's hard to be humorous, and some of those writers are great at it. I see other writers try to be humorous and it just comes off as . . . well, I don't know what. I don't know if they just aren't aware how to do it well yet, or maybe the era's changed, where now you come up and everything has to be critical. I do know this can be a tough town, but most towns are when it comes to sports. Still, a Mike Downey is able to ruffle some feathers when it's needed, but even then he usually does it with great insight and humor. Mike is a columnist for the *Los Angeles Times*. He's a brilliant writer. He's also fair. One of my pet peeves is that a lot of young writers apparently don't know the difference between being a columnist and being a reporter. They tend to want to put their opinion on everything when they should be just reporting.

Talk radio? Basically, a joke. And a bad one. I understand that ESPN did a piece on the affliction of talk radio recently, and the main theme was that these people viewed themselves as entertainers who usually try to be as outrageous as humanly possible, but don't give one whit about consequences — that for all its zaniness, talk radio is starting to seriously affect people in the sports profession. They might pass themselves off as being wild and wacky (and able to bring in ratings), but the ESPN report noted that it was actually having a serious, often harmful effect on coaches' and players' professional and personal lives. Unfairly, I might add. They confronted several of these talk-show rabble-rousers with statements they'd made which were patently untrue. ESPN told them what the actual facts had been in issues they'd ranted about. Virtually to a man, these people just ignored the facts ESPN presented, just kept dancing and prancing around it, sluffing off anything so incidental as the facts. So much of it is bogus. One time I heard a guy call in and say he was a homeless person. But he had access to talk radio. Right. You'll also get people criticizing me and saying they're from UCLA, but in some cases you start to suspect they might be USC fans just trying to cause trouble and vice versa. I do know this: It's an open forum for any human to express his opinion — nice concept — but so much wild and unsubstantiated stuff is bantered about that it becomes a freedom exercised without any responsibility. And there are a lot of people driving down the road with their radios on who believe what they hear. It permeates and spreads, and it can get out of hand.

Like I say, there are some in the media you can trust. And I do — even though I might not necessarily agree with everything they say. The ones you trust are those who have proven themselves to be fair-minded, people who have a rationale behind their criticism and are consistent in their views. I would approach them if I had a problem with something they'd done. I mean, I've sat down with some of them and said something if I thought they hadn't been fair. And we've talked back and forth. But it's never done with acrimony. You can disagree without being disagreeable. I've told *L.A. Times* writers "you're like the Bible, so please scrutinize some of the things you're doing." I'm not so sure they agree with a lot of what I want scrutinized. They want to have the freedom to say whatever they want to say, anytime they want to say it. So I don't know. Sometimes the line is pretty murky between what's OK and what's not.

Sometimes it feels like the newspapers are bashing the home team. People, including recruits, read all this — and it makes your job just that much more difficult. If I didn't talk to the media, their jobs would be more difficult. But I do.

There have been some articles so nicely done that I've gone to the writer and told them how much I appreciated it. For example, Gene Wojciechowski of the *L.A. Times* wrote a sensitive article on Tom Asbury's daughter, who died of anorexia nervosa. It was just a beautiful piece, and I wrote him a nice note, thanking him and complimenting him on it. Tom was my assistant, and successor, at Pepperdine. In a case like that, I want the writer to know it was appreciated.

With the writers who seem born to be negative, however, I keep a firm commitment to myself. There always seem to be three or four writers, usually young, who are out to make a name for themselves. In most cases, I never let these types know if I don't appreciate what they've written. I learned that at Utah State. Never let 'em know how you feel. Not those types. Not when it's just bad stuff. I am not going to let them get to me. No sir. They're not going to put me in a funky mood. Uh-uh. Not going to let it happen — because I never want my players to listen to or be around negative people. You should never let that happen to you, whether it's a writer or someone down your street. Get away from them, because it puts you in a bad, negative thought pattern yourself. I want my players thinking positive thoughts. And it's the same with me. So I'm not going to let a sportswriter do that to me.

Lord knows they were doing it in droves after Tulsa. But you know what? As clamorous as the call was for my job in some circles, as widespread the criticism that prompted my athletics director to respond in print, I don't think one writer or TV personality or talk radio host was aware that UCLA's lopsided loss to Tulsa had something of a precedent.

It happened in 1963.

In the first round of the NCAA Tournament.

To John Wooden.

UCLA played Arizona State in the first round that year and John Wooden was down 31 points at halftime. UCLA came back, much like we did, but lost by 14 points, 93-79. I remember asking Coach about that game once and he just said, "They had Jumpin' Joe Caldwell. They were better than us." The irony is, John Wooden went on to win his first national title the following season — same as what would happen to me. You know, when I think about it, sometimes the similarities between us are spooky. Like me, Coach was only the third or fourth choice at UCLA before getting the job. Both of us married our childhood sweethearts. Both of us were high school English teachers for nine years. Both of us came from east of the Mississippi. And both of us were high school coaches before making the leap to the college level. Don't get me wrong. I'm not comparing myself to John Wooden's genius. When I cite those things, I do so with that idea of fate and destiny again. It intrigues me.

There's one other item I should mention. In 1981, the year after Larry Brown took his 22-10 UCLA team to the NCAA title game, he lost by 23 points in the second round. It happens, folks, it happens.

Still, the embarrassing loss to Tulsa did weigh heavily. I haven't told anybody this, but long before the 1994-95 season was to begin, I put a videotape on my desk. It was a tape of the Tulsa defeat. I kept it there as a reminder, because I had a plan. On the 15th of October, the first day of practice, I was going to show it to my players. It was trimmed down, and it would only take an hour to show, but — you know what? — I never did. Never put it in the VCR. It really ran against every principle I'd ever preached, that you build on positives and you don't rip into people when they're down. So, as the summer wore on, I said I'm not going to do that because we always forget the past and think about the future. That's what I count on. So the tape was never run. But I'll tell you something else. It didn't leave my desk until a month after we'd won the national championship. It was always there, waiting in the wings.

CHEMISTRY, CHARACTER AND CHARISMA

3

One of them came from Czechoslovakia. Two of them had to grow up without their mothers. Two came from the same family. All of them shared something special. When I look at the roster that comprised our 1994-95 national championship squad, I'm struck by what a bright and exuberant group it was. "Chemistry" is the term we sports guys use like a blanket, an easy way to cover all the intangibles that transform good, even great, teams into something even greater.

You'd like to be able to reach out and capture whatever it is — that spirit, that essence, that feeling that something extraordinary is going on here — but you never can. All you can do is establish the environment in which it can happen, and recruit the kind of players whose character suggests they can come together and create something special. With this team, that's what happened.

One of the raps against UCLA teams in the past was that they were soft, that they often were more concerned with indi-

vidual glory and were quick to break down when the road got
rocky. These players were well aware of those labels. And that
can lead to a negativity that feeds on itself — producing an ugly,
self-fulfilling prophecy. Maybe that's what bothered me most
about all these unfair attacks on players' personalities. The very
ones yelling that UCLA was a bunch of losers were the ones creating the psychological climate for losing to happen. I don't care
who you are, if you hear something enough times you are vulnerable to start believing it — even though it runs contrary to
what you know deep in your heart about yourself. If you're not
strong, and not very aware of that possibility, you'll lose track of
your essence.

I get the feeling that, most times, sportswriters never understand why coaches tend to react — and yes, maybe overreact
in some cases — to any hint of negativity. Well, this is why. Negativity is a luxury maybe the media can indulge in (if not, in
some cases, take downright glee in producing). But it's one that a
coach, and his players, can't afford. Sometimes I think the media
in town either don't know or don't care that all the players I recruit are reading their articles or listening to their comments. Do
they *not* want our team to be good?

As far as labelling UCLA soft, this team not only stayed
positive, it also used all the negative comments as a motivating
factor. Something to prove. You channel anger constructively, fo-
cusing on the mission rather than the messengers of bad vibes,
and you can get a lot done. Remember, this was a team born out
of adversity. That Tulsa loss had an effect, and even though we
had some key freshmen who weren't around for it, they could
feel the resolve the veterans had at wanting to erase the Tulsa
memory.

In many ways, this was a team that refused to fold because Ed O'Bannon just made the decision that it wasn't going to
happen. Certainly Ed was the rallying point for everybody, but,
like that chemistry tag, it falls way short in explaining everything. You mix in the incredible heart of a Tyus Edney, or the
steely determination of a George Zidek, or the ability to sacrifice
that Charles O'Bannon showed. Then you add the glee of a kid

like Toby Bailey, or the take-no-prisoners maturity of a J.R. Henderson or solid confidence of a Cameron Dollar. But how does it all come together? You can quantify some of it, but mostly it's just this beautiful mystery — this merging of minds and hearts into something that's greater than the sum of the parts.

That's what this UCLA team was like. It's easy to throw around words like "character" and "charisma," and the good Lord knows we abuse those terms enough as it is. But these guys had it. When you consider all the criticism that preceded them, all the doubters and all the critics . . . and then when you see how they won 31 of 33 games and met these challenges with such perseverance . . . maybe then you can understand why I think that extraordinary character and charisma are labels these players earned.

One of the interesting things to me is that for every hardened look of determination there was a wink as well. We tell our players to go out and have fun, and also to compete to the best of their ability. These players did both. They enjoyed themselves, and their company together, but they also played with the kind of resolve that said they could look in the mirror afterward and know they'd given their best. That's what I always stress.

I know a lot of people have marvelled at how crisp our passing was against Arkansas, how well we seemed to play together and rocket that ball around like a pinball machine. It was no accident. And frankly, we played that way pretty much all season long. That's the best physical evidence of the rare blend of intangibles these young men brought to each other.

You know, I've played several rounds of golf with the fathers of Tyus Edney and the O'Bannons and, believe me, that doesn't mirror the normal relationship between coaches and parents. Players come out of high school wanting to play in the NBA and their parents think they should already be there. But an Ed O'Bannon Sr., or a Hank Edney, is the kind of man who always told his kids that what the coach said is what goes. They're like me: throwbacks — men who grew up in an era where if you were disciplined at school, you knew you were going to get twice the discipline when you got home.

Chemistry? Oh yes, we had beakers full of it. Charisma? The audacity of a Tyus Edney or the high-leaping exuberance of a Toby Bailey exemplified that. Character? Everywhere.

So before we look at the 1994-95 season and I tell you my own story, let me share a little about these players. Let me give you some hints at the intangibles these guys brought to the table.

George Zidek — One of my favorite stories about George came out of our team's summer tour of Italy in 1992. All the players had their Walkmans and music going, of course, and George was no exception. But my wife Sally was curious. "George," she said, "let me hear what you're listening to." So George put his earphones on my wife and what she hears is Beethoven. A little later, some Bach.

When we go through St. Peter's Basilica, we didn't need a tour guide. There's George, lecturing his teammates about all the paintings and the statues, talking about their history and their meaning. And our guys are looking around and grinning at each other like *"Who IS this guy?!?"*

Well, just about the most intelligent and hardest-working fella I've ever been around, *that's* who. I think George speaks about four different languages. Frankly, when George first came to UCLA we never thought he would be much of a player. But when a guy is seven feet tall and weighs 250 pounds . . . well, that kind doesn't come around very often. Last time I checked, you still couldn't coach a player to be seven feet tall. And when you come across a guy that big whose intellect, and heart, are every bit as big, that's an even rarer find.

George had played on the Czech national junior team, but his skills were not at the level of big-time college basketball. I remember when the Czech team was playing in the World University Games and Sally came over to watch him play. George looked just awful. Sally elbowed me in the ribs after the game. "George isn't very good," she said. And I was just sick all summer, thinking there was no chance of him ever developing. But in our second exhibition game, I decided to start him. He goes out and gets 20 points and 10 rebounds. That gave him some confidence. He wasn't a player yet, but he just improved and improved.

As strong as he was academically, George struggled at first because he didn't have a great command of English (if you can call a 3.67 grade point average as a freshman struggling). But it truly was a difficult time for him. He worried so much about his studies and his oncourt play that he couldn't sleep. We'd have to send him to the sleep clinic at the UCLA Medical Center, he was putting so much pressure on himself.

Well, suffice it to say that George wound up with a 3.8 GPA in Economics for his career at UCLA, and went from a marginal-at-best prospect to a first-round NBA pick by the Charlotte Hornets. I'd like to say that George became my project, but the fact is that George made George his own project. He'd work out five to six hours a day in the summer. And he never gave up, even though those first two years were a slow progression for him. He was discouraged at times. I wanted to redshirt him his sophomore season but he didn't want to. And at one point in that sophomore year, he was discouraged enough to consider returning to Czechoslovakia. Thank God he didn't.

By his junior year George was a starter, although I split playing time between him and Rodney Zimmerman. He was clearly becoming a factor — and it began to show in his leadership qualities. He was always the first guy at practice and the last guy to leave. Guys would go over for a drink of water and George would still be out there shooting 50 hooks, 50 jumpers, a hundred foul shots . . . and they all would be looking at him. Those kinds of things rub off on other players. This was an unselfish team, and a lot of that came from George. This was also an aggressive team, and George again was one of the catalysts.

George would walk up to guys and say, 'Hey, you're not working harder than I am today. I'm gonna work harder than you.' You know, kind of challenge them. And that kind of thing is really good for your team.

George started shooting his windmill hook shot in his sophomore year. As a freshman he'd shot nothing but jump-hook, jump-hook, jump-hook. Then, next season, one day at practice I look down at one end of the court and there's George shooting this old-time, sweeping hook and I said, "Wow! Look at that!" I mean, it was just such a natural for him. It looked beautiful. No force to it. Great touch. He just plain had it. So I went down to that end and started working with him on it. We worked his right hand, then his left. And of course, by his senior year that hook shot was a potent weapon for us in many crucial games — thanks in great measure to our assistant Mark Gottfried, who spent endless hours working on it with George. Zidek's defensive brilliance against Arkansas' Corliss Williamson in the title game marked the finest performance of his career. In fact, I don't think he ever played better than he did in the semifinals and final.

Perhaps you already know the story of how George was a demonstrator in Czechoslovakia during the tumultuous months leading up to the fall of communism. At one particular rally that began peacefully but turned violent, George found himself hemmed in by soldiers and feared for his life. He persuaded a soldier to let him go. Many who didn't get out in time were badly injured in the melee that followed.

But perhaps you don't know another aspect — far more tragic — of George's life under communism. His mother, a physician, died when George was only 13. She used to lie out in the sun quite a bit. George and his family firmly believe that she died as a result of the Chernobyl nuclear reactor incident — the dangers of which, as I understand it, the Soviet Union didn't bother to inform people about in the Communist Bloc countries. George is convinced that his mother was unwittingly exposed to radioactive material during her frequent trips to the beach.

George's Czech name is Jiri — same as his father, who was an assistant coach for the Czech national team — but he's always preferred George. I'll never forget when he first came over. Every year at the start of the fall term we have a softball game: coaches, dads and managers versus the players. George had never caught a ball or swung a bat. It was funny. He grabbed the bat with his hands way apart. He just didn't have a clue.

Now he's a first-team GTE Academic All-American, and a

Phi Beta Kappa with a $5,000 NCAA post-graduate scholarship and a fat NBA contract. Someday he'll be doing something of major significance, I have no doubt, for the Czech Republic or for this country. He'll be productive, whatever he does. And I have to tell you, to see someone like George excel academically and come out of nowhere athletically to contribute like he did . . . well, that's one of the things that makes my job so worthwhile.

Cameron Dollar — In retrospect, I guess I shouldn't have been surprised at the incredible job Cameron did in replacing Tyus in the championship game. He is a sophomore in name only, and I don't mean simply as a basketball player.

When Cameron came for his recruiting visit in 1992, at a time when my contract had not yet been renewed and there was a lot of speculation in the media, I found out quickly that this was not your average high school kid. I'll never forget it. Cameron gets off the plane wearing a three-piece suit, just looking magnificent and exuding all this poise. So we go over to my office and he says "I want to talk to the athletic director." By now I am just a tad bit impressed, not to mention taken aback. So we go up to Pete Dalis' office and I introduce him and I leave. Now it's Cameron one-on-one with the A.D. Well, Pete just fell in love with the guy. Said later that he'd never, ever had a kid come in and conduct himself the way Cameron did — to see a guy look so nice, act so nice and speak so well. What did he want to know? The future of Jim Harrick. The longevity and everything.

Pete just thinks the world of him for it. Here was a kid who stepped forward and was a man at that moment, and he hadn't even graduated from high school. Cameron has such a great attitude, and there's a kindness to him which belies his demeanor on the court, where he is 100 percent pure-bred bulldog. I mean, he'll just bite your nose off. Terrific defensive player. Son of a coach. Incredibly tenacious.

But offcourt, he is just a pleasure to be around. He's heavily involved with the Fellowship of Christian Athletes and, like so many of our players, is exceptionally bright (he had a 3.43 GPA in the winter quarter of his freshman year). And he's also worked with the Promise Keepers organization. They had 73,000 men at the L.A. Coliseum and Cameron was one of the speakers. He's just a dynamic young man.

But it couldn't have been easy for him. Like George, Cameron lost his mother at an early age. In fact, he was only three years old when she was murdered. So he grew up without a mom. To turn out the way he has is a great tribute to his father, Donald. The raising of his son is a special, special thing.

You know, I think Cameron and George are probably two of my wife's all-time favorite players, because I think she realizes what they've been through having to grow up without their mothers. Sally goes on all the road trips with us so she got to know them, and she has a great feeling for the kind of young men these two have become. How could you not? I mean, those two guys are what college athletics are all about. Or *should* be about, anyway. Neither has a car. They either walk everywhere they go or bum rides. (Well, at season's end George had a car, if it can be called that. It looked not quite as long as George is tall, a 1978 clunker that's all beaten up and everything. He got it as a hand-me-down from Richard Petruska.) But they really are something. Both are terrific students and very, very dedicated. You have to have a special place in your heart for guys like that.

Tyus Edney — They made the movie probably before he was born, but Tyus is the prototypical Little Big Man. He is also a wolf in Smurf's clothing. Cute as a bug's ear (now *there's* a West Virginiaism for you) but full of fangs as a competitor. Still, I've got to admit that when I was recruiting him out of Long Beach Poly High School, another prospect in the L.A. area intrigued me a bit more because he was bigger than Tyus. I went to this player's home, made my presentation and asked him what schools he was going to visit. He said, "Well, you know, I've got 10 more people to see and after that I'll make a decision on what five I'm going to visit." I said, "We're right up here at UCLA." And he said, "Well, I'm still going to wait."

So the next night we went to Tyus Edney's home. Up close, he's just a whisper of a guy. So I'm sitting there and I'm getting ready to open my folder and give my spiel and his mother and dad got up from their seats right then and there and said "No, no, coach, don't worry about that. We want to come." So here's a 3.0 student with a beautiful family, a great kid and a solid player and I'm thinking, *They want to sign. So which way do I go?*

So now I'm walking out of the Edneys' home with this decision on my mind, and there are four of us, a couple of my assistants and Edney's coach, Ron Palmer. I've got tremendous respect for him, but I'm not ready for what happens next. Ron says "Jim, I want to tell you something. He's the best guard I've ever coached." Whoa! Wait a minute here! Ron has coached Tony and Chris Gwynn (yes, *that* Tony Gwynn, who could have played pro basketball had he chosen to) and both were terrific, terrific high school players. And he'd also coached Morlon Wiley, who played with the Dallas Mavericks. So I about fell down on the grass when he said that. "Come on, Ron, who do you think you're talking to?" I demand. "I can't believe that." "Jim," he says, just as firm and as calm as can be, "I'm *telling* you." Well, we wind up signing him that fall. Tyus didn't even visit another school.

Now it's spring and I go to a CIF championship game and he is absolutely horrible. I think he got four points. He was terrible. I'd taken a friend who I play racquetball with, who's not really into basketball that much. We get in the car after the game and we drive about 10 or 15 minutes and neither of us says a word. Finally, he leans over to me and says "You gave that guy a scholarship?" I was so depressed.

All summer I don't talk to Tyus on the phone. Now it's fall practice and there's Tyus in a UCLA uniform. So we run this defensive drill where four guys are out shooting threes and three guys have to get out and contest the shot. The ball's moving around and Tyus gets it and shoots it and makes it. Then he gets it and shoots it and makes it again. Gets it and makes it a third time. And I just stop practice. Right then and there. I yell out: "Who IS this guy? Who IS this guy?" Then we run a fast-break drill and Edney is a blur and I'm thinking, "Holy mackerel, is he quick or what?" And then I notice that all the other guys are just lighting up because they love playing with the guy. It wasn't long after that that Coach Wooden visited a practice and called me over and pointed toward Edney. "Jim, he sees the court better than anybody else you've got," Coach said.

And the rest, as they say, is history. The kid is magic. Gets ping-ponged this way and that and just adjusts his shot in midair, or flips up some audacious scoop that finds the net, or dishes to somebody. Lightning. Not to say that he wasn't just as effective defensively as well. His whole senior year, Tyus made life miserable for the opposing guard. Not every night, but just about.

The only thing that interrupts his brilliance over his entire career is a string of injuries, but always he bounces back, plays maybe sometimes when he shouldn't, always conjuring up some kind of play that leaves you open-mouthed. You know, he won four games for us at the buzzer his sophomore year. He was absolutely brilliant.

People say Tyus truly came into his own as a senior, but really he was already there as a junior. The only thing that kept him from showing it on a consistently brilliant basis was a series of injuries. Tyus started off 1993-94 with a back injury — he missed our first 10 days of practice — and then he got tendinitis and then he suffered from a bad shoulder. It all culminated when he had that terrible back spasm at Oregon in practice the day before the game, our last of the regular season. All season, I'd say Tyus was able to play at only about 80 percent of his effectiveness because of injuries.

And it was an injury the following season, of course, that kept him out of the biggest game of his life. But the fact he couldn't play in the NCAA title game didn't take away one whit from the enormous contributions he'd made. In fact, I truly believe that up until that night, he had been the most outstanding player on any of the 64 teams in the tournament.

Ed O'Bannon — I'm biased, but I couldn't think of any player more deserving than Ed when he won the Wooden Award as the nation's most outstanding collegiate player. It's easy for a lot of people to forget now just how difficult a road Ed had to travel — to recover from a horrible knee injury. No hyperbole here. Horrible is the word. It was a difficult and uncertain journey from a mishap that easily could have ended his career, and it took him five years.

Ed was named the National High School Player of the Year by *Basketball Times* in the spring of 1990, and when we signed him I thought we were putting ourselves in a strong position to have a legitimate shot at a national title — given that by the time Ed was a sophomore he'd have plenty of seasoning and be playing alongside the likes of Don MacLean and Tracy Murray. Considering how good he was, it wasn't out of the question, of course, that he would step right in and be a force as a freshman.

That's what was on our minds when my assistants and I met in Palm Springs on our annual planning retreat, five days before practice was scheduled to begin for the 1990-91 season. And that's when our trainer, Tony Spino, called with the news. He told us that Ed tore up his left knee in a pickup game. He painted a gloomy picture. At first, I just refused to believe it. We drove back the next morning and there wasn't a sound in the car. Not one guy talked the whole drive back to L.A. We were just stunned. Then we went to see Ed and the feeling was devastating.

It's called a torn anterior cruciate ligament. In Ed's case, substitute destroyed for torn. To repair his knee, surgeons had to borrow an achilles tendon from a cadaver. The surgery lasted five hours. The road back lasted 15 months. Ed had to redshirt the 1990-91 season and didn't see his first action in a UCLA uniform until January 16, 1992, in the eleventh game of the season. That's a whole lot of rust.

Basically he was out two years. Even in that half-season as a freshman he saw only limited action because he had not been able to practice much during his rehab and didn't really know the offense. He wasn't in that great of condition, but we just brought him along slowly. Everything he did at that stage was on natural ability. Then, all the way through his sophomore season, I could sense he was really off balance. He was always landing on one leg. It was just a slow process. And once he got over it physically, you didn't know if mentally he'd recovered. But by his senior year, it was no problem at all.

Obviously, I saw Ed go through enormous changes. But perhaps the greatest was his assumption of leadership from the Tulsa loss on. You might not know it from the way he performs oncourt, but Ed is an extremely sensitive, almost shy, guy off the court. Very thoughtful.

What's important to remember about Ed's ascension to being named the nation's best player is all the adversity he had to overcome. That's why he's so special to me, because I have it so ingrained in me that challenge is what life is about. You set goals, you have a plan and you overcome adversity. To the casual observer of linescores in the newspaper, Ed's career might have seemed smooth sailing. I mean, he got 30 against Arizona his sophomore year and in his junior year he had a few monsters, some brilliant games. He was always a good, often excellent, player. But he wasn't a dominant player. I remember I kept telling his dad, "You know, I remember him as a high school player. He's good, but he's not yet the player he was."

About halfway through his senior season, however, Ed just bolted from the pack and dominated every game. The key thing to remember about Ed is that he did this while never straying from the team concept. He was like mom in the kitchen to all the other players, somebody they could turn to, someone they always counted on. The reason he is such a great player is because he's so team-oriented. I know that the NBA scouts were impressed because when they were with him all he talked about was winning. He doesn't talk stats or what's in it for him, and that's what impressed them the most.

There's another thing that made Ed special. Several times in our championship season, Ed would come out of a game and I'd tell him, "Great job." Well, Ed would drape his arm around me and say: "Hey, Coach, you did a great job of coaching out there." In 35 years, he is the only player who's ever said something like that to me. It showed not only how complete a leader he had become, but also how thoughtful and considerate a man he had grown to be.

There was another troubling time for Ed, and the way he handled it just increased my admiration for him. It was during his junior year that he found out he was going to be a father. And while the news wasn't public, it came out on campus and a lot of people knew. I think it was hard sometimes dealing with other people's reactions. I don't know for certain how it affected him personally, but I know he's a very, very sensitive guy. And I certainly saw how it affected his play. His shooting percentage dropped from 54 percent to about 44 percent, roughly during the same period we were dropping from being a 14-0 team to one that went only 7-7 in its last 14 games. It wasn't until the Tulsa game that he truly broke free of it on the court.

At one point I talked to him. I told him that everybody was going to love him regardless, that he should never worry about how other people judge him. I told him that he knew what kind of person he really was, and to embrace that. And Ed turned it into a positive. His son, Aaron, was born shortly after his junior season. Soon after that, Ed granted a newspaper interview and for the first time publicly talked about becoming a father. I think maybe it was the therapy he needed. He accepted it as a positive in his life.

When Ed walked onto the court with his 10-month-old son in his arms on Senior Day before his final home game, and raised him high above his head while grinning as the crowd roared . . . well, that pretty much said it all. Ed O'Bannon endured a lot in his five years at UCLA and emerged all the better for it. A champion, in more ways than one.

Charles O'Bannon — This might surprise you, but as talented as Ed's younger brother is, I think he needed to learn a little bit of how to play basketball once he got to college. And it really wasn't until this season that he began to absorb the lessons. Once he did, he was a significant factor in our team's rise from a very good team to a great one.

Why did he have things to learn? Because in high school, things probably came too easily for him. Charles was quick enough and athletic enough where he could make a mistake and recover. If a guy got around him he was quick enough to block it from behind or recover and block it — but on the collegiate level you can't get away with that. He comes to college and suddenly he's having to learn how to get through single screens and double screens. And it took him a year and a half to get to the point where he was a top-flight player.

When he first got to UCLA, something happened that I wish hadn't. He got 22 points and 12 rebounds right out of the chute, in his first-ever collegiate game against Loyola Marymount. He must have thought this college game was easy.

Understand, though, that Charles has as fine a character as any player I've ever had. He would never lie to me and, any time I tell him something — whether it hurts or not — he tells me the truth and does things right. (I asked a lot of Charles and how he delivered helped this team jell.)

Charles spent his freshman year adjusting to this new level of play. He was always a terrific open-court player, but not that skilled in the half-court game. And in the second half of the season, we were involved in a lot of half-court games. So it was a typical up-and-down freshman kind of year for him. But by the second half of this past season, Charles had developed into a solid, solid player. In fact, I think he has the chance to be one of the top players, if not the top player, in the country over the next two years.

Where Ed is basically reserved and quiet off the court, Charles is just the opposite. And there was no problem with sibling rivalry. That's because their family is immensely close — and that very fact wound up playing a major role in landing him at UCLA.

Recruiting Charles was no easy assignment, because so many schools were after him, and a lot of people thought Kentucky with Rick Pitino was going to get him. Rick, in fact, was the speaker at Charles' high school team banquet — and there were a lot of other coaches, including Arizona's Lute Olson and Michigan's Steve Fisher, in attendance.

It was some night. Rick, remember, has to be very careful in his speech because he can't talk about recruiting or make any direct mention about it regarding Charles, even though he's courting him heavily. As usual, Pitino did a superior job of speaking. Outstanding. So the evening is going along and I'm wondering if Rick's speech drove a nail in my coffin. Then Charles is named his team's MVP and goes up to accept his trophy.

Now, the O'Bannon entourage has two tables there, and sitting around them are maybe 20 from the family in all. Charles begins to speak and there's Ed with his chair turned around facing his brother, and there's mom and dad and grandma and grandpa and aunt and uncle and Charles starts talking about his family and the support system he's had . . .

And he starts crying.

I just about did, too, 'cause I knew right then and there I was going to get him. I knew how strong the power of a good family is. I've always preached that the single reason you are put on this earth is because of the family unit, that the single most important thing you're put on this earth for is to get married and replenish the earth. And the O'Bannons typify that closeness of family. So when Charles broke down and cried, I knew we were going to get him.

I go home and go to sleep. At 1:30 in the morning my phone rings. It's Charles. He's all excited and says, "Coach, I want to be a Bruin." Now this is about as good a piece of news as you can get, but when you get to my age even great news takes a while to permeate through the fog of sleep. So I try to muster up enthusiasm to match his. "Charles, that's great. I'll talk to you to-morrow." But no, I stayed on the line a little longer. You know why? Because I had gotten emotionally involved with recruiting him. That's a cardinal sin, because you know you're going to lose some of the ones you want. But knowing Ed and his parents, I couldn't help it. In retrospect, when you consider what these two guys contributed to raise us to a championship level, I sup-pose I should have been emotionally involved regardless.

Toby Bailey — Right at the time Ed O'Bannon was about to make his decision to come to UCLA, I was also watching Toby Bailey play eighth-grade ball. There was a tournament out at Ed's high school in the morning and that afternoon they had the junior high games. That's when I first saw Toby play. Maybe you remember another coach (Bobby Knight) who became intrigued with another junior high kid named Bailey (Damon) a few years ago. Well, I had the same feeling about Toby, so I tracked down his dad, John, and started talking to him and Toby (because he wasn't in high school, you weren't prohibited from talking to the kid), and I told them the story of Knight and Damon Bailey and how by the time he was a junior in high school, Damon just came out and said he wanted to go to Indiana, that he didn't want anybody else to try to recruit him.

So I look at Mr. Bailey and I tell him "I'm looking for a player someday who just wants to come up and go to UCLA and I don't have to go into the home to convince him." (This was before Tyus did that very thing.) I'm trying to lay a little groundwork, because even then I could tell Toby had the potential to be something special. I watched him play over five straight days. He was a point guard then, a good little player.

Time flies by and now Toby is awaiting his senior year at Loyola High School in Los Angeles, but there were seven outstanding guards that we were in the hunt for. Which one to take is always a dilemma. Lo and behold, on July 1, before recruiting actually started for the fall, Toby calls me up and says he wants to come to UCLA. Most of the time the philosophy in recruiting is "A bird in the hand is worth two in the bush." So we took Toby and the other guys — several of whom were ranked ahead of him — went to other schools. And this time I never had second thoughts, because Toby had an outstanding senior season. Playing center and forward because he was 6-feet-5, he averaged 26 points, 14 rebounds, 6 assists and 2.7 dented ceilings per game (the kid can jump!).

While J.R. Henderson was the freshman who became a starter first during our march to the championship, it was Toby who replaced him in that role late in February — and his insertion proved to be the final piece to the puzzle. Toby's offensive fireworks — in particular, his 26 points against Arkansas — were obviously a major factor, but the thing I liked about him most out of high school was that he guarded people, and that he really played hard. He seemed to me to have a little bit more of that hungry spirit than some of the other guards we'd looked at.

As it turned out, Toby began to display a real love for crucial situations. He was an uncommon freshman in that regard. The bigger the game, the more he seemed to relish it. Believe it or not, my biggest concern after Toby signed was that he wasn't a strong enough shooter. But he worked hard on that during the summer. People say he had a great title game, and there's no disputing that, but it's important to remember that he had four or five games like that. He got 26 against Connecticut in the West Regional final. More important than those big-scoring games, though, he made just about every shot when we really needed it all season. He gets 19 points and seven rebounds in his first-ever trip to Arizona (where usually all you get is condolences over a defeat).

Toby's got a great sense of humor and loves to do imitations of his teammates (not to mention me and my West Virginia caints), and that effervescence is, I think, the key behind his ability to play so big when the occasion is big. To him, that kind of challenge is just plain fun. He doesn't have any jitters. Hey, when you consider his real name is John Garfield Bailey, that might explain why the brighter the stagelights, the more brilliant his game.

J.R. Henderson — We'd watched J.R. since his ninth grade. I used the word "watched" advisedly, because you didn't ever get into much of a conversation with J.R. He'd come to our football and basketball games and would never say a word. Pretty much a yes-no kind of kid. In July before his senior year in high school, I'd call him and try to engage him in conversation and eventually hang up thinking I'd just got finished playing a game of Twenty Questions.

A lot of people interpreted J.R.'s brevity as sullenness, and it might even have cost him a chance to play in the McDonald's All-American Classic after his senior year, when he'd averaged 27.3 points, 14.0 rebounds, 5 blocks and 6.3 assists at East Bakersfield High. But when we landed him the previous fall during the early signing period, things weren't so cut and dried.

The reason is that during summer play that year, J.R. just didn't do much. A lot of other schools thought he was just laying down, that he was a tired and lazy player who wouldn't listen. A lot of people began to shy away from him. But it just didn't add up. He'd led his team to a state title as a junior and he was the kind of player who was always taking charges and diving on the floor. So while we too were a bit worried about how uninspired he'd played in the summer, we weren't going to give up on him. I decided to go on how he'd played the previous winter.

Still, the mystery lingered. What kind of player would I be getting? When we gave all the players physicals last fall, the mystery was answered. The doctors discovered that J.R. had asthma. So they gave him medication and it just changed his whole life. Suddenly he had energy and strength.

We wound up starting J.R. in early January and he held down that spot for 13 consecutive games. And when I finally replaced him with Bailey, he handled it well. Not that he wasn't a major factor for us the rest of the way. J.R. was able to play at several different spots, and it allowed me all kinds of flexibility. When Toby would have one of those freshman valleys, J.R. seemed to counter it with a freshman peak. And vice versa.

At 6-feet-9, J.R. has a bright, bright future. He's a solid human being and a very good student, and underneath all that quiet is a pretty good sense of humor. After the championship and after Mark Gottfried got the head coaching job at Murray State, we all signed a card for Mark. When J.R. got it he wrote this: "I've signed enough things already. This is it!" That was his parting shot for Mark.

The Assistant Coaches — I'll miss **Mark Gottfried**. He was with me through my first seven years, the last three as a full-time assistant, and he helped head up our successful recruiting the past few years. Mark was a great player at Alabama, hitting 47.8 percent of his three-pointers in his senior season in 1987, and he's a sharp guy in all respects. Mark is the one who worked hardest with George Zidek in developing his hook shot. It's no surprise to me that he wound up getting a head coaching position.

Lorenzo Romar paired with Mark in our recruiting efforts. He's a tremendous competitor, but also a great guy to be around. Lorenzo is to our coaching staff what Toby Bailey is to our players' lineup: the team mimic. He can be with you for five minutes and if you walk out of the room, he'll be imitating you to a T. It's hilarious. Lorenzo played with Mark for Athletes in Action before they became coaches here. All through his career, Lorenzo displayed great tenacity. He was always getting cut from his teams. But he wound up getting a junior college scholarship, then was signed by the University of Washington. He struggled at first at Washington, but became a seventh-round draft choice of the Golden State Warriors. And wound up making the team. He played four years in the NBA, then played eight years with Athletes in Action. So he's always been an underdog who made it — just the kind of spirit you want your team to have, and something Lorenzo can instill. He spent hours and hours helping Ed O'Bannon develop his three-point shot, and he's a great communicator, with strong Christian beliefs.

Steve Lavin was a restricted earnings coach, but we've moved him up to full-time since Mark left for Murray State. Steve got valuable experience while a graduate assistant at Purdue, and he's been with us for four years. He also got some valuable experience from Coach Wooden. One day we were having breakfast with Coach and Steve was talking about his father, Cappy — who's a member of the San Francisco Prep Basketball Hall of Fame. Steve said of his dad: "He's just an English teacher in high school now." Well, you know what that meant. Coach Wooden got that mischievous grin on his face and said: "Ooooh, *just* an English teacher, huh?" Coach was an English teacher for nine years at South Bend Central High and I was an English teacher nine years at Morningside High. So now, every time Coach sees Steve, he says: "He's just an English teacher, huh?" Steve just grins back and shakes his head. We kid him about it, but Steve understands. He won the Scholar Athlete Award as a sophomore at San Francisco State in 1984, and he's an excellent leader.

The Supporting Cast — As a 6-10 freshman, **omm'A Givens** was the first player we ever signed who was selected to play in both the McDonald's Classic and the Magic Johnson All-Star Game out of high school. The adjustment to college has been a big one for omm'A — socially, academically and athletically — but he's got great, great skills. His distinctive first name comes from the mantra (omm) with the "A" added for uniqueness by his deceased Choctaw Indian father.

With George gone now, **Ike Nwankwo** is our brightest student. We just hope he can fill George's athletic shoes as well as his academic ones. He has tremendous athletic skills and his time may be coming soon. Ike's parents are both from Nigeria and his father is an English literature professor at Tennessee State. He was a medical redshirt his freshman year when he suffered nerve damage in his left arm after accidentally putting his arm through a window.

I thought **Kevin Dempsey** was going to be a terrific player in our program, and he still can be, but his progress was slowed by a back problem in his second year. Kevin came off the bench as a freshman and hit three consecutive three-point shots in our near-upset of Michigan in the NCAAs. He has what's called Scheuermann's Disease, which is the growing together of vertebrae, and he's been struggling with that ever since. I hope he'll get better. He has a lot of talent, and he's a very likable young man.

Two years ago our players came back to school and at all their workouts they kept telling me about **Bob Myers.** He was a solid player and a solid student, so we let Bob walk on. A year ago we had only 11 players, so Bob gets to make the traveling squad. This year, same thing. Now, all the players call him Forrest Gump, because he's popped up everywhere. Jay Leno, Disneyland, the White House . . . there's Bob Myers. He's had a great two years.

Last, but certainly not least, is **Kris Johnson.** The son of former UCLA great Marques Johnson, Kris was another freshman we thought might make a significant contribution. But he tore cartilage in his knee while diving at a swimming pool in the summer, requiring surgery, and he got off to a slow start in the fall as a result. I remember getting on him once, as I do with freshmen from time to time, and I listed him dead last on our squad chart. So we have an intra-squad game after that and Kris comes off the bench to get 18 points and 13 rebounds.

That really opened my eyes. I thought we'd get a solid year from him. But he developed a stress fracture in his foot that kept him out until the first of January. So now it takes another month for him to get into playing shape, and by then it's February and our team is pretty much formulated. So I didn't use him much. But we have great expectations for him in the future.

As it turned out, Kris did indeed contribute. He was the guy on the bench who kept everybody involved (and usually laughing). It was Kris who came up with that Ali Baba and the Forty Thieves look from some turban-veil contraption he made with a towel — his symbol that we were taking no prisoners, I guess. Now some coaches might discourage that sort of thing (and I'm a guy who, because I'm Lebanese, was called "Towel Head" as a kid), but the last thing I want to do is to keep my players from having fun and enjoying their sense of humor.

There's a line you can cross, of course, but I didn't think he was hurting anybody. He wasn't abusive, and as long as that's the case I'm glad they can bring that sort of playfulness to the game. Really, that's what college is all about, letting a young man express himself.

Funny thing is, I got tremendously more grief about the length of our players' shorts than anything else. Believe me, I'm no fan of these uniforms where the guys look like they're wearing mini-skirts instead of basketball shorts. But that's the trend, so when Ed O'Bannon came in and said the team wanted to redesign the uniforms to make the shorts longer, I didn't say no. We didn't change the design, of course. UCLA has been very, very traditional in its uniforms and there was no way I was going to change the basic look. But we did get the length they wanted.

When we first broke them out, we got a tremendous number of letters, most from women, telling me things like "Get hold of your team!" or "What are you doing?" or "Have some discipline!" or "Show some leadership!"

Two things. The first is, having Ed come in with such a request was a good sign to me, because it underscored that he was becoming the leader of this team. And the second is this: While I draw the line at those things going down below the knee, if you look back at pictures of those old UCLA teams that won national titles, those short, short pants look pretty crazy themselves.

Oh, and one other thing. Since we've won the national championship, I haven't heard any complaints about the uniforms.

Too bad that wasn't the only controversy I've had to face during my time at UCLA. It's been a long, sometimes weird, sometimes frustrating — and always challenging — road. As I go back through the years and reflect on how I got to this point — and share with you some of the ups and downs of the season that finally brought the title back to Westwood — it's important to remember what these players did. They're the ones who made the journey ultimately so worthwhile.

FINAL
FORESHADOWING

4

December 3, 1994 — The John R. Wooden Classic, Anaheim: UCLA vs. Kentucky.

There's definitely something intense swirling around. It's a Final Four feel, this doubleheader extravaganza that's drawn an overflow crowd to The Pond, the beautiful new arena they've built here in Orange County. The games also have worldwide television coverage with a potential audience of 60 million households in 80 countries.

As I get ready to take my team onto the court, Final Four-caliber electricity has already been generated in the first game of the inaugural Wooden Classic. Seventh-ranked Kansas has just finished putting an 81-75 blemish on Massachusetts, which came in with the nation's No. 1 rating. Now it's time for us to take on third-ranked Kentucky. We're ranked No. 5 in the wire service polls (and I'm still trying to figure out why in the world *Sports Illustrated* picked us No. 1 in its pre-season issue), even though our only accomplishment to date is an 83-60 win over Cal-State Northridge.

Tension? You bet. It's early, but a game like this is a lesson in preparing yourself for the NCAA Tournament. And this is the first time UCLA and Kentucky — I guess the two biggest names in the history of college basketball — have met in 20 years. The last one came in the 1975 NCAA championship game in San Diego, where Coach Wooden won his last title and then retired. So, you can bet this is a big-time matchup.

(Tulsa!)

Yes, and also a chance to maybe put the death knell on a certain, nagging memory.

It's not just that, Jim. Don't forget that Tulsa's coach, Tubby Smith, was an assistant to Pitino at Kentucky. Hmmmm . . . wonder if they've been talking. Whatever, it doesn't make the Tulsa memory any less distant.

I know this game can have an enormous psychological effect on our players — especially if we lose in a big way. The impact of a loss like the one we had against Tulsa can stay with a player a long time, particularly when its ramifications are repeated over and over again in the media. And our guys have the sense that there's a big mass of critics out there who don't believe they've got the right stuff — or that I do either, of course. (Said one writer of the four coaches — Roy Williams, Rick Pitino, John Calipari and me — gathered here: "Harrick is to this high-profile quartet what Ringo was to The Beatles.")

These 40 minutes are going to tell me a lot about the character of this club.

And it's just about time for the clock to start ticking.

*   *   *

The Wooden Classic was the brainchild of Randy Ryan, an entrepreneur who put it together in the face of tremendous adversity, particularly from the television people. I think they regarded it as an affront to them, how he stepped in out of nowhere to join their parade. He had no corporate machinery to get the thing going, just his own dream and perseverance.

When Randy first bounced the idea off of me a couple of years earlier, I told him he was crazy. One individual trying to put all that together doesn't usually have much of a chance. But I did approach Coach Wooden about the idea. Without his approval, obviously there wouldn't be an event, regardless of Randy's determination. Well, you know Coach. Initially he was reluctant, simply because his nature is so self-effacing. "Does my name really need to be perpetuated in college basketball?" That's what he'd say to me.

What eventually changed his mind was that the more he thought about it, the more he believed it would be good for West Coast basketball. Virtually all the big tournaments are east of the Mississippi and for years the impression has been that the West Coast is basically left out of the power equation in college hoops. So Coach thought maybe it could serve a good purpose. Then, too, he was won over when he learned that some of the proceeds from the Classic would go to charities.

Once Coach Wooden gave his blessing, getting teams to participate proved easy. All four of us had to juggle our schedules, but were quick to do so. That's a tribute to the man, of course. When Randy contacted UMass coach John Calipari, John simply said: "If it's for Coach Wooden, we'll come out. Just tell me the date and the time and we'll be there." John said yes even before he knew who his opponent would be.

When they held a special ceremony for Coach on the court during the Classic, he got this tremendous standing ovation that threatened to never stop. I watched as I saw this embarrassed grin cross his face. He began moving his hands downward, trying gently to shush the crowd. "Time out! Time out!" he said into the mike with that slight grin, clearly feeling awkward at all this fuss being made over him. He is such an example, a man who accomplished more than any other in our profession, yet so grounded in humility. You can talk that word, but John Wooden is one of the few men I've seen who walks it so consistently and inspiringly.

*   *   *

Buzz in the air now, and a buzzsaw out there on the court in Kentucky. It's fierce, but it's not particularly well played on either side. Figures. This is early December. Even so, we're looking worse off than Kentucky. For some reason, Edney is not having his normal game. He's dribbled the ball off his knee a couple of times. I'm aware that some of this is due to Kentucky with its harassing, attacking defense — but, hey, that's Tyus out there. It's nothing he hasn't seen before.

It doesn't end there. We're putting up free throws like we're shooting them in the Bermuda Triangle. They disappear everywhere but into the rim. (We'll wind up making only nine of 18, and in one stretch we go 4-for-10.)

Now it's late in the half and we're still struggling, but we're taking it up a notch and there — look there! — a Kentucky player trying to in-bounds the ball can't find anybody and he's just stepped over the line. He pulls back his foot and throws the ball in.

Somebody call it!

But there's no whistle. I jump up, angry. One of the officials is trotting by. "You know, there are only 18,000 people who saw it, but not you guys! How can that happen!?!" I am one syllable shy of a technical foul and now I see Kentucky come down and nail a three, and now I'm 100 percent bona fide livid. My assistants have to calm me down or that T is a certainty.

We never get the lead in the first half. But there's Tyus, finally revving up and dropping in a three-pointer with eight seconds to go. Kentucky doesn't score again, so I walk toward the locker only five down, 38-33. Given all that's gone wrong, I feel we're in pretty good shape.

Just make a few adjustments here and there, Jim, and we can win this.

We go over what we're going to do in the final 20 minutes. Now we're heading back to the court, and it's a long walk from the lockers, and as I turn a corner I bump right into one of the officials.

Oh, great! Fancy bumping into you here. You would have to be the one I'd yelled at the most.

He just shrugs. And, without me bringing up the play again, he says: "Jim, I didn't see it." I give him a pat on the rear. "Hey, that's OK. You'll get the next one."

Second half starts. Edney picks up where he left off. He hits a short jumper in the lane to bring us within three. Then it happens. Kentucky is out on a breakaway and Rodrick Rhodes is racing for the basket. Easy two. He's at the top of the circle, flying, and BOOM! Charles O'Bannon comes out of nowhere and just hammers him. It's a foul, all right. But wait a minute. The official is calling Rhodes for walking! Terrible call. Now it's Rick Pitino who gets the chance to go bonkers. And he *doesn't* calm down. TWEET! Technical. Tyus hits both free throws, we get the ball out of bounds and now here's Ed drilling a three. Big-time turnaround. From five down to start the second half to two up in nothing flat. Seven-point swing on two possessions.

(Later I'll review the tape of this game and see five or six obvious calls that were mishandled by these three officials, all of whom are among the best in their profession. Which just goes to show you that December isn't tuneup time for just the teams. It is for all of us. The stripes just had a bad game. It happens.)

We're back in it now. But Kentucky regroups well. This is turning into some battle. Then I see Charles pick up his fourth foul and I want to take him out, but Ed's already out of the game because he's having to change his shorts after getting blood on them. Can I afford to have them both out right now? Thirteen seconds later, the whistle blows again. It's Charles again. Fouled out. And there's 11:11 still to play. Big mistake on my part.

I've got to replace him with a freshman, but which one? Toby Bailey or J.R. Henderson? Well, J.R.'s 6-9 and quick, Toby's 6-5 and plays 6-11. I decide on J.R. But it doesn't seem to matter much, because we're out of sync with Charles gone. And Kentucky's on a hot run. The clock shows 10:12 to go, and we're down 10.

Well, it's truth or dare time. Are we gonna get blown out of here and have this kind of embarrassment piled right on top of last season's parting stinker? Are these guys going to set a tone that just might haunt us from here on out? Don't let it happen, Jim. Time to strangle that possibility right now.

"Time out!"

The players come over to huddle, and I lay it on the line. "All right, listen up," I say. "The time is now. If we're ever going to be a quality team, if we're going to beat Kentucky, we need to turn it up a notch defensively. We need five straight stops! We can't wait. We have to do it now!"

I like what I see. Everywhere the ball goes, we've got a guy hawking it. We are darting and attacking and challenging everything Kentucky tries to do. From here on, even if they score, they're getting nothing cheap. They're having to work hard at it. And Tyus is starting to get great dribble penetration, either scoring off it or dishing off to a teammate for easy baskets.

Something else is becoming apparent. Kentucky doesn't have anyone bulky enough to handle Zidek. And they're trying to guard him one-on-one. With Tyus causing such a stir, it's setting up Big George inside. George keeps scoring. It's crunch time, and he scores seven straight! And this last one, a five-foot hook, cuts Kentucky's lead to 81-80.

Clock? Eighteen seconds! C'mon now! One more stop! Crank it up! We need that D one more time!

And we get it. Rhodes takes an in-bounds pass against our press and hurriedly tries to pass out of a trap, the throw too hard and too low. It bounces off Mark Pope and out of bounds to us. I call another timeout. I tell Tyus to penetrate and look to dish to Ed, who's going to come off a screen. If it works, he gets either a layup or a short jumper.

It doesn't work. Kentucky comes after Tyus big-time, and Edney has to reverse his dribble out toward the wing. But he spins, and darts back toward the lane. Whoa, quick! Now he rifles a pass to the baseline opposite his side of the lane. J.R. goes up and gets whacked. Foul.

With six-tenths of a second left.

And my heart somewhere up in my throat.

In our exhibition game against Athletes in Action, J.R. had

five free-throw attempts and missed them all. He'd had a really flat shot. So every day after practice, he and I worked on the problem. Nothing major. I had him put more arc on the ball. He'd shoot, I'd shag. He must have shot 400 extra free throws between that exhibition game and now.

So here he is, the freshman called in only because Charles had fouled out, stepping up to the line. As he waits for the official to give him the ball, he turns over to our bench. Our eyes meet.

You're a great shooter. GREAT shooter! You've worked on your form, you know how to arc it, you're a machine out there. It's all concentration now, son. Just concentrate.

That's the vibe I'm sending out, and in his eyes I can tell J.R. understands. We'd prepared for this moment, even if neither of us could have imagined it would be quite THIS kind of moment.

Swish.

We're tied now. Pitino calls a timeout, trying to ice J.R., but in our huddle I can see it in his face. That No Problem, Coach face. What do I say to him? Absolutely nothing. He goes back out, hits the second free throw pretty as you please and this game is ours, 82-81.

You know, Jim, come to think of it, Ringo laid down a pretty good beat for those other guys. What were their names again?

*   *   *

A lot of important things came out of that game. For one, the tremendous defense we played over the final 10 minutes set the tone, I think, for the rest of the season. In fact, when times arose that we needed to step up our intensity on D, we'd refer to our "Kentucky Defense" as the guiding light. My whole theme from then on was "Let's build on that," because I knew that defense is what wins championships. As the season progressed, we continued to go after people with a vengeance.

Winning a high-profile game also helped us establish our identity, and certainly helped shed any lingering image left from the Tulsa loss. Most important, these guys showed they weren't going to lie down when it got tough out there — particularly with Ed O'Bannon now clearly a leader, one his teammates knew would lay down the law if he saw something he didn't like. Which he did in the post-game locker room celebration. Toby Bailey was moping, no doubt because he didn't get a chance to contribute much while J.R. wound up the hero. It was Ed who saw Toby standing apart from the others. "Bailey, get over here and get in this huddle!" Ed yelled. "Be happy for your team. Your day will come."

I also realized that against certain teams, George Zidek was going to be a key factor. His hook was consistent and deadly now, and with his size some teams would have trouble containing him. Of course, I didn't know it at the time, but you'd have to say that George was our unsung hero of the season. I'm a firm believer that you rarely, if ever, win championships without some bulk in the middle. And George began to give us consistently strong efforts, including his defense. Never would that be more apparent than in the Final Four, when he played what I think were the two greatest games of his career.

But that's another story. I also realized after the Kentucky game that Ed had put any lingering worry about his knee completely behind him, that he had the chance to be the dominant player I'd always expected him to be. He scored 26 against Kentucky, even though he missed five free throws.

As it turned out, this game foreshadowed a lot of things — our ability to come back against adversity, as we did against Missouri and then Arkansas in the Final Four; our need to have a freshman step up and deliver in crucial moments, as Bailey did against Arkansas and Connecticut, and on other key occasions; and George becoming an unexpected major factor, just like in Seattle.

I don't mind telling you that one thing I'm glad this game didn't foreshadow was another matchup with those guys in blue-and-white. As the season went on, I became more convinced I didn't want to face Kentucky again in the NCAAs. I thought they were the best team we played all season. Also, I remember losing badly to Indiana in the 1992 tournament after having beaten them handily in December. You don't like to give teams a second shot. They have the edge.

After the game, one of the writers asked me about the contrast in styles between me and Pitino. He said that Rick and I seemed complete opposites, like Old World vs. New World. Well, I never see a game as a battle of coaches. I always chuckle when I see it written up like that. It's not Jim Harrick vs. Rick Pitino. It's UCLA's athletes vs. Kentucky's athletes. I didn't score a single point for us, and I'm pretty sure Rick didn't make the boxscore either.

So, to answer the writer's question, no, I just didn't think much about any contrasts. I really don't know Pitino that well, anyway. About the only thing I can say with some certainty is that he's a New Yorker and — decades in L.A. notwithstanding — I'm just a guy who came out of Charleston, West Virginia. Which will never, ever, be confused with Manhattan.

*   *   *

Back in the old days, the great pool players would barnstorm around the country, hitting cities big and small, participating in tournaments, giving exhibitions, hustling. Money was tight for everyone back then, and this was one more way to make a few extra bucks. Charleston was one of their regular stops. The pro would come to town and put on a dazzling show, then finish up with a series of marvelous trick shots. But as interesting as the exhibition and the trick shots were, it was just a prelude to the real highlight of the evening — the challenge match.

Prior to the pro's arrival, the locals would get together and pick the best pool player in town. How they did this is anyone's guess, but they did. Displaying the best pool hall diplomacy imaginable, they'd choose their top player, knowing that the visiting pro would close out his performance by challenging the town's best to step up and take him on. This was the moment the locals had been waiting for. In unison, true brothers in arms, they would push their guy forward, sending him into battle, the pride of the community resting on his artistry with a cue stick. David against Goliath in a smoke-filled room.

And that's how my father came to play the great Willie Mosconi.

Two things about this story bear remembering: It may or may not be true (my father said it was, but . . .), and my father was more than comfortable in the world of hustlers.

In truth, my father was something of a hustler himself — which figures when you consider this: he lived to be 84 and never once collected a paycheck. Of course, he never thought of himself as a hustler; he probably saw himself as an entrepreneur more than anything else, even before that word was in vogue. But that's being polite, calling him an entrepreneur. My father, Major Harrick, was a real character, a small-scale hustler with big- scale dreams. (If you think about it, even his name could be construed as something of a con. It had nothing to do with the military; Major just happened to be a favorite name in Lebanon, so that's what his parents named him.)

Dad was one of those men who tried his hand at every-thing. Bars, restaurants, pool halls— he owned them all during his lifetime. And nothing he tried ever succeeded. He really thought he was good at what he did, but the sad truth is, he wasn't. Part of the reason he failed is because he was just a little unlucky. Maybe some guys are born under an unlucky star, and he was one of them. But the bigger, more important reason is that he wasn't a driven man. He didn't have that spark — that light inside that's so necessary for success. My father was a ter-rific guy. He had a big heart and he was capable of great acts of generosity and caring — he always showed Mother, my sister, Dee, and me plenty of love. But when it came to business, his failures far outnumbered his successes. He was a dreamer whose dreams went unfulfilled.

My mother, Helen, was the complete opposite. She was a rock, the real strength that kept it all going. She had one of the greatest personalities of anyone I've ever met. Without her courage and determination, I shudder to think what might have happened. She was a worker — she had to be because my father's income wasn't always steady, and when it was, it didn't usually amount to much. During the really hard times, it was my mother who supported us. If she were a young woman today, with her spunk and intelligence, she would have been one successful lady. But the timing wasn't right. She grew up in an age when few women were encouraged to develop and utilize their talents and intellect. That's sad. But if there's one consolation, it comes from the successes my sister and I have achieved. We inherited her drive, her personality and her willingness to work hard at whatever we do. That was her greatest gift to us.

Both my parents grew up in non-English-speaking homes. Their parents came to this country from Lebanon, right outside Beirut, and never learned to speak the language. Not a word. I remember my father's mother. She lived right in Charleston, lived to be 95 and never uttered a word of English. She would go into town, do the shopping, and even though she couldn't speak or understand the language, she'd somehow manage to make herself understood. She was a real terror, that gal. I have many great memories of her.

Of my four grandparents, the only one I didn't know was my father's dad. He died before I was born. The others were around quite a lot, and they played a big role during my formative years.

My mother was born and raised in Pittsburgh. We used to go there fairly regularly. I probably spent a month there every summer during my first 18 years. My cousins and I used to play up at Duquesne on the bluff. Those were some of the most fun times I can remember.

My parents met in Pittsburgh and were married on October 16, 1935. Dee was born on October 10, 1936. I came along two years later, on July 25, 1938. We had a strong family unit, even though we weren't very well-off financially. My parents never owned a house, so we always lived in an apartment. A two-bedroom apartment. But it was a good home, very neat, very clean, certainly nothing I was ever ashamed of. They did have a car, a Cadillac they paid on, and that was a source of great pride. We lived in what I like to call a chicken-and-beans environment . . .

one week we ate well, the next week, not so well. It was a constant struggle, but we were never really poor. Not like a lot of other people I knew.

Most important, there was tremendous love in our house. Tremendous caring and respect. A family that doesn't have love and respect as its foundation is poor, regardless of how much money it has in the bank. Looked at in that context, I would say we were wealthy.

It's hard for me to imagine a better place to grow up in than Charleston. Most people probably don't realize how big Charleston, the state capitol, is. They seem to have it in their minds as some small hick town. I think a lot of people have a certain stereotypical picture of West Virginia. Whenever I tell someone that I'm from there, the first thing they want to know is if I worked in the coal mines. I hate to shatter the stereotype, but I've never set foot in a coal mine in my life. I don't know any of that stuff about country, hillbillies and coal mines. Anything other than a pool room and I'm unfamiliar with it. At the time, Charleston had a population of about 100,000. If you include the surrounding valley, that number swells to more than 350,000. That's not a small town.

The primary industry was Union Carbide, the second-largest chemical plant in the country. Because Union Carbide was important to the war effort, during World War II we used to have air raid drills. The lights would go out, the siren would blow . . . it was just like the real thing. The police would go around and canvass the neighborhood. I was pretty young at the time, but I can still remember hearing one of the policemen yelling, "Get that light out!" to someone who didn't follow the rules.

Those were the days when certain items were rationed. Tires, gasoline, butter, things like that. Mom would always send me to the store whenever she needed butter. She would give me a coupon, then send me off down the street. Carrying that coupon always made me feel important.

The things I remember most about those childhood days are the family dinners and going to the movies. The things we did together as a family. Television didn't come to Charleston until about 1952, so the radio was our biggest source of entertainment. We listened to the radio for hours. *The Lone Ranger, Fibber McGee and Molly,* all that stuff. Today, when I tell my players that I grew up before television, when every car had a standard transmission, they look at me like I'm some ancient character from a different planet. They have no idea how different the world was back then.

I was eight or nine when sports entered my life, and once they did, things were never the same. The playground became my second home. I practically lived there. Both my parents were off working, so I became what is known today as a "latchkey" kid. In the summer, the playground was open from eight or nine in the morning until nine or 10 at night. We'd play everything — baseball, basketball, football, horseshoes — it didn't matter. We played them all.

One summer our playground supervisor was Hot Rod Hundley. He was about three years ahead of me and already he was the big hot shot basketball player in town. He did all that flashy Pete Maravich stuff with the basketball long before "Pistol Pete" was even born. There was nothing he couldn't do with a basketball. It was amazing. I just loved Hot Rod. I thought he was the greatest guy in the world. He and I became great buddies, and we still are to this day.

Back in those days, we were still very much a segregated society. I never went to school with black kids; integration didn't take place in Charleston until the year after I graduated from high school. But that didn't mean I never played against blacks. I did. Quite often, in fact. Every Tuesday we'd load up in a car and drive over to Donnelly Street and play ball against the black guys. Then on Thursday, they'd come over and play against us. Out of that we developed friendships, respect and great rivalries. That was the first time I realized that sports — athletic competition — is a way to bring people together, a way to bridge cultural and racial differences. In all the times we played, I can't remember a single nasty incident that occurred because it was a "blacks versus whites" situation. We got angry at each other and we had a few disagreements, but none of it was ever racially motivated.

Don't get me wrong, there was a lot of razzing going on in those days. A lot. *Everybody* teased everybody. I know I took my share. As soon as they found out I was Lebanese, they'd call me a camel driver or a towel head. I'd walk into the classroom and "camel driver" would be written up on the blackboard. Those guys were crazy. But it was always in good fun. In no way, shape or form did I ever experience genuine prejudice or discrimination while I was growing up.

Charleston was a great city for prep sports. There were two high schools in the city and 14 others out in the county. Those 16 teams made up the Kanawha Valley Conference, which was, year in and year out, an outstanding and competitive league. A lot of great players came out of the KVC, including Jerry West, one of the greatest basketball players of all time. There were city schools, county schools and Catholic schools, so the competition was always fierce. Since there were no professional teams anywhere close, high school sports were the big deal. The local newspapers gave more coverage to the area high schools than they gave to West Virginia University.

Most of my buddies rooted for the Cleveland Browns in football and the Cincinnati Reds in baseball. Because of my Pittsburgh connection, I was a big Pirates fan, even though they never won. My boyhood hero was Dick Groat. I liked him because he was as good at basketball as he was at baseball. He'd been an All-American at Duke in both sports. He was a shortstop, I was a second baseman. He was a guard, I was a guard. Dick Groat was tops.

Many years later, I had an amusing incident involving Dick Groat. It happened in the early '80s while I was at Pepperdine. The University of Pittsburgh was playing on TV and Groat was the color guy. When I saw him I was absolutely stunned. He'd lost all his hair. A couple of years later, in 1982, we played Pitt in the NCAA Tournament. My first game as head coach in the NCAA. I was being interviewed the day before the game and I just happened to mention that Dick Groat had been my boyhood idol. Then I added, "He's bald now, you know." The next day I walk into the arena at Washington State University and the first person I see is this bald-headed guy coming toward me, shaking his head, grinning from ear to ear. It was Dick Groat. He must have razzed me for the next 30 minutes.

By the time I got to Lincoln Elementary School I was the best athlete in my class. I'd groomed for it, spending endless hours playing all the sports. I was a very hard worker, dedicated to reaching my full potential as an athlete. It also didn't hurt that I grew so fast. I was almost 5-10 by the time I was in eighth grade. Unfortunately, I never grew much more after that, so many of the guys who weren't as good as me at the time eventually passed me by.

Lincoln Junior High was made up of three grades — seventh, eighth and ninth. Our coach was Al Ball. He was not only a great coach, he was also one of the big influences on my life. I loved the man, even though I was scared to death of him. He was 6-2, maybe 6-3, but he looked 6-9 to me. I thought he was a monster.

Back then, teachers and coaches were highly respected. When they told you to do something you did it, no questions asked. Their word was The Law. Next to your parents — and maybe in some instances, more than your parents — they were the dominant forces in the lives of young people. It was a lot different than it is now.

I was a hot-tempered kid, one who could have gotten into trouble had it not been for my love of sports. I ran the streets from the fourth grade on. I knew the west side of town like it was the back of my hand. And I usually ran with a gang, which didn't help matters. We weren't hoodlums or anything like that, but we did some things we shouldn't have done.

Because of my love for sports, because I respected (and feared) the coach, I managed to avoid getting into any real trouble. I was one of those kids who always listened to the coach. If he said be home by nine, I was home by nine. If he said be in bed by 10, I'd be under the covers when 10 o'clock rolled around. Al Ball was a strict disciplinarian — the first guy to ever discipline me. One time I did something he didn't like, so he sat me down and wouldn't let me play. Boy, that was traumatic. From that time on I was the most dedicated guy he ever had. I didn't want it to happen again. (I didn't realize it at the time, of course, but I learned then that my greatest ally as a coach was the bench.) Also, I knew that if I got a whipping at school, I'd get two whippings when I got home — further incentive for me to keep my nose clean.

Lincoln won the county junior high championship during my eighth- and ninth-grade years. My eighth-grade year, we were really good, going undefeated in the regular season. That team could play. If I'm not mistaken, that was the only time in history that West Virginia held a Junior High State Tournament. It was played on the afternoon of the high school state finals. We made it all the way to the semifinals before we got beat.

The next year, when I was in ninth grade, we came back and repeated as league champions. I was voted captain of the All-City team that year. Those two years were testimony to what hard work, desire and the outright love of competing could bring. I'd learned what it takes to be a winner, and Al Ball is the man who first taught me.

Stonewall Jackson High School was the second-largest school in West Virginia at the time. The Stonewall Jackson Generals. I played three sports, and actually had a moderate degree of success as a football player. I started at safety during my junior year and at quarterback when I was a senior. Our coach was Russ Parsons, one of the football coaching legends in West Virginia. I remember getting pretty upset at him my final year because he wouldn't let me play quarterback and safety. I loved to play defense — you could gamble and anticipate — but this was about the time when specialization and platooning were becoming popular, so he decided that I would just play quarterback. I was a fair quarterback, pretty fast on my feet, with decent passing skills. I couldn't throw the ball long, maybe 30 to 35 yards, but I made up for it with great accuracy.

But I was really more of a basketball player. That was my first love. We had two really fine coaches at Stonewall Jackson back then, two men I feel fortunate to have played for. Pud Hutson coached the varsity and Sonny Moran coached the junior varsity team. Or the "B" team as we called it back then. Both were to play a big role in my life. Pud is about 95 today and still lives in Charleston. Sonny eventually moved up to head coach for one year, then took the job at Morris Harvey College, where he would be my coach for two years.

I played on the B team my sophomore year and we finished with a record of 20-3. The varsity was very strong that year, making it all the way to the West Virginia state tourney. When the jayvee season was over I was in for a pleasant surprise — Coach Hutson called two players up to the varsity. I was one of them, which meant that I got to make the trip to Morgantown. That was a big deal for all of us. We went into that tournament with the attitude that it was us against the state of West Virginia.

My junior year we were 24-2. A lot of people gave us a good chance of winning it all, but it didn't happen. We lost in the first round of the tournament. That just broke my heart. I was a starting guard, more of a defensive specialist than a scorer. My average that year was 11 points a game. I'd played well and the team had been strong, but it all ended on a down note.

One of my rivals all through school was Jerry West. We were in the same grade, so we played against each other from junior high until we graduated. I got to know him a little back then, but it wasn't until a few years later, in the late '50s, when we were teammates on a summer team called Blossom Dairy, that we became good friends. Those games were played outside in front of two or three thousand fans. I'll never forget what an influence he had on me in those games. I never wanted Jerry to get on me, so I concentrated hard and played so well that I began to think I was a really good player. I went back to college thinking "Boy, I'm pretty good." Until I got on the floor, that is. I'd just been playing beyond my capabilities in the summer because of Jerry's presence. I just didn't want to make a mistake. West was the kind of player who made you step up and perform at a level beyond your ability. (Just as Ed O'Bannon exerted a similar influence on my UCLA team.) The summer that I got married and left for California, Jerry went to Rome for the 1960 Olympic Games.

When we were both sophomores, Jerry broke his leg and couldn't play against us when we played his East Bank High School team. The next year, when we won the KVC championship, we played East Bank and beat them. When we won the league title, they gave each player a small gold basketball. I gave mine to Sally. She made a necklace for it and wears it to this day.

Going into our senior year, East Bank had never beaten us. We played them early in the season and won, 64-62. We played a great game against them that night, especially on defense. That win kept us in first place in the league standings. Later that year we had to go to their place and play. We knew it would be a real war, but we'd whipped them before, so we had all the confidence in the world that we would do it again.

When we got there, the East Bank fans were waiting for us. They rocked the bus, screamed at us, held up signs . . . they were ready. So were the East Bank players. They just beat the living daylights out of us. I always guarded Jerry, and most of the time I did a fairly good job on him. But that night he got 45 points. He just ate me for lunch. Jerry had developed into a truly great player. There was no stopping him. And there was no stopping East Bank, either. They went on and won it all.

*   *   *

My father finally found his calling in 1962, my second year of teaching in California. He bought a hotel, which he would run for the next 20 years. It was a lower-class hotel right across the street from the Greyhound bus station. The most expensive room cost about three bucks, so it's not hard to imagine the clientele. But that was his business, hotel owner, and I guess I'd have to say he was more successful at that than anything he tried. If nothing else, it was the job he stuck with the longest.

There are numerous stories to tell about what went on in that place, about the colorful characters that came and went. Something wild was always happening. One night while Sally and I were visiting — it was during the summer — the phone rang at three in the morning. It was from the night manager, telling my father to come to the hotel immediately. Dad came in, woke me up and said, "Come with me." I had no idea what was happening. I jumped out of bed, got dressed and drove my father to the hotel. By the time we arrived, there were police cars all over the place, lights flashing, and a crowd of onlookers standing around. I go inside and there's this dead guy lying on the floor. What had happened was, the guy came in, pulled a gun and demanded all the money in the cash register. The night manager reached into the drawer, but instead of getting the money, he pulled out a gun of his own and shot the guy. I remember saying to myself, "Oh, my heavens, what am I getting into?"

*   *   *

I first met Sally Marple when I was a freshman and she was in the eighth grade. We met at a party, and I guess it's safe to say that we've been fairly inseparable ever since. I don't know what it was that so attracted me to her, but something did. She knocked my socks off, that I do know. In no time she became the great love of my life.

Sally and I went to different junior highs, then ended up going to Stonewall Jackson together. Strangely enough, although we lived within three blocks of each other we'd never met until that night at the party. Once we did meet, it didn't take long before we were serious about each other.

Our relationship wasn't looked upon with great joy by her family. I suppose it had to do with our ethnic differences. I came from a Lebanese-Catholic background, Sally was Presbyterian. This was in the mid-1950s, before John Kennedy was elected president, when many Protestants had negative feelings about Catholics. Kennedy's election changed that, I think. But maybe it wasn't just the religious or ethnic differences.

Maybe her dad looked at my dad and decided that I wasn't the kind of guy she should marry. Whatever the reason, Frank and Grace Marple were less than thrilled at having me court their daughter.

Our backgrounds were different in another way as well. I came from a family dominated by love; she came from a family dominated by fear. That's not to say there wasn't love in her family. There was. But her father was a very strong-minded man who ruled by fear. All five of his children turned out to be shy, a little backward and not particularly outgoing or forward. In other words, they avoided confrontation at all costs. In all the years I've known Sally, only once have I seen her get mad and challenge someone. Other than me, of course. Factor that in and it brings the average way up.

Something else about Sally: She has one of the sweetest dispositions of anyone I've ever been around. She's easy to like. In fact, I've never met a person who didn't like her.

Back to her father. I was absolutely terrified of the guy. Just the sight of him petrified me. Talk about fear of confrontation . . . I wouldn't even think of going to their house unless I was certain he would be gone. He was the meanest guy I've ever known in my life.

Fortunately for me, Frank wasn't around all that much. He worked for the government as a civil service employee at HUD. His job kept him very busy and on the go a lot, which was more than fine by me. I had no desire to bump into him!

I have always felt that their attitude toward Sally and me is one of the reasons we made it. It was just so anti-everything. They kept saying, "You can't, you can't, you can't," which, of course, led to us strengthening our resolve to defy what they were telling us. They used the wrong psychology. If a parent tells a kid not to do something, chances are the kid will do it. Flip that over and tell the kid he can do something, and he might not. Sometimes it works, sometimes it doesn't. In our case, the fact that so many people thought it wasn't a good deal probably helped to spur the whole thing on.

*   *   *

In 1956, the year I graduated, I was named the co-winner of the Most Outstanding Athlete Award at Stonewall Jackson. It was a nice honor, and in a way I suppose it brought to a close my glory days as an athlete. I hate to admit it, but I reached my peak as an athlete when I was 16 or 17 years old.

I decided to go to Marshall University in Huntington as a walk-on. Like most walk-ons I didn't get much playing time. But I was in the gym, around other athletes, doing something I loved, so it wasn't all bad. Hal Greer was a senior when I was a freshman. He was a great player, one of the best I've ever been around. I remember playing touch football against his team. He played safety and would be the only guy in the secondary. I saw that and thought to myself, This is a piece of cake. But it wasn't; he was so strong and so quick that he covered the whole field by himself. Hal just dazzled me with his great talent. There was no way I could play against athletes like that.

I had the desire to play, but I quickly discovered that I wasn't good enough. So I became a socialite. That's when my dad said, "Get your little butt home, pal. I ain't paying any more money down there."

After two years at Marshall I moved back home and enrolled at Morris Harvey College, now the University of Charleston. It was a smart move. Living at home forced me to become a more dedicated student, and consequently I did much better academically. My grades at Morris Harvey were outstanding. I got a little playing time while I was there, but not much. Again, it was just a matter of the other players being better than me. Maybe I could have had a better career, but I wasn't all that dedicated to the game anymore. I'd joined a fraternity — Tau Kappa Epsilon — and was really into the college life. My social life became more important to me than my basketball life.

A few years ago I was elected to the University of Charleston Hall of Fame. They had a nice ceremony, a dinner . . . it was a tremendous honor for me. I told the people who were responsible that I had one restriction — they could never make my career statistics public. I didn't want everybody to see what a lousy player I was. That got a pretty good laugh.

Mostly, I was happy to be back in Charleston because I missed being separated from Sally. She attended West Virginia University for a year, then moved back to Charleston and went to business school. When I left Marshall and came back to go to Morris Harvey, we were back together again. I couldn't have been happier.

When she was at WVU and I was at Marshall, I went up to Morgantown one weekend and we got "pinned." That was big in those days. I gave her my fraternity pin, so from that time on we were semi-engaged.

I earned undergraduate degrees in speech and physical education from Morris Harvey in 1960. That was without question one of the proudest moments and greatest achievements in my life. Three of the best things that ever happen to you in life are getting married, having children and earning a college degree. It was doubly eventful for me because I was one of the first two members of our family to graduate from college. My cousin Phil, the same age as me, graduated from VMI that same year. It was just unheard of for someone in our family to get a college degree. That was a real milestone.

I have to give my father credit for the opportunity to go to college. Coming from a poor, non-English-speaking home, having grown up during the Great Depression, survival, not education, was foremost on his mind. Yet, when I had the chance to attend college, he was all in favor of it. Both my parents were very encouraging. Although my father had only an eighth-grade education, he knew how valuable a degree was. He may not have had much formal schooling, but he did possess a certain amount of wisdom. "Be the best you can be." He must have said that to me a thousand times when I was growing up.

During the spring of my senior year, when I started applying for jobs, Sally and I started talking about getting married. People tended to marry at a younger age in those days, much more so, I think, than kids do today. I know that of our three sons, one was 30 when he got married, another one is 30 now and not married, and our youngest is 26 and really not even close to getting married.

Sally wanted to get married in April, but I said no, let's wait until after I graduate. Once we made the decision to marry, I had to go see her father and ask his permission. Well, I didn't have to, I wanted to. I wanted everything to be just right. That was one of the scariest days of my life. I had to finally sit down and confront the man. I'd talked to him only four or five times through all the years I'd been going with Sally, and now I had to face him, man to man, and tell him our intentions. I asked him for his daughter's hand in marriage, just like in the movies. By now he knew it was out of his hands, that she was 21 and I was 22 and it was inevitable, so he said OK.

I could never have imagined it in my wildest dreams at the time, but Frank Marple ended up being one of my best friends. Really, our whole married life, he adopted me. And Grace was always very good to me, too. She's the only one of the four parents still alive today.

Frank had been a pretty fair basketball player himself when he was a young man. His high school, Sutton High, won the state championship back in the '20s. Somehow, the game ball got signed by President Calvin Coolidge. They kept it in the school trophy case for many years. When they closed the school, the ball ended up in the College Basketball Hall of Fame in Springfield, Mass. In 1991, when we played Indiana in the Tip-Off Classic in Springfield, I flew Frank and Grace up for the game. We went to the Hall of Fame, got that basketball and had our picture taken in front of the statue of Dr. James Naismith.

Frank passed away six weeks later.

When we won the NCAA championship, I thought about how sad it is that my parents and Frank Marple weren't there to share in one of the great moments in my life. I know they would all have been very proud. And certainly my parents, if they were still alive, would be sitting on top of the world. They'd have bragging rights in Charleston for a year.

As I was finishing college, I made 50 inquiries into business jobs and 50 into education. At no time during that process did the thought of coaching ever enter my mind. I graduated in May, then worked that summer for the Libby Owens Bottle Company. On August 20, 1960, Sally and I were married.

And that was the beginning of this wonderful life we've shared.

BRING YOUR ATTITUDE

5

The win over Kentucky was a springboard for the rest of December. We won our next four games to finish 1994 with a 6-0 record and a No. 2 national ranking. Still, it wasn't time for optimistic projections. At that stage, the only certainty was that a tough Pacific-10 Conference schedule awaited. Our team was far from emerging into what it ultimately would become. That wouldn't happen until about halfway through our league schedule. No surprise there. Chart the course of any team over a season and you'll see Charles Darwin's theory in action. The trick, of course, is not to devolve. Given the previous season, I'm sure plenty of people thought it would happen again.

Following Kentucky, we beat Cal-State Fullerton at home, 99-65. All through December, our starting lineup was Tyus and Cameron at guards, George at center, and the O'Bannons at the forward spots. Ironically enough, we didn't settle on Edney and Dollar together as starters in the backcourt until late in pre-season practice. When we put them in at the same time, things just flowed. We had incredible quickness in the backcourt defensively, and both were just whizzing the ball around, getting it to the open man. And that's why I decided to open the season with Cameron joining Tyus at guard.

LSU was the next real test. We'd beaten LSU by 20 at home the previous season, but that only gave me greater concern now that we had to meet them on their turf. They had Randy Livingston and Ronnie Henderson, and some real good inside players, not to mention 14,000 very raucous fans in the Deaf Dome. I told my team before we left for Baton Rouge: "Hey, Custer never knew what was coming, but I know what's coming." Turns out, I didn't. With Cameron and Tyus forcing 19 turnovers out of their guards, we just dominated, winning 94-72. But it was tight in the early minutes, which is when I found out something about Toby Bailey. I brought him off the bench and he hit three consecutive three-point jumpers to give us a nine-point lead. From there, it was a rout. And from that point on, I knew Toby Bailey was a basketball player. It would take more time to fully see that the bigger the game, the better he played, but to operate as he did in LSU's hostile environment was a telling moment.

Remember how Toby had moped after not figuring in the Kentucky game, only to have Ed get on him? After that, Mike Warren (his daughter was dating Toby) took him to Coach Wooden's house for a long talk. Coach told Toby that, although he didn't know when, he was certain that sometime during the season Toby would be needed. Well, here was the first example — though none of us could imagine just how huge a need he would fill in March.

Next was George Mason at home, and The Disease. That's what I call it, the kind of game that Paul Westphal gets you into. I'm sure you'll remember Paul's teams at Loyola Marymount, which would always score a jillion points to the opponents' zillion. I was coaching at Pepperdine when he had his great club with the late Hank Gathers and Bo Kimble, and we were in the same league. When Paul first came into the league, he played conventional basketball. But he began to develop "Paul Ball," which is pretty simple but can be pretty devastating. Put simply, it's putting the ball up as fast as you can, creating a game designed as much to infect the opponent with a kind of anarchy as it is to score a lot of points. When he had Gathers and Kimble, he wound up upsetting Michigan by something like 148-123, and Paul Ball began to catch on at some other schools. After a stint as a pro coach with the Denver Nuggets, Paul came back to the college ranks at George Mason. Playing against that style . . . well, The Disease is the proper name for it. It's contagious. It can take you out of everything you're trying to do as a basketball team. If you catch it, you're in danger of getting beat, even against lesser talent, because that's the way they play every time; but it's not your way. So you have to adjust your game a bit and try to control tempo, at least somewhat.

You try, but once we tipped it up against George Mason, my guys were suddenly getting every shot they'd ever wanted in their lives. We had all the symptoms, but fortunately we didn't suffer from them. We won, 137-100. Problem is, The Disease doesn't necessarily go away quickly. On December 28, when we played North Carolina State at home, we still had it, and we didn't play so well. We struggled, but won, 88-80. Not pretty, but it was a good game to get us ready for the league. Although we'd finished 1994 unbeaten, I wasn't overly excited. I remembered the 14-0 of a year ago, and what ultimately happened.

George Zidek's father came over from Czechoslovakia for Christmas. The North Carolina State game marked the first time he'd seen George play in a UCLA uniform, and it was nice to have George's dad around. He stayed through the New Year's holiday, then made the trip with us to Oregon.

Where a volcano named Mt. Not-So-St. Harrick was about to erupt.

January 5, 1995 — Eugene, Oregon: UCLA vs. Oregon
Well, here's another fine mess we've gotten ourselves into. Figures. They don't call this place The Pit for nothing. The place where Tyus Edney's back blew up last year. The place where we lost by a single point and lost the league title and went from there to . . . Tulsa time. The place where the fans are packed like sardines, yell like banshees and don't mind rubbing elbows — or maybe throwing a couple. All the hits Dick Enberg used to take while backed up against the fans, trying to

broadcast games from here when he was UCLA's announcer . . . he probably should have earned a letter sweater.

But that was then, and now is now, and it's frustrating out there. What were we up? Thirteen? Yep, 56-43 back when there was 14:44 to go. But we haven't been playing well since. They've killed us on the boards. The last time we blocked out on the offensive glass, I can't even recall. And now we're about to get beat. Down four with 45 seconds left. We need to make something happen. Soon.

And we do. Tyus comes streaking down, penetrates, pulls up and dishes to Ed for a layup. Great pass.

Still got a chance. If we can jus — Wait a minute! What's he calling?

What Steve Wilson, the official, is calling is walking. On Tyus. Before the pass. Before the shot by Ed that would have cut Oregon's lead to two. No basket. We're still down by four, and now only 37 seconds remain.

What in the world is he thinking? All game, the officiating's been great — and now this? Swell, just swell. The game's out of reach. An official takes the game out of the hands of the players. An official decides the game.

Rightly or wrongly, that's what's running through my mind as I stand and dispute the call. I do not think I'm complaining vigorously. My voice can boom, but Steve Wilson knows that, and it's hard to be heard above the crowd's roar without raising my voice. I've known Steve a long time. He does not let coaches affect him. I've watched him work for years. I've never seen him give a technical foul to anybody. Saw one coach follow him and call him every name in the book one time, but Steve didn't throw a technical. I keep complaining.

And hear his whistle go off. He's slapped a T on me. Wonderful. You know how you always seem to *not* get a speeding ticket when maybe you deserve one, but you get one when you don't think it's deserved? That's what this technical feels like.

Un-bleepin-be-lee-vuh-bul!

Steve walks toward the scorer's table to assess my penalty. I walk up that way to give him my assessment. At no time do I curse at him or try to show him up. I'm inside the coaching box. I'm not out of the box, but I am out of patience. I let Steve know what I think. He lets me know what he thinks: another tweet, another T. I'm outta here. Automatic ejection. Oregon gets four technical free throws. Orlando Williams makes 'em all. One of their players will get a technical himself for taunting at the end, but the game's long over. We lose 82-72. Their fans, mostly students, rush the floor, and several of my players say they were shoved or struck during the Oregon celebration. It is not the best of times.

And now it's time for the post-game media lovefest. Somebody asks me if I intentionally went after a technical. (*Are they kidding?*) "Heavens sakes, no!" I hear myself saying. "Gracious sakes, no!" But they won't stop. They keep asking me about the T's. Keep wanting to know if I meant to get thrown out. What do they want, a confession? They want me to confirm what they've already decided in their own minds? "The answer's no," I say. "How many times are you going to ask me? Next question."

And so it goes. We are no longer unbeaten. And I am once again under the media gun.

*   *   *

"HARRICK: ALWAYS A QUESTION" is the headline in a follow-up story in the *Los Angeles Times*. It is ostensibly a news report, but it has as much commentary as it does reportage. For instance: "Ask this question: If Harrick didn't know he was about to draw two loss-clinching technical fouls, is that another indication of a man who sometimes gets lost in the habitual chaos of pressure-cooker basketball? Another question: Is his team's disjointed performance down the stretch . . . and in other high-profile powder kegs of the recent past — at least in part reflective of its coach?"

Well, it was beginning to look like another season of serious scrutiny. I don't know, getting thrown out of a game is not what I'm about, but I honestly did not think Steve Wilson was going to react the way he did. I had no verbal warning before the first technical. Once it was called, whether you think we were out of the game or not beforehand, we were definitely out of it then. The second one only made things embarrassing. But I can take criticism from just about everybody — except Sally. She's harder on me than anybody with a word processor. She talked to me, and so did Pete Dalis. I expected that. I was out of line. You don't want to let those things happen. But getting a technical at UCLA seems to generate a lot more heat than I see happen to coaches at other places. Maybe that's because Coach Wooden never got any. And maybe that's not such a bad tradition. But I felt the resulting attention and inferences made about me were out of proportion. Suddenly, I was a coach whose ability was suspect again. It's always somethin'.

Our next game was at Oregon State, and never let it be said that God doesn't like to test you. In this game — all in succession — we get three of the worst calls I think we've ever had. Boom, boom and boom again. Now what do I do? My hands are tied. I've got handcuffs on and my tongue's tied, too. Oh my heavens, I was wanting to at least get an opinion in. But I didn't. I said, well, if it happens, it happens; if we get beat, we get beat. I'm not going to say a word.

As it turns out, we play a pretty good game, rallying from a 41-35 halftime deficit to win, 87-78. Particularly noteworthy: I started J.R. Henderson, and he would remain a starter for 13 consecutive games. We just hadn't been getting much offensive production from Edney and Dollar as a guard tandem. And we'd also gotten pounded badly on the boards at Oregon. Oregon had shot only 37 percent, but had out-rebounded us 45-37, and absolutely whipped us, 25-10, on the offensive glass. At 6-9, I figured J.R. would help us immeasurably from that standpoint. Against Oregon State, J.R. played 35 minutes and responded with 16 points, six rebounds, three assists and three steals. And we owned the boards, 34-22.

That got us back to Los Angeles, where we had Washington and Washington State next. We beat Washington 75-57, but I was noticing a disturbing trend. We had trailed Washington something like 20-12 and were sloppy throughout the first half, which ended with us ahead only 28-25. We'd also played some pretty tough teams (Oregon's record was 9-1 after beating us) and we'd not been nearly as emotional as I felt we should have been. Consequently, I got on my players the day after Washington. And the next day against Washington State, they responded. In defense of Washington State, they were playing without two starters who had broken curfew. But my team was cranking it up to a higher level. We came out and annihilated them. We were up 30 at one point and won, 91-78. Tyus, who had never dunked in a game his entire career, did it in this one. It was kind of a coming-out for him. And for our team.

*   *   *

It was during this period that I had a long talk with Charles O'Bannon. I'd been sitting him during key stretches of some games. Finally, he comes into my office and says, "Hey, Coach, what's up? I'm on the bench in crunch time." And that's when I told him. I said he was doing nine or 10 things really well for this team, but there were three things that were hurting us. I put on some videotape, and then I pulled out the stats chart. In particular, I pointed out how many threes he was taking and how few he was making. I wanted him to bring his game in closer to the basket, instead of being way out, beyond his range. We sat down, and I pointed out all the things he was doing well. Then I pointed out the things he wasn't doing so well. "What am I supposed to do, Charles?" I said. "I can't let you continue to hurt this basketball team. You've got to eliminate these three things. Hey, just bring your game in a little bit. Let's do what we can do. Then, next summer, we'll work on the things we're not good at yet."

Well, he just blossomed after that. Charles had hit only two of 14 threes in his first nine games, was four-of-23 through his first 20. But over our last 22 games, Charles attempted more than one three-pointer in a game only once — and he tried only two on that occasion. To come into full blossom takes some time, and it would in this case, but almost from the get-go after our talk, Charles' willingness to corral his game began to bring results and help develop our team. To his credit, Charles bought into my argument. He just got better and better and better — because he'd listened. A lot of guys don't. A lot of them go home and listen to their dad or to their summer league coach who tells them to shoot, shoot, shoot, because, the argument goes, you've got to score to get into the NBA. Well, I knew that wouldn't be the message coming out of the O'Bannon household. But the credit goes to Charles. He would develop into a force in all areas of his game. He would be terrific, the last third of the season in particular, hitting around 55 percent from the floor, rebounding, passing well and defending extremely well.

The talk didn't come a minute too soon. We were 9-1, but we were about to head for the Arizona desert — where our greatest challenges to date awaited. Arizona had won 112 of its last 115 games at home. They'd beaten us by 19 and 24 there the last two seasons. Meanwhile, at Arizona State, Bill Frieder had his best-yet team since coming to the school in 1989. Led by Mario Bennett, Arizona State was ranked among the top 15 teams in the nation, and they'd be sky-high for us. They'd never beaten us in 11 games with Frieder as their coach, and they knew this would be their best shot.

All that was on my mind when I talked to my team.

                    *   *   *

January 18, 1995 — The locker room in Pauley Pavilion after the last practice before the Arizona trip.

"Fellas, it's time to develop an attitude. I'm not going down there to Arizona to get beat. I'm not taking you guys down there and see you get your living brains beat out of you. We're going down there to compete. If you're going to compete, come on. If you're not, then just don't go. Don't get on the bus for the airport. Don't get on the plane to go to Arizona if you're not going down there to compete. I don't care about winning and losing. That's not the point. I'm going into McKale Center to compete. Bring your attitude! Bring your attitude if you're going to go with me."

Take no prisoners. That was the attitude I wanted, and that was the way we played. We beat Arizona 71-61, the worst Pac-10 home defeat they'd had during Lute Olson's tenure at Arizona — and just about the worst ever. Lute had lost a home game by 12, to Tennessee, but that was in his first season at Arizona, in 1983.

Several major developments came out of this game. For one, Tyus Edney showed once and for all that he belonged in the same upper echelon as Arizona's Damon Stoudamire, whose career had generated more attention. Not only in the same echelon, but maybe ahead of Stoudamire on a given night. Don't get me wrong. I think Damon is terrific. I had the pleasure of coaching him as an assistant for the USA team in the World University Games, and I fell in love with him as a player. He's a tremendous guy. I nicknamed him "Nails," after Lenny Dykstra of the Philadelphia Phillies, because he's so tough and hard-nosed. I never knew the guy to be hurt or injured, and he was just so quick with the ball. But I also believe Tyus Edney had had to play in the shadow of Damon Stoudamire, and unfairly so. I also knew how Tyus responded to challenges. Well, in this game, Edney was unbelievable. First play, Tyus gets the ball, goes into the corner, beats Damon on a baseline drive and scores. They miss, Tyus takes Damon one-on-one to the basket and scores again. We're up 4-0 and we go up 9-2. I rested Tyus and some others late in the first half until, finally, Lute took Stoudamire out with three or four minutes to go. I put Tyus and the others back in and we go on an 8-0 run for a 35-26 halftime lead. They would come back, but they could never catch us.

In the end, Tyus had 19 points, nine rebounds and five assists. He also did a super job on Stoudamire defensively, holding him to 6-of-21 shooting and a telling 1-of-12 from three-point range. The game was on ESPN, and all through it Dick Vitale had been extolling the virtues of Damon Stoudamire, in a manner only Dick can do, but he finally realized that the story here was Tyus Edney. He just controlled the game. Afterward, Ed

O'Bannon — who had 21 points and 11 rebounds — was called over along with Tyus for an oncourt TV interview. But the TV guys said there was time for only one of them. "Hey, take Tyus Edney," Ed said. "He's the star of this game." Just another example of Ed developing into a special leader. He was really setting the tone for this team.

There were other significant aspects to the win. Namely, Toby Bailey. He'd had that great game at LSU, but really hadn't done much since. Against Arizona, however, Toby came off the bench and just went wild above the rim, grabbing 12 rebounds, five on the offensive boards. He also scored nine points, and scored them at crucial times. Every time we needed a big bucket, Toby got it. He also had a big steal that he took all the way downcourt for a layup. On the road, in the conference, in a huge game. He'd done well at LSU, but Dale Brown's team had proven not to be a top-20 club. But here Toby was, just dazzling in the desert, and it was no mirage.

We were drained, emotionally and physically, after that win. We went on to Arizona State and I figure, well, if ever there's a time we're going to lose, this is it. This was the best Arizona State team I'd seen since I'd been at UCLA. Maybe we'd spent ourselves against Arizona. We'd brought our attitude, all right, but had we used it all up?

Not at all. We beat Arizona State, 85-72, opening the second half with a 14-2 run to break a 42-42 halftime deadlock. Again, Toby was great off the bench. He scored 19 points, had six rebounds, and notched two assists and two steals. But the biggest development involved J.R. Henderson. He'd been playing well all along as a starter, but circumstances made me make a change with J.R. that brought exciting results.

Keep in mind that I'd installed a 1-2-2 offensive set for this club — Tyus at the point, Charles and J.R. on the wings, Ed and George Zidek inside. Now, you're not doing bad when you can have a 6-9 player like J.R. able to play outside (and, like Toby, can even play point guard in a pinch). Against Arizona State I found out something else. But let me set up what happened to bring it about. Early on, we fell behind by 11 points. Ed and Tyus looked like zombies. I took them out. And the game is so fast-paced that George Zidek gets in foul trouble. I need a big man to spell him. I put in Ike Nwankwo, who's 6-11, and he did OK, but he gets his mouth busted and has to come out. So now what do I do? I decide to go with a freshman, omm'A Givens, who's 6-10, but Mario Bennett takes him for a couple of dunks. And now it's decision-making time for Jim Harrick.

I decide to move J.R. from one of the wings to one of the two inside spots. I decide to let him try George's post position. Well, he had a marvelous game, 12 points and eight rebounds. He'd played inside in high school, but we'd always used him on the perimeter. He'd never much practiced with us from an inside position. Oh, he did a little. I'd told him to learn it and know what we wanted to do from that spot, but he'd spent very little time working on it. It's a credit to J.R. that he could step in and master it in the heat of battle. Let me tell you, J.R. Henderson just has a great understanding of this game. And what I learned from moving him inside was that, as brilliant as he could be on the perimeter, he was the best inside big man we had.

A major missing piece to the puzzle of this team fell into place. I learned right then and there that, my lands, this guy, he could do it from anywhere. He took Mario Bennett out to a wing and he just waved everybody off, faked left, drove right and took Mario inside for a layup. He could post up, too. Suddenly I had a much more versatile team. I realized that if I'm going to have to substitute for George — and George's effectiveness could vary depending on the pace of the game — I'd put J.R. in there for him. Combining his performance with how Toby was starting to excel, it was the first inkling that this team might evolve into having J.R. as a sixth man — with George and Ed up front but J.R. the first sub for either of them. From off the bench or just switching J.R. from the wing to inside if I needed to, the option settled us into a basketball team, right then and there. He could rebound and was a great defender. And his quickness made us quick everywhere on the court if I put him in for George. It gave us a much greater dimension.

Meantime, Charles O'Bannon had probably the best game of his career to date against Arizona State. Just solid in all phases with 23 points, 11 rebounds, two assists and one blocked shot. Things were really starting to jell. We went back home, checked the tape, and I saw a team that was unbelievably quick with J.R. inside and either Toby or Cameron out on the wing. With that lineup, we had five guys who could all handle the ball, pass, dribble, shoot, take their man one-on-one and . . . whoa! Did I ever like what I saw! We watched that tape, and it was just obvious. And we still could exploit slower teams inside by calling on George. We had Cameron and Toby off the bench, and J.R. a highly movable chess piece. We had a whole lot of options, and all of them looked good.

It was a huge leap in possibilities — and, yes, part of it was the result of luck. Circumstances had forced me to try J.R. down low. I ran out of guys and finally put him down there. And when I did, I saw a light go on with this team. It was so obvious. I mean, I've been coaching a hundred years, and things like that stand out like a sore thumb. When we looked at the tape, one of my assistants said, "Wow! Look at this team." The light was on, all right. Down the stretch of the season, we often would go 20 minutes with Zidek and 20 with Henderson. It would depend on just a feel for whatever the team needed. And having a feel for things is crucial to a coach. With J.R., I'd had a feeling building that I might want to try him down low. Basketball is in many respects a feeling game. You go into the game, you've got to make me have a good feeling about you, on an instinctive level. If I don't, you're going to come out. Sometimes I take guys out and they ask why, and I have to tell them, "Well, I don't really have an answer for you." It's just a feeling. Granted, it was mostly circumstance at Arizona State that finally prompted me to act on the hunch about J.R. As I learned from Tommy Lasorda: You change pitchers and if he strikes the guy out, you're a hero. If the guy hits a home run, you're a bum. A lot of it is intuition, the choice you make. You make a lot of decisions in a game. And sometimes you do it on feeling. That's how it is. All your experience through the years and your observations in the thick of the action help that feeling arise, I think, but often it just comes down to what you trust in your gut. With J.R., the end result was huge.

We'd survived the desert — and learned volumes in the process — and then came home to survive Stanford. We had 'em down 14 at the half, but got in trouble after that. We trailed 74-73 after Dion Cross nailed us for a three-pointer with 1:07 to go. But George retaliated with a great play. He missed a hook shot, but fought for the rebound and was fouled going back up. He hit a pair of free throws at 0:32 to put us back up by one. And then Cameron Dollar, quick as ever, drew a charging foul to get us the ball back, and Tyus hit a couple of free throws over the final 24 seconds and we won, 77-74. George figuring prominently was another example of our versatility. With Stanford a somewhat slower team, we called on George and he responded with 17 points, second to Ed's 23.

We were 12-1 and still ranked second in the nation. After the Arizona trip, the media was suddenly tossing roses our way. "ANY CRITICISM OF UCLA AND HARRICK NOW IS FOR THE BIRDS," one headline said. "HARRICK'S BRUINS WOR-THY OF SUPPORT," read another. But I knew that I was only one gaffe, or misstatement, or whatever, away from getting drowned in ink again. The criticism after the technicals at Oregon was still fresh in my mind. I knew this was an up-and-down relationship with my critics, and the downside could get overblown if not downright brutal. After all, I'd been at UCLA for seven years. I'd seen plenty of that.

*   *   *

When I took the job at UCLA, I sat down with Sally for a talk. I'd seen what had happened in the 13 years since Coach Wooden left, seen Gene Bartow hanged in effigy and Larry Farmer leave in frustration. I'd seen Walt Hazzard and the an-tagonistic relationship he had with the media erupt into storm after messy storm. I'd seen all this and more. I knew I was step-ping into a pressure-cooker where the only remaining UCLA tradition seemed to be this self-defeating attitude of "Well, here's another one who'll be here a couple of years and out." You wondered if maybe they should have taken the championship banners down and hung revolving doors in their place. Seeing how most people considered me a consolation prize at best and a booby prize at worst, I knew the darts might start flying early. I also knew that, despite my having been so close to the program and having lived in L.A. so long, and despite having talked with Coach Wooden about the UCLA job, I could never fully realize its demands until I actually sat in that seat. And now I was about to. All of that was on my mind when I talked to my wife.

I told Sally this: "Whatever happens at UCLA, I will be a better man for it. And we'll go on and survive."

My objective for the school was to bring consistency and continuity. But I'd be doing it, according to many observers, at a place that seemed desperate for the quick fix, trying to recapture the glory of the past in an instant. That was reflected in the cattle-call search for a big-name coach, or so the commentators — editor/publisher Larry Donald of *Basketball Times* in particular — suggested. True or not, it was certainly something for me to be aware of. My personal objective was to stay at UCLA the rest of my working life. My philosophy was that if it didn't happen, I'd still be a better man. I would have learned from it. I guess it says something that even from the start, I had that kind of speech rehearsed in my head if the ax found me like it had so many others.

If it came down to it, I'd always be able to go back to high school. I'd never had a blemish on my teaching or coaching record in any way, shape or form. From that, you can never give anybody a reason not to hire you. So I could always get a job doing something.

If that sounds a little far-fetched for somebody just named the head man at UCLA, well, maybe you forget the post-Wooden history of UCLA, and maybe you forget where I came from. I sure hadn't. It had been a long, hard climb up the ladder. There's a saying back among the West Virginia and Eastern Kentucky hills: "Don't get above your raisin'." Well, I'd never done that. I knew who I was, and I was proud of it. I'd earned this shot, and I would earn a living somewhere else if it didn't work out. It's funny. One of the writers criticizing me after Tulsa was attacking every point people had used in my defense. To the idea that nobody understood the pressure I was under at UCLA, he wrote: "Maybe nobody cares. Pressure is trying to feed a family of five on a $20,000-a-year salary." Well, I'm sure the writer didn't appreciate the irony, but I did. I'd had a family of five and spent years making it on twelve-five a year. You come up that way, you don't forget.

The heat never got to scorch-level during my first four years at UCLA. There seemed to be a recognition that the program was pretty much out of shape and the talent pool was relatively shallow. After our team got into the NCAA Tournament in my first season, I think people were more willing to listen to my constant preaching of continuity and consistency.

Still, taking on the job was quite a change.

The most overwhelming aspect was the incredible number of people wanting a piece of my time. I had people wanting to pull me in all different directions, and that took some getting used to — knowing when to say yes and when to say no. The media crush alone could be awesome, but I'd known many of the writers in the area over the years, so that was helpful. But there were eyebrow-raisers from time to time — things that said "Welcome to UCLA" in the same way a 260-pound linebacker smashes you in the mouth to say "Welcome to the NFL." In my second year, we lost five games in a row in the Pac-10, including home losses to Cal and Stanford, the first time either had ever beaten us in Pauley. It was a dramatic and traumatic time. But I learned something. We wound up making the tournament and beat Kansas and then played a great game before falling to Duke in the Sweet Sixteen, and people were happy. They'd basically forgotten about the string of losses. It hammered home the fact that, as upset as people might get in the regular season, it's March that counts. December through February, they don't much recall.

Even though my first four years at UCLA were relatively free of controversy and criticism, I think I was often trying to be somebody other than myself. It was a new experience, and something I obviously wanted to get right. That can make you ignore your own instincts, maybe trying to please everybody, being all things to all people in a job where that's just not possible — as if it is in any situation. As a result, I think I was tentative in some cases. At any rate, the general atmosphere of constant expectation was one reason I made a point not to read or listen to a lot of things. (What I've always wanted to tell somebody who really gets on my case is, well, if you feel that strongly about it, you ought to go out and get your own team — see what it's like.) I made a vow that I wasn't going to let the peripheral stuff beat me, because I felt it beat the other five guys. I wasn't going to let the media take me out of my focus, which is coaching and recruiting. Those are the meat and potatoes of any program. Anything else is superfluous. And that includes speaking to groups, doing clinics, running summer camps, listening to talk radio, reading newspapers, watching TV reports. If something was going to get me, it was going to be based on my coaching and recruiting.

In some ways, I was fortunate to take over when I did, because the expectations were tempered by the reality of the last few years. Entering my first season (1988-89), UCLA had been to the NCAA Tournament only twice in the previous seven years. And, thanks to some injuries — including an accident when Gerald Madkins was hit by a car while driving a motor scooter, forcing him out for the season — I wound up with only seven scholarship players I could use. Consequently, people were more willing to listen. My stated goal of having UCLA capable of being among the final 16 in the NCAA Tournament on a regular basis — with the idea that, from time to time, we'd have good shots at going farther — seemed to be accepted. (Expectations might have been tempered, but some newspapers were already in the bullpen warming up. Said one headline: "BRUINS SETTLE ON PEPPERDINE COACH.")

I wanted a well-rounded, solid program, and that included contacting former players who hadn't gotten their college degrees. It was important to me to re-establish a family feeling at UCLA. My teaching background also made me want to do it. I didn't make any big deal out of it. I was grateful, however, when Mark Gottfried, in an interview with the *Daily Bruin* in January of '95, pointed it out. "Most people . . . don't know that when Jim got the job at UCLA, he went back and convinced 14 guys, who didn't play for him, to come back and try to get their degrees — and nine of them did," Mark said. It was nice of him to point it out, and I've always felt a sense of satisfaction that those guys got their degrees.

When I looked at the 1988-89 squad for the first time, it was a bit of a shock. Right after the press conference when I was named coach in the spring of '88, I met with the players. And I'm looking at this outfit and I've got seven guys looking back, and I'm saying, holy mackerel, holy Toledo, no way we can win. Then I hit the recruiting trail.

Don MacLean was my top priority. I'd had a good relationship with Don, knowing him from my Pepperdine days. He'd visited the school on an unofficial basis as a favor to me. Not that I thought I could get him. But, you know, maybe a standout goes to a school and doesn't like it and wants to come home. Maybe then a Pepperdine has a shot. Just about every major school in the nation wanted him. I think Don's high school coach told me that Georgia Tech must have made 33 trips or so out to L.A. to see him. Can you imagine that? I knew Bobby Cremins, and he'd come by Pepperdine to visit me on some of his trips. Bobby kept telling me, "Jim, he's not going to UCLA." And I said, "Well, you know, that's fine." But suddenly I'm the coach at UCLA, and I'd kept that relationship open with Don over the years, and he chooses us.

In the papers, someone asked him if he'd been considering UCLA before Walt was fired. "It's hard to say," Don told the reporter. "I didn't really like the way the players were reacting to the leadership of Hazzard. There was a lot of dissension. That's not what I wanted to step into. I wanted to step into something positive, and Coach Harrick made it positive." Darrick Martin, meanwhile, had committed to UCLA but said he was going to go somewhere else after Walt was fired. Perfectly understandable. But by Memorial Day, we'd finally convinced him to still come.

Trevor Wilson had been rumored to be transferring. Thank God he chose to stay. Wilson, Pooh Richardson and Kevin Walker were the only ones with a lot of talent from the group I inherited. Wilson was absolutely terrific. He was only about a 50 percent free throw shooter, but I love him like anything because he had a big heart and he played his heart out. He was a big reason for our success that first season. But I guess I had special admiration for Pooh Richardson.

The previous year, I was one of the trials coaches during selection for the U.S. team in the Pan-American Games — the team that Denny Crum would coach — and I got the chance to meet Pooh. We kind of hit it off. We'd fly back to L.A. together and I'd drive him to his dorm and things once the trials were over. On the day I was named coach, I had my press conference at 11 a.m. and went to see the team at 1 p.m. I met them and said: "I'm going to be your coach, and I want to meet with each one of you and we'll talk about some things. And I hope you give me your complete dedication and desire . . ." and I don't remember the rest. Anyway, after the meeting, Pooh Richardson grabbed me and said, "Come here." He took me around the corner and into my office and shut the door. Then he hugged me and started crying. "I'm so happy for you," he said, "and I know we're going to do well." I was moved by what Pooh said, but I was also stunned. His emotional reaction gave me an idea of the kind of pressure and difficulty some of these players had been feeling.

The months flew by, and it was time for my first practice as UCLA coach. I couldn't believe it. Guys were gasping and struggling to keep up. One guy goes over and hyperventilates and another was throwing up in a trash can. And this practice wasn't anything I hadn't done in high school or college. We'd just had what I call a John Wooden practice, and I'd finished it with a few sprints.

But Pooh was right there, leading the way. He was something. Every time we had a team meal, Richardson would eat with the coaches. And we'd sit and talk all the time, just how you want a coach-point guard relationship to go. He'd want to know what was going through our minds in relation to what we'd been doing as coaches. We'd have a rough practice and Pooh would say: "Coach, I couldn't believe that. That was the greatest practice I've ever had in my life last night."

You always know the difference between guys who mean it and guys who are just trying to get on your good side. With Pooh, the difference was obvious. I called him a hardballer. Never got hurt, never missed practice. We'd practice two hours, four hours, six hours, and he'd just keep giving us more. Pooh was never a guy to put his hands on his shorts and bend over. He'd just look you right in the eye and say, "Let's go." One time I ran him in 4-17s, which means running from one side of the floor to the other 17 times in a minute. I ran him four straight times, and he'd never bend over. He'd just give me that look: "Gimme some more. Whatever you want. You want to practice at midnight? Four a.m.? Noon? Let's go." I tell you, he just busted it. And he had a great year. At one time in February he led the nation in three-point shooting, and he spoon-fed MacLean and Wilson to the point where he was making the game easy for them.

I learned a lesson early in that first season. I remember going to North Carolina and getting hammered, 104-78. Being the poor sport that I am, in the post-game press conference I make the comment, with sarcasm dripping: "Well, you know, Dean Smith . . . he's got 12 All-Americans on *his* team." Never mind that Dean had been a friend and had actually spoken for me when I campaigned for the UCLA job. I'd just gotten my brains beat out and I wasn't feeling very good about it, so I made a ridiculous comment. Later, somone said, "Dean heard that and just looked at you like, 'What are you talking about, why would you *say* something like that?' "

Over the years, I've learned that that's the whole idea, pal. You darn well better have you some players on your team or you're going to get clobbered. I learned right then and there. I asked Coach Wooden about it and he said, "You'll never have enough good players. Don't ever worry about over-recruiting." I've since apologized to Dean. Told him what a stupid, inexperienced thing it was to make a statement like that. You'd *better* go seven, eight, nine deep because if somebody leaves early or somebody gets hurt, you'll have enough to cover your bases. Because nobody cares what you did last year. As time went by at UCLA, I'd learn that more and more.

One thing I found out about my first players: They were cocky without being confident — whereas I want players who are confident without being cocky. They just had no self-esteem. They certainly hadn't accomplished anything to be cocky about, so I think it was a front. We began to work on correcting that. With Pooh leading the way and the incoming freshmen contributing, we won our first three games. We would finish with a 21-10 record. More significantly, we beat Iowa State in the first round of the NCAAs and then met none other than North Carolina again. This time, we actually led by eight. And we were in it until the end, losing 88-81. Carolina would go on to the Southeast Regional semifinals, losing a tight one to Michigan, which was on its magical mystery run to an NCAA championship under Steve Fisher, who'd taken over the team just before the tournament started when Bo Schembechler fired Bill Frieder. Bill had announced he would leave for Arizona State after the tournament. Bo, angry as all get-out, basically told him he could enjoy the desert a little earlier than scheduled.

Anyway, Ron Rapoport, a columnist with the L.A. *Daily News,* wrote after our near-miss against Carolina: "Give Jim Harrick a little bit here and a little bit there, and it is possible that nobody would today be talking about Steve Fisher." I thought that was overstating the case, probably by a large margin, but what couldn't be overstated was the significance of how my guys had played. After losing to Carolina by 28 earlier, we'd actually led them, and come close to winning. On the plane ride back to L.A., all I saw on my players' faces were smiles and a sense of pride. We hadn't won, but we'd accomplished something. I think we'd turned the corner in establishing a sense of real confidence, a feeling that UCLA basketball was going places. We'd played our guts out.

I was very pleased with that first team. In an article in *Sport* magazine, one unidentified player said of me: "Coach came off a little like a policeman at first. Or like a drill instructor.

As it turned out, he is extremely demanding, but in a fair way. No favorites, no teacher's pet driving his car. And you know what? Underneath, he's also a great guy." As long as they feel that way, I'm doing the right thing.

And what of Pooh? In pre-season magazines, they'd rated him maybe 33rd among point guards. He wound up the 10th player taken in the NBA draft. I think he'd tell you that his senior year was one of the most gratifying of his life. I think it helped make him what he is today, a guy with a $2.7 million contract over seven years. Pooh still comes back, still sees our games. And he donated $100,000 to our basketball program. Does anyone not understand why I have a great love affair with Pooh Richardson?

There were a couple of things I couldn't do as a coach those first couple of years. We didn't have much depth. Consequently, it was not easy to bench what talent I had, even when I felt they needed benching. A guy like Trevor Wilson, so high-spirited and effective, was terrific, but there were times he needed to sit on the bench to learn a lesson. He wanted the ball, and he'd let his teammates know it. I've always wanted our best player to have the ball, but when you scream for it and I give it to you, you'd better be productive. I really loved Trevor. His aura of competitive greatness was beyond almost anybody I've ever had. But he went overboard sometimes. Well, I had a choice to make. With no real backups, either I can bench him and run the risk of going 12-17, or I can play him and take a little bit of the things I don't like, and go 21-10. I decided to go 21-10. From that, I think, some people perceived that I wasn't much of a disciplinarian. I prefer to think I was a realist, even if I didn't like the situation.

The 1989-90 season did little to change my sense of growing optimism. We had those losses to Cal and Stanford in Pauley, but we finished with a 22-11 record. And we got all the way to the Sweet Sixteen in the tournament, beating Alabama-Birmingham and upsetting Kansas 71-70 before a hard-fought loss to Duke, 90-81. Still, I knew the expectations would grow. I told one writer: "If we don't get a Pac-10 title or a visit to the Final Four by the 1992 season, at the outside, then people will be gunning for me."

Sometimes you just hate to be right. Sure enough, in my third season, '90-91, the bloom was starting to fade. That's when Ed O'Bannon wrecked his knee in the pre-season, and even though we went 23-9, we were upset by 13th-seeded Penn State, 74-69, in the first round of the NCAAs. One columnist wrote: "When it came time to find a new coach, they didn't go to Indiana or Arizona. They went to Pepperdine." Guilty as charged. Another writer said: "No, it is not time for fans to start calling for Harrick's head . . . Let's bring Harrick to trial next season." Resting up for the big push, I guess. But all in all, there was not a great outpouring of catcalls. Not yet, anyway.

It was in the 1991-92 season, the senior campaign for MacLean, that the heat was really turned up. It didn't start out that way. We played Indiana in the Tip-Off Classic in Springfield, Massachusetts, to open the season, and we won convincingly, 87-72. I had the best depth I'd ever had, and the most experience. If there was a fault to this team, it was that we didn't have a true big man in the post. But it was a very good team. We finished the regular season with a 25-4 record and our first Pac-10 championship. We became the first UCLA team to rate a No. 1 regional seed in the NCAA Tournament since 1979 (I know, because that's when I was an assistant), and we advanced to the Elite Eight, facing none other than Indiana in the West Regional title game. Which is when somebody pulled the plug. Indiana just totally handled us. It was bad. The final score: 106-79, a 42-point swing from the start of the season when we'd beat them by 15. Our final record was 28-5.

And the big, bad ball of criticism was suddenly rolling in earnest.

I have to say that it wasn't just the magnitude of the loss, or the setting in which it occurred. Earlier that year I'd made maybe the biggest mistake of my career. It had started innocently enough, but it set me up for the criticism that would erupt in the wake of the Indiana loss. It happened in early February. I granted an interview with Ron Rapoport, the *Daily News* columnist and a guy I'd rarely talked to. In fact, I've probably seen him three times in the seven years I've been here. Well, we're in a room and the conversation is rambling here and there. And in responding to some questions, I let it out that I was frustrated because my contract had not yet been extended, and I'd not gotten a raise in my time at UCLA.

Next day, on February 5, 1992, the headline read: "HARRICK WANTS TO BE PAID LIKE A WINNER — COACH WONDERS ABOUT UCLA'S PLANS FOR FUTURE." The column took this tack: that Larry Brown, who was about to take the coaching job with the L.A. Clippers, would be in the right spot to return to UCLA "if Jim Harrick quits in a dispute over his salary."

Oh, Lord.

Rapoport quoted me as saying: "My only reservation is about money. The position I don't want to be in is for someone to make me an offer I can't refuse. Money is not the most important factor, but it sure is second." Well, yes, but I thought I was making it clear that I didn't want to leave UCLA, that only if a huge offer came might I be tempted to do so. And yes, I thought I deserved a raise.

I also said: "I need to know the philosophy here. Don't you think they have some responsibility to step up? They sure think about firing you when you don't do well." I had only two years left on my contract, and that's why I'd wondered when the administration was going to meet to talk.

I also noted the difference in the offer they'd made Larry Brown compared to what they'd offered me back in 1988. But in making my point that my performance justified a reward given what they'd wanted to pay Brown, I uttered words that would haunt me. "I've beaten Bobby Knight, Lute Olson and Denny Crum this year," I said. "You want me to beat these guys? Of course you do. But you don't want to pay me what these guys are getting."

Well, to talk off the cuff and get your frustrations out is one thing. To do it with a writer is quite another. And to see it in the cold light of black-and-white print gave it a momentum that I still shudder to think about. But I have to say, it was my fault. It had been a rambling conversation, the guy led me down the path, and I just jumped on it like a kangaroo. *Dumb and Dumber,* the original version.

The immediate reaction was predictable. Like: "JIM HARRICK HASN'T EARNED THE RIGHT TO WHINE" or "LET'S PASS THE HAT FOR BRUINS' COACH." One writer, tongue planted firmly in cheek (or was it wagging as it gave me the raspberries?), suggested everybody send me a dollar, in care of the Jim Harrick Relief Fund. You get the idea. Worse, of course, was that the administration was offended. I can understand that. They asked Pete Dalis for a comment, and he said he was somewhat disturbed by my comments. And that he'd told me if I could find a better-paying job, UCLA wouldn't stand in the way. The only thing I wanted right then was a hole to crawl into.

Actually, things died down rather quickly, but when we lost to Indiana, everybody was talking about the contract thing again. Even Bobby Knight made a sarcastic mention of comparative salaries after he beat us. The magnitude of the loss was big enough to cause a tidal wave of criticism, and my contract comments six weeks earlier just multiplied their intensity. At season's end, I was having to deny rumors that I was considering the Villanova job. Bill Walton was questioning the toughness of my team, and my own toughness. And in the fall of 1992, when I entered the next-to-last season of my original contract with no word on an extension, we didn't land a single recruit in the early signing period.

It was not until a little more than a year after that original, explosive column that Rapoport came out with an explanation of what had gone down. On February 22, 1993, he wrote: "As the guy who helped get Jim Harrick into all this trouble in the first place, I want to say enough is enough." He went on to write about how he'd known the Clippers were getting ready to hire Larry Brown, and wanted to ask me how I felt about Brown coming back to L.A. And how I'd said that, sure, I'd been lucky that Brown turned down the UCLA job in 1988. And he said how the conversation had turned to this and that, and then I had said I felt unappreciated at UCLA. And how that was the genesis of that Bobby Knight-Lute Olson-Denny Crum quote. And how all hell broke loose after the Indiana loss. "It has become The Quote That Wouldn't Die," he wrote. "To Harrick's credit . . . he never complained. He didn't say he had been misquoted, he didn't say our conversation had been off the record, and he didn't stop being honest and cordial with the press . . . In the flush of victory he made an unfortunate remark, one that had made him an easy target for ridicule when things turned sour . . . I would like to make a modest proposal. We retire The Quote That Wouldn't Die once and for all."

Good idea. But its aftermath nearly killed me. I'd lost four starters entering the 1992-93 season, hadn't gotten any recruits by the early signing date, and still hadn't heard anything about my contract. In *Basketball Times*, Larry Donald wrote: "On the same day Mitchell Butler's driving layup delivered UCLA an upset win over Florida State in the Preseason NIT, a columnist in the *Los Angeles Times* was suggesting athletic life in that city would be more pleasant if Larry Brown was the Bruins coach." Donald added that there was "what seems to be a bubbling undercurrent of discontent with the four-year coaching performance of Jim Harrick, a development I find rather astonishing even given the consideration that we're speaking about UCLA basketball."

Donald also wrote that "neighboring USC got so excited about George Raveling's two winning seasons in six, they decorated his life with a new and lucrative long-term contract last spring. It would be rather difficult to blame Harrick for feeling a bit underappreciated these days." He suggested that when coaches like Dean Smith, Denny Crum and Eddie Sutton said no to the UCLA job over the years, "they weren't running from the Wooden legacy . . . [they] simply couldn't afford the cut in salary or the cost of living in Los Angeles." He finished by saying that "it would be both telling and unfortunate if [UCLA's administration] didn't step forward and reward Harrick for the stability he's brought back to UCLA . . . He's done exactly what he promised to do."

Of course, by then I was in a corner that I only wanted to get out of — a corner I'd helped paint myself into. Besides, there was a team to coach, and that's where my focus stayed. But there were distractions. "PRESSURE COOKER TURNING TO 100." That's what one headline said in early December. And it had. In our second game of the season, we jumped out on Texas-El Paso but Don Haskins, the old fox, just pulled in the reins and took control of the game, changing its tempo. We fell behind, and our fans started booing us. It was not a pretty sight, and we had to make a late comeback to win, 72-71. Tyus saved us at the end with one of his length-of-the-court drives. It was not the last time my players would be booed at home that season.

As the season wore on, my contract became an even hotter issue. On January 18, 1993, Pete was quoted as saying that my contract would be reviewed at the end of the season. The newspapers contacted me. "I'm a hired hand, that's all," I said. And I avoided further comment. "I don't talk about that [job status] anymore. It seems like every time I say something, it doesn't seem to come out the right way, and I get criticized." Still, I couldn't turn around without being asked.

On January 24, the *Daily News* displayed prominently a quote from a UCLA "booster" — no name given. "As soon as the team starts to go downhill — which is where I think they're headed — he's in trouble," the quote read. The *Times* ran an article on the situation, the headline saying: "HARRICK-BASHING IS AFFECTING TEAM, BUTLER SAYS." That would be one of my players, Mitchell Butler. By then things have escalated to the top of the mountain. After a game at USC, reporters rush in and Butler steps up and says: "Hey, wait a minute, wait a minute! Quiet!" And they all hush up. "I want all you guys to lay off our coach!" And Ed O'Bannon — who's a sophomore then — seconds the motion. And I'm telling you, I felt that from that moment on, things started to subside. With only a few exceptions, everybody who was jumping on me jumped off.

In fact, as the season progressed a lot of circles picked up on Larry Donald's theme. Dick Vitale criticized the lack of a contract renewal. Several newspapers began to scrutinize it. A headline on Doug Krikorian's column in the Long Beach *Press-Telegram* said: "HEY UCLA FANS, GET OFF HARRICK'S CASE ALREADY." Mitch Chortkoff of *The Outlook* in Santa Monica wrote: "Shame on UCLA Athletic Director Pete Dalis and anyone else . . . responsible for not giving Jim Harrick a contract extension last summer . . . Now the Bruins play tight . . . Harrick's status dominates (their) thought process." And Denny Crum came to my defense. "Harrick must be a hell of a coach if he's not recruiting and he's still ranked in everybody's top 25," Denny said. I won't tell you I didn't appreciate the support, but the whole thing was such a mess. I wasn't feeling so hot and I'm sure the administration wasn't having a joyride, either. And there was still a team to coach. It was a really hard year.

As it turned out, our team did well. A key game came at home against Washington State late in the season. We were down 23 points in the first half, and were still in deep trouble late, but we scored the game's last nine points, Tyus hitting both ends of a bonus with two seconds left for a 71-70 win. We finished with a 22-11 record, beat Iowa State 81-70 in the NCAA's first round and then had that ferocious overtime game against Michigan, losing 86-84. But I really believe we'd have been more like 28-5 again if, before the season, Tracy Murray hadn't left UCLA early to go to the NBA.

The contract renewal? It wound up coming shortly before the end of the regular season. We were getting ready to go to Duke, and Chancellor Young was having an open forum with the students, a monthly deal of his. Well, several students jumped him about my contract. They asked some tough questions. Suddenly the forum isn't about any direct, student-related issues, it's about athletics. I imagine that as a result, Chancellor Young decided it was time to get things done. Shortly thereafter, they called me in and said they were going to renew me for four years — a three-year extension on what was left of my original pact.

In the aftermath, Mike Downey wrote: "They hit him with their best shots . . . They evaluated him, undermined him, submarined him, second-guessed him, third-guessed him, backstabbed him, back-doored him and suggested his successor before he ever needed succeeding . . . I don't know if Harrick will ever coach UCLA to a national championship, but I am quite sure that he never will have more trouble winning anything than he had in winning the contract extension through 1997 . . . The man lost two NBA first-round draft choices [MacLean and Murray], lost his best defender [Gerald Madkins], had his best blue-chip recruit [O'Bannon] convalescing from serious surgery, and still kept UCLA among the West Coast's top college teams. And people wanted him fired. I would have extended his contract to 2097."

You already know about the 1993-94 season. Tulsa was a No. 12 seed when they upset us, and the howling began again. Rapoport was one of the ones calling for my firing after the game. (But after we won the NCAA championship, he absolved me. Go figure.) After the season, Coach Wooden had a talk with Bill Walton. He kind of chastised Bill, telling him he was wrong for "commenting on a member of our family." Finally, in August of 1994, Bill called me. He apologized, and he was very sincere. I told him, "Bill, I accept your apology. I think it hurt me and our program greatly, and there's one thing you should do. You've got some fences to mend, not with me, but with our players and our assistant coaches. You'd do well by doing this throughout next season, when you're around."

Bill does four or five of our games for television, where he's a color commentator, so he comes to some practices. You know, Coach Wooden said that as a player Bill was always negative about something and always fighting some kind of battle, but I know Bill and I understand him. And I admire him now, because during this '94-95 season, long before we would win the title, Bill came around and talked to the players and my assistants. I wound up having him give the team a pep talk before one of our tournament games.

Sometimes in this hectic environment, things turn out just fine.

CALIFORNIA BOUND (AND GAGGED)

6

January 28, 1995 — Pauley Pavilion: UCLA vs. California.

Who are those guys? Are they ever going to miss?

We haven't had a home loss all season, but I look out there and see California playing lights-out, playing like it wants to become the first conference team to ever beat UCLA in Pauley Pavilion three consecutive years — which is exactly what they can do with a win now — but also playing as if something more is driving them. We're not doing much offensively or defensively, but I've got to give Cal its due. They're playing some inspired ball.

Not that this is unexpected. There's little love lost between these two programs. Toby Bailey said it best, even though Toby is new to firsthand experience with the Cal rivalry. "We hate losing to Cal more than any team in the Pac-10," he'd said to one newspaper. It all goes back to a bunch of personal rivalries. A lot of guys on both teams have played against each other in the Southern California area since junior high, and the recruiting

battles for them always seem to generate some acrimony between the two schools.

One of them, Tremaine Fowlkes, a freshman fresh out of
Crenshaw High, is giving a first-rate demonstration of how emotion can lift your game. Todd Bozeman brought Fowlkes off the
bench and he's been killing us ever since. We're 14 down and it's
still the first half.

*This is embarrassing. Somebody better step up or we're in deep
trouble.*

We look lackadaisical, especially Charles. During a timeout, however, I see something I like. It's Ed. He's in his brother's
face. Charles has missed a couple of easy putbacks and now,
right on the bench, Ed is on his case. "Start playing!" he yells.
"And quit shooting the ball like a sissy and get it up there!"

As the game progresses, so does J.R. I love his game. A
silent assassin, that's J.R., looking like anything but a freshman.
Of course, neither do Fowlkes (he will finish with 24 points) and
Jelani Gardner (18 points) for Cal. It's halftime, finally, and while
we have made a comeback, we're still seven down.

We go on a 15-3 run to rally for a 61-58 lead, but we've ex-
pended a lot in overcoming the deficit — and Cal jumps right
back with a pair of three-pointers by Fowlkes and Randy Duck.
"Dig in! Dig in!" I tell my players. But Cal simply won't fold.

They're on fire. Like demons possessed or somethin'.

The nine-minute mark now, and I have a decision to
make. Ed has four fouls and is sitting, but we can't afford to keep
him out any longer.

*You know the risk. He might foul out early. Never mind. If
we're gonna lose, we're gonna lose with my best player out there.*

Ed goes back in, but he's tentative, worrying about that
fifth foul, and Fowlkes knows it. He pounces on the situation.
First a couple of free throws, then a dunk, then a trey and then an
eight-foot jump hook. Nine straight points. We're down 11. We
won't come back. The final is 100-93.

I check the post-game stats. Ed has 23, J.R. 22 and Tyus 21.
Big numbers. You ought to win when three guys put up those
kind of numbers, but we just couldn't overcome their bench and

those two freshmen. They were playing like banshees out there. Their bench outscored ours, 52-3.

Time to face the music. The post-game press conference. My favorite thing in life! You just wait, Jim. Somebody's going to ask if this is the start of another UCLA tailspin.

But they don't really get into that aspect much. They've got another theme to latch onto. They're telling me that Bozeman was upset. Says we disrupted his practice yesterday.

What? You gotta be kidding me.

It's no joke. Bozeman says that our players came out onto the court early and were laughing and heckling his players. Says we didn't show them the respect they deserve.

I think I'm gonna gag on this! It's ludicrous! The man is making a mountain out of a mixup. C'mon, guys, get real. You ever think maybe it was just Bozeman's way of looking for an edge?

I don't state the case that strongly, of course. I just tell them we had no intention of disrupting anybody's practice. We weren't there to heckle or harass. To do that would be just plain stupid.

Besides, who needs this sideshow? You just got beat at home, Jim, and you can't let this team slide into the abyss a lot of observers are expecting will happen now. Time to get this train back on track. Real quick.

*   *   *

As for that Cal "controversy," here's the deal: When we're at home, we practice every day at 3 p.m. On the dot. Been that way since I got here. On the floor at 2:50 for stretching, then practice begins. On this occasion, my guys came out, Cal was still on the floor, so we went over by the steps to stretch. We didn't talk to them, they didn't talk to us. And my guys are usually big talkers, too. Chatterboxes. But not this time. This time they stayed pretty much silent until Cal left the court. This happens all the time to us on the road, the home team coming out before we finish. Especially during shoot-arounds, something Bill Sharman started back in the early '70s. Usually the players visit with each other while the coaches chew the fat. No big deal, right? So you would have thought this time.

The Cal loss ended a five-game win streak and dropped our record to 12-2. Bouncing back off the canvas after a disappointing knockdown is the hallmark of a good team — a fighting team. And we didn't have the luxury of bouncing back slowly. Road games against USC, Washington and Washington State wrapped around a non-conference home game against Notre Dame faced us, and that was just the warmup act. After those four games we would face the real test: a five-game stretch within a 10-day timespan, and against rugged opposition. We needed to get back accustomed to firing on all cylinders and winning. Which we did.

We started the string at USC, another big rival and a team that had beaten us at its place four of the last five years. We beat them this time, 73-69, and the significant aspect was that we did it without Tyus Edney. He was sick with the flu and didn't play at all. So I started Dollar in his place. Ed and Charles each scored 16 for us, but Dollar was the big story. He scored nine points but, more important, he had just one turnover in 32 minutes. That's exceptional, particularly in a hostile environment. Looking back, the fact Edney was sick and Cameron got that experience — and handled it so well — just might have played a role in how well he took over for Tyus in the national championship game. The last thing I wanted at the time was for Tyus to be sick, but it might have proved a blessing in disguise. Fate again.

Next was Notre Dame. For several weeks leading up to that game, we'd worked almost exclusively on our man-to-man defense. We'd almost forgotten about our press. It was just tucked away somewhere in a corner. When the first half ended, we were leading by only a deuce, 29-27. Just pathetic. I decided it was time to resurrect our press. Even though we hadn't practiced it much, it was absolutely outstanding against a mediocre team like Notre Dame. We outscored them 63-28 in the final 20 minutes for an easy 92-55 win. Edney took a hard foul in the game, knocked into a backboard brace, and Ed ran the length of the court and got in the face of the guy who'd sent Tyus flying. Gave him a little push. He got a technical for it, but Ed was protecting his teammate. It was another example of his leadership. I don't like for it to surface that way, but Ed knew the value of Tyus to our team, and he just wasn't going to let people do that to Tyus without knowing they'd have to answer for it.

I also learned something. We were a much better pressing team with J.R. in place of George in the lineup. His quickness made us mongoose-quick everywhere on the court. In particular, with him and Cameron in the game together we had an excellent press.

Our road games against the two Washington schools had me seriously concerned, mostly because I was afraid we'd look ahead to Arizona and Arizona State. Although I wasn't overly thrilled with our performance at Washington, I did see some things I liked. We won 74-66 and showed some grit by holding off their run after they cut it to five. Washington shot just 33 percent, and our defensive intensity was impressive. I was starting to really like the way we got after people.

While we were in Seattle, I loaded the players onto a bus, then whispered to the driver to take us to the Kingdome. The players had no clue where we were going. We'd just finished our shoot-around, so I assume they thought we were going back to the hotel like we always do. But I wanted them to get a look at where the Final Four was going to be played. Maybe by seeing the place, the Final Four would become more real to them. Something tangible. Maybe the vastness of the Kingdome would underscore the vastness of our possibilities. I wanted them to start dreaming bigger dreams.

I'd called ahead and set up the tour with Vern Wagner, the Director of Operations at the Kingdome. Vern and I go back a lot of years, to when we were both at Morningside, so when I asked him to give us the nickel tour, he was only too happy to oblige. When the bus pulled up at the Kingdome, the players wanted to know what was happening. I told them we were going in for a little tour, that it wouldn't take more than 30 minutes. There was a lot of groaning. They weren't excited at all. They wanted to get back and eat and do the things that young guys do on the outside.

But once they saw the enormous expanse inside the place, they began to perk up a little. They started paying attention. There was an RV show going on, and there must have been 500

RVs in there. The guys were having trouble visualizing the place as a basketball arena, but once Vern started describing the layout, where the court would be, the seats, the press tables, I could see their eyes getting bigger and bigger. Now, they were *really* interested.

I'd wanted to plant a seed in the back of their minds, a feeling that, "Hey, wouldn't it be nice to come back here?" I think maybe it did.

We went up to Washington State and beat them 98-83. We played an outstanding game, handing them their first home loss of the season. They played well, we played better. We shot 62 percent from the field and that was the difference. Along with our defense. We went zone on them late in the game, and I think that threw them off. Tyus dominated. We spread the floor and he just picked them apart, finishing with 18 points and 11 assists. George got in early foul trouble, so I decided to use J.R. down low. He responded with a huge game, scoring 28 points. Toby came off the bench to score 15, and Ed and Charles each had 13.

This game helped me solidify my thinking in regards to rotation. From that moment on, I started using seven guys. Later, I would make one final change, but the pieces of the puzzle were starting to fall into place.

When we won at Washington State, I began to think that we had a chance to be a really good basketball team. I thought that was a pivotal game. Despite my growing confidence, I knew there was still much work to be done. There were hard times ahead. No worry. I was used to that. I'd had hard times in the past.

*   *   *

How does a person get from Charleston, West Virginia, to California? Easy. Just get in the car, aim it toward the setting sun and take off. Simple as that. The road that followed, however, was anything but. We were California-bound, with no idea of the twists and turns awaiting us over the next several years.

Sally and I left for California on the night we were married. We loaded everything we owned — mostly the wedding gifts we'd just received — into a U-Haul trailer and took off, two young kids heading to the Promised Land. Neither of our families shared our adventurous spirit, but I think they understood it was something we had to do, crazy or not. After all, they had been young once.

At the reception following our wedding, Sally's father pulled me off into a corner and handed me an envelope. Inside was a hundred bucks. Big dough in those days, let me tell you. A few minutes later, my father sidled up to me and slipped me another C-note. Then he handed me something else — a car payment book. "This is all yours now, pal," he whispered. "See that you take care of it."

I was now the proud owner of a 1960 Chevy Bel-Air. Stick shift, and no air conditioner. Nothing fancy, just a car. I didn't have a place to live, and my job situation was shaky, but I did have a monthly car payment. Welcome to the real world, Jimmy-boy.

The money we got at the wedding, along with what we'd been able to save from our jobs — I worked nights in a local factory; Sally, having graduated from business school, worked for the telephone company — was the sum total of our nest egg. Leaving for California with no more than what we had was a risky move. No wonder our parents were so concerned.

California hadn't necessarily been our first choice; it just turned out that way. Sally and I had several options, several other places where we could have chosen to live. Or we could have stayed home. One job I almost took was with a business machine company in Charleston. There were two or three teaching jobs that I almost accepted, one of which was in Cleveland, up at Shaker Heights High School. For whatever reason, I turned those down, choosing instead to travel across the country.

Why? In the end, I always seem to come back to that question. Maybe it's that fate thing I always talk about. I've said a million times that fate has guided my life every step of the way, and I truly believe it. Those other jobs were good ones, maybe even for more money, but I declined each and every one. What was the reason? I can't give a clear answer, except to say that perhaps some force I wasn't aware of was leading me. Fate. It's the only word I know that begins to explain it.

The instrument fate used to draw me to California was my cousin Bob. He was the one who first planted the seed. His parents had divorced a few years earlier and he had moved with his mother to California. They lived in the Los Angeles area, in El Segundo. During my junior year in college, Bob and a friend of his graduated from high school, then drove back to Charleston to spend a few days with us. While he was there, he kept telling me, "It's sweet out there, Jimmy. You ought to come." He must have said it a hundred times. I didn't give it much thought then, but later, when I began a serious job hunt, his words kept creeping into my mind.

During my final year at Morris Harvey, I signed up with a teacher's agency that came to the school's placement bureau. Ironically, the first offer was from Smith River, California. I'd been waiting and waiting to hear from somebody, really starting to get antsy, when I finally got the call. When they offered me the job, I quickly said yes. The big reason was money. California teachers made about a thousand dollars more a year than West Virginia teachers. Most of my buddies who taught in West Virginia were really struggling, making somewhere in the neighborhood of $3,500 a year. My first job paid $4,700. Wow, man, that was big time.

After accepting the job, the first thing Sally and I did was get out the map. We had no clue where Smith River was. Turns out it's about 15 hours north of Los Angeles, right on the Oregon border. Our families were even less thrilled when they heard that. They had counted on us being near my aunt Gladys and my cousins, Bob, Phil and Diane. Instead, we would be living in a place where we didn't know a single soul — and a long way from L.A.

On the night of August 20, 1960, after saying goodbye to our family and friends, we left West Virginia. The future was uncertain, but we were young and in love and filled with a great sense of adventure, so we weren't worried. Things would work out.

*   *   *

We took our time driving across the country, stopping along the way to check out the sights, most of which we'd only heard about or seen in the movies or on TV. Coney Island in Cincinnati, the Grand Canyon, the Mojave Desert . . . it took us about six days to make the trip. Crossing the Mojave Desert was some experience, let me tell you. Remember, that 1960 Chevy didn't have an air conditioner. Driving across that monster in late August isn't at the top of my list of fun things to do. But at the time it was nothing, really — just a small fragment of the overall adventure. Looking back, I remember it as a wonderful time for us. The possibilities seemed endless.

People have always asked me if I had to do a big selling job on Sally to persuade her to make the move to California. I didn't. She's every bit the adventurer I am. Maybe even more so. When I told her I had a job offer in California, all she said was: "Let's do it."

We drove to El Segundo and spent a few days with Aunt Gladys (had to let our folks back home know we were safe) before making the trip to Smith River. The thing I remember most about the trek north was driving across the Golden Gate Bridge. I had no way of knowing it at the time, of course, but that spectacular view with the bay to our right and the Pacific just off our left was a sneak preview of the Smith River experience. Not the view. The water.

Our first home was actually a garage that had been converted into an apartment. A shotgun shack divided into three sections — living room, kitchen, bedroom — all very small. You could look from one end of the place to the other. It wasn't much, but it was warm and dry — and staying dry in Smith River isn't something to take lightly. The average rainfall is about 127 inches a year. It rains buckets in that place. They don't have a monsoon season; they have a monsoon *year*. Unbelievable.

Because our place was so small, we had to put most of our things in a storage room, including many of the gifts we received at our wedding. Bad mistake, given the amount of rain. Everything we had in storage got mildewed. I mean, *everything*. It was a disaster.

I taught at Smith River for a year. A self-contained classroom, seventh grade, all classes. English, science, math, making bulletin boards — I did it all. I even taught music. Imagine me teaching music. In college I hit notes so sour that my fraternity brothers wouldn't even let me sing in the Mother's Day pageant. Now I had to teach it. Bet those kids never listened to music again.

Becoming a coach still hadn't entered my mind. I was a teacher and I was going to be a teacher all my life. My only concern was making it to the end of the month. To make it to the 30th, that became my operative phrase. Putting food on the table was my priority. My take-home pay was $291 a month. That's all. Sometimes, when things would get really desperate, we'd wonder if that paycheck was ever going to arrive. We'd sit around hoping it would show up before the cupboard was completely bare. Later, after we had our three sons, we'd *pray* for it to show up.

The way things have turned out, I guess it's somewhat surprising I hadn't entertained thoughts of becoming a coach by then. Given my sports background, it would seem only natural that I would have come out of college with coaching at least on the list of strong possibilities, if not as my life's goal. Many of my college buddies knew they wanted to become coaches from day one. Not me.

Each step along life's path is a learning experience, whether or not we realize it at the time. Though coaching was the last thing on my mind in Smith River and through the next few years, once I did get into the profession I immediately recognized how valuable those years of "just being a teacher" were. They taught me how to teach. I had to make a lesson plan every day as a teacher, and I still do as a coach today. You have methods and discipline, subject matter . . . the very things I had back in Smith River when I was standing in front of a bunch of eager-eyed seventh-graders. Teaching instilled in me many of the principles and habits I still carry. I have never considered myself anything other than a teacher. The only difference is that now I'm a teacher of basketball and the court is my classroom.

Everything that's happened to me as a coach goes back to my roots as a seventh-grade teacher. It's that fate thing again. "The Lord never put me in a situation I couldn't handle," my mother always said. "Wherever you are is where He wants you to be." I believe that with all my heart.

Maybe that's why I started my career as a seventh-grade teacher. Maybe it was the Lord's way of saying, "Better learn what you're doing, pal, before you go on to the next level."

*   *   *

When we were in Smith River, we spent our Christmas vacation with my aunt in El Segundo. Stayed with her 12 days and just had a great time. We loved the place. School was supposed to start back on January 2, but I didn't make it. Too many things were happening that I didn't want to miss. I called in sick, then went to see the Rose Bowl parade and the Rose Bowl game. Afterward, we drove back to Smith River. When I got back to school I found out that they docked me a day's pay. I told the principal, "Hey, but I called in sick." He looked at me and said, "No, no, we know what you're doing." That was a great life lesson.

At the end of the school year we packed our U-Haul again, drove to El Segundo and rented an apartment. I had no job and no guarantee I would find one. It was another risky move, but one we again felt compelled to make. Smith River was a nice enough place, but we'd fallen in love with the Los Angeles area during those 12 days. Once we spent time in L.A. and got to know it a little, Smith River didn't have a chance.

On the Tuesday morning after we arrived in L.A., I went to the Board of Education building and filled out an application. Then I sat there from nine in the morning to four in the afternoon. I talked to everybody, telling anyone willing to listen that I'd take any job — *any* job — they had to offer. I wasn't certified to teach at the high school level, but I was ready to take any junior high job available.

About four o'clock a guy came out of his office and told me to go to a certain school, that they'd be waiting for me. I drove over, walked in and talked to them for about an hour. When we finished, they offered me a contract on the spot. I said, "Well, let me take this and I'll think about it." I might have been desperate, but I felt compelled to explore all my options — like maybe finding something a little closer to home.

On Wednesday I went to Inglewood and El Segundo; on Thursday, Pasadena, Glendale and Burbank; and on Friday, the Long Beach City School District. I had applications all over the place. Every couple of hours I would call home and check in with Sally. At noon on Friday I called and she said, "Come home, you've got a contract." It was from the Hawthorne Intermediate School right in Hawthorne, just a couple of miles from El Segundo. I drove over there later in the afternoon and they hired me. The next day we got in the car and drove to West Virginia, cross country, non-stop. We would make that drive five times in our lives. Five is plenty.

Living in Southern California took some getting used to. The vastness of the city was overwhelming at first. Jim Murray, the great sportswriter, once wrote that Southern California had changed drastically since he first came, the population having swelled from eight million then to something like 32 million now. Well, we thought there were 32 million in 1961. I stayed lost for the first year. Maps were everywhere in the car, yet I never knew which way I was going. I learned my way around by trial and (mostly) error.

That summer I began work on my master's degree at Southern Cal. Tuition was pretty cheap, about $27 a unit, which I could afford. Coaching played no role in my decision to get a master's degree. Again, it all came down to money, to being able to better provide for my family. When you choose teaching as a profession, you know you're never going to get rich. That's a given. However, having a master's can mean another 30 grand or so over the course of your teaching career, and that's a big boost.

I also took a job with the Mattel Toy Company, where I worked for two summers. I'd take classes from seven until noon, go home and study for about three hours, then work from four until midnight. I was a foreman at Mattel, in charge of an assembly line that made automatic water rifles. All the workers were women. We were expected to crank those things out, too — 4,000 per shift. If we failed to make our quota, the big shots would let us know about it in no uncertain terms. Getting those ladies angry wasn't a wise thing to do, though, because at the end of the assembly line each rifle had to be tested, and if you were on their hit list they'd drill you. I've seen them drown guys who got on their bad side.

After two years I made a couple of changes. I quit graduate school, choosing instead to start work toward a teaching credential from UCLA that would qualify me to teach high school. (I later returned to the master's program; by 1966 I had my master's and my principal's credential.) I also left the soggy demands of Mattel and went to work for Northrup Aviation in the paint department, putting primer on all the parts before they were painted. Another tough job. I smelled fumes all day. I hated the work, but by now our first son, Monte, had been born, so I needed the extra money. I made $4,700, $5,100, $5,300 and $5,500 my first four years of teaching. That's the kind of thing you never forget.

*   *   *

My involvement with sports at this time was strictly peripheral. I played four or five nights a week in an industrial league, but mostly I was just a spectator. The Lakers had recently moved from Minneapolis to L.A., and I used to watch them play all the time. Attendance wasn't all that great, maybe 4,000 fans a game, so it was easy to get tickets. I used to get them for a couple of bucks at the grocery store. One year, my friend Bob Green and I saw 41 of 42 Laker home games. We'd sit up in the nosebleed section watching Jerry West and Elgin Baylor play. And yes, it dawned on me that the guy I'd guarded in high school was down there, a star in a Lakers uniform, while I was up in the rafters with the pigeons.

Occasionally, I would check out a UCLA game. I say occasionally, because in those days watching a UCLA game took some work. You never knew from one game to the next where they would be playing. Finding them was a real challenge. UCLA didn't have its own gym. This was several years before Pauley Pavilion was built, and they were the nomads of college basketball. Real gypsies. I can remember watching them play at Santa Monica City College. Once or twice, I saw them in the old Shrine Auditorium. They were all over the map. Venice, the downtown Sports Arena, everywhere. And this was when UCLA was on the verge of starting to win it all, when Coach Wooden was bringing in the players who would lay the foundation for those championship years that were just around the corner. Guys like Gary Cunningham, Walt Hazzard, Fred Slaughter, Gail Goodrich and Keith Erickson. Coach Wooden had his first Final Four team in 1962, and he did it without having his own home court. That's incredible. They practiced in a gym that only had two baskets. They shared the gym with the volleyball team, the gymnastics team and the cheerleaders. It must've been a circus in there. When I think about the success he had under such difficult circumstances, I just appreciate him all the more.

Mainly, I kept up with UCLA by watching them on television. Their games would be taped, then replayed at 11 p.m. Years later, after I got into coaching, we'd finish our game, go out and buy some pizza, then run home to watch the Bruins. Dick Enberg, one of the best sports broadcasters ever, did the play-by-play. Watching those UCLA replays became a ritual for us.

During my first two years in L.A., I began to ease into coaching, but only on a small-scale, non-paying basis — Little League baseball in the summer, Pop Warner football in the fall. I did it for fun, for the kids. It was my way of paying back all those guys who spent time coaching me when I was growing up. Really, though, I was too busy to get very involved with much of anything. Teaching, studying, working part-time jobs, being a husband and father . . . that was more than enough to keep me on the go, 25 hours a day. Not once did I think about becoming a coach. I didn't have time to think about it.

But all that changed in 1964. I guess I was enjoying those Little League games more than I realized, because the coaching bug finally bit me big time. I knew that Morningside High

School in Inglewood needed an assistant coach, and I decided to apply. Then I got a call from Lee Smelser, the head coach at Morningside. He knew about me, so he called and invited me to his place for an interview. I was interviewed by Eldon Boyd, the principal, and Russ Wiley, the assistant principal. Lee was also present. We had a great talk and they hired me to teach English and driver's training, and to coach the junior varsity basketball and baseball teams. Jim Harrick and the coaching profession had finally collided.

I was 26 years old.

*   *   *

Let me tell you a little about being a driving instructor. There's nothing that really quite compares. Mainly it's one adventure after another, a series of near-death experiences. To understand the true meaning of fear, try sitting in the front seat while a 16-year-old kid tries to negotiate L.A. traffic. Being scared doesn't begin to describe how I felt. Coaching in the Final Four was a piece of cake compared to that. I'd rather face Arkansas a hundred times than spend another hour in a car with a student driver behind the wheel.

And I did it for nine years. Why would any sane person subject himself to that kind of torture? For the money, that's why. Twenty-five dollars a week extra. That's a hundred bucks more a month. Man, that was big money. When I found out I was going to be the driving instructor, I rushed home, jumped on the table and blurted the news to Sally. We both cheered. And we both *really* cheered when I quit nine years later. I told her: No more driver training, no matter how poor we are.

One of the funniest things that ever happened to me occurred while I was teaching driver's ed. Well, it's funny now; it was humiliating at the time. We had stopped for a red light at the corner of Manchester and Prairie. A student was behind the wheel, and I was sitting next to her with my foot on the special brake the car had for the teacher to use. While we're waiting for the light to change, a big Lincoln Continental pulls up alongside us, not five feet away. I glance over and . . . it's Jerry West. My heart sank like Atlantis. I turned my head and slowly slumped down in the seat. No way I wanted to say hello to him. I just couldn't have him see me in that situation. That would have been too embarrassing. He and I were contemporaries, we'd been opponents and teammates, we'd known each other fairly well — and now he's this great star with the Lakers and I'm this anonymous JV coach teaching driver's training on the side. So there we were, me trying to nonchalantly blend into the dashboard and Jerry sitting there in his Lincoln. We may have only been five feet away from each other, but I think it's safe to say we were miles apart.

Over the years that gap has closed somewhat. Don't get me wrong, I'm not saying I'm nearly as famous as Jerry West. He's a legend. But we are on a more even keel now. We occasionally talk on the phone, or we'll bump into each other at a game. He's always been very, very good to me. While I was at Morningside, I asked him to come over and speak to our entire student body. He did, and he was terrific.

The thing about Jerry is that he's such a great guy. Smart, too. There's not a sharper, more shrewd general manager in professional sports. You never know what he's thinking. I don't know if Jerry is a poker player, but if he is, I'll bet he's a good one. In a way, I think Jerry's a little like Coach Wooden. I know for a fact that they share at least one important quality: Both have remained humble even though they've risen to the highest heights of success. That's not easy to do.

But believe me, I wasn't thinking about any of that when he pulled that Lincoln Continental up next to me. I just wanted to disappear.

*   *   *

Every coach I played for made a lasting impression. I learned plenty from all of them, just as I learned from the many coaches I later came in contact with. Once I dedicated myself to being the best coach I could be, I became a sponge, soaking up everything I heard, regardless of whether the speaker was John Wooden or a fellow JV coach. Some things I kept, some I discarded. But none was ignored.

Learning strategies and philosophies, various offenses and defenses, different presses and ways to attack a press — those are certainly important elements to being a successful coach. But coaching involves so much more, dozens of intangibles that have nothing to do with what kind of offense or defense you employ. Few coaches are successful unless they master the little things. Without the ability and the insight to do that, a coach is doomed to failure.

Lee Smelser taught me how to coach, how to work on the basketball floor. Much of the work ethic I now have came from him. His influence on me was enormous. Lee worked like a madman, and if I wanted to keep up I had to work equally hard. We would open the gym in the morning and stay there all day, working with the kids; teaching them, talking basketball. Always we talked basketball. We spent endless hours discussing, arguing, breaking it down, comparing the different things we'd picked up. We worked at it year-round, too. The gym was never closed, even during the summer. I remember one summer our team played 62 games, more than twice as many as we played during the regular season. Those were games I coached but didn't get paid for. Never mind, it didn't matter. I loved what I was doing. It may have taken me a few years, but I'd finally found my true calling.

I was a coach.

My first JV team is one I'll always remember with great fondness. That was a special group of guys. When our second son, Jim, was born, the players pitched in and gave me $20. I'll never forget that. It's one of the nicest things any team has ever done for me. That's the kind of thing that binds you to coaching. The highs of winning and the lows of losing come and go, but moments like that stay with you forever.

Lee is the man who really got the Morningside basketball program rolling. The success I later achieved there was the result of the great foundation he laid. I like to believe that I took the torch from him and carried it to an even higher plateau during the four years I was at the helm. I know we were very successful. In the nine years I was at Morningside — five as Lee's assistant, four as head coach — we never failed to make it to the C.I.F. (California Interscholastic Federation) tournament. It was a great run.

More than anything, though, Lee became one of my closest friends. He and his wife, Joan, had three sons who were born in exactly the same years that our three sons were born. Through the years we've all supported each other. It's been a close and special relationship.

After five years at Morningside I decided it was time to make a move. Although I loved it there, I felt that Lee would be the head coach forever, and that if I wanted to become my own man, maybe it would be best to leave. My parents thought I was insane. My father said, "You've got it good here, so why would you even think of moving?" He was right, too. I did have it good. But it wasn't a matter of being miserable or terribly unhappy; I had a yearning to be a head coach, that's all. I wanted to be the guy who made decisions rather than suggestions. I wanted to find out if I could cut it, if I could handle being the top guy. The only way I would ever answer those questions was to put myself in that position, so I applied for the job as head baseball coach at Sonora High School in Orange County.

They offered me the job, but I kept putting them off. Since this was in January and the job wouldn't begin until the following fall, I felt no great sense of urgency to give them an answer. I don't know why I stalled them, I just did.

Then, out of the blue, Lee gets hired as head coach at College of the Canyons Junior College, where he still coaches today. Suddenly, the Morningside job is up for grabs. Naturally, I think the job should be mine, no questions asked. So do the players, all of whom had played for me on the junior varsity. They're lobbying like crazy on my behalf. Problem is, we'd changed principals and the new guy, Sam Zackheim, was in no hurry to make up his mind. February and March pass, still no decision. Then we get into April, and by now I'm *really* starting to sweat. What's going on here? I've been the assistant coach for five years, who else could he pick but me? I was the logical choice. The *only* choice.

To make matters worse, the situation with Sonora High was coming to a head. Tired of being kept on hold, the principal called to let me know he wanted a definitive answer, yes or no, by five o'clock that afternoon. No more waiting. This was on the Friday before Easter Sunday. How appropriate. Seldom have I been in more agony.

At noon that day I walked into the lunch room just as Sam was leaving. He passed me without saying a word, then turned around and called my name. "Oh, by the way, you're the new basketball coach," he said. Then he just spun around abruptly and walked away. That's how I found out that I was the head coach at Morningside High School. I immediately ran to the office, called the folks at Sonora High and informed them that I wouldn't be their baseball coach. I'm sure they were tickled to death to be rid of such an indecisive guy.

Like everything in life, when one chapter ends another begins. Now I was the head coach, athletic director, chairman of the P.E. department, and, of course, driver education instructor. I'd gotten exactly what I had asked for. All the responsibility now rested squarely on my shoulders.

*   *   *

As I mentioned, much of my coaching philosophy derives from the men I played for — Al Ball and Pud Hutson in Charleston, Jules Rivlin at Marshall and Sonny Moran at Morris Harvey. They all did many of the same things — tough man-to-man defense, a lot of pressing, an up-tempo, fast-breaking offense, and break-you-down dribble-drive penetration. Just old-fashioned, in-your-face basketball. While I was the JV coach, Lee wanted me to run the same offense he used with the varsity, which I did. It was the Doggie Julian Shuffle, a slower style that was the antithesis of what those other four guys did. So by the time I took over at Morningside, I had been exposed to several different styles and philosophical systems, out of which evolved my own approach.

Two other men had a major impact on me — Coach Wooden and Pete Newell. I used to attend all of Coach Wooden's clinics, regardless of where he held them. If he had one, I was there. Sometimes as many as six or seven a year. Same with Pete. And I read every book those two guys ever wrote, primarily studying Pete for his defense and Coach Wooden for his offense. Over the years, the majority of what my teams have done came from those two men.

When I was younger, I probably thought I was a lot smarter than I really am. I would tinker around with Coach Wooden's high post balanced court offense, thinking that somehow I was going to improve it. How dumb was that? Here's a man who won more NCAA championships than any coach ever, and some young punk coach who's never won anything is going to make the man's system better. Crazy. After awhile, I finally came to my senses and said: "Hey, who am I to change anything Coach Wooden does? Just learn it and learn how to teach it."

My first year as head coach we did nothing but run a series of set plays. Everything was called. I didn't like doing that because we'd be in those crowded gyms where we couldn't hear each other and we'd be forced to hold up big cards with numbers on them. That's how we called the plays. With signs. I solved that problem the next year when I switched to the UCLA high post offense, which I've run every year since. I also began to stress conditioning, fundamentals and being unselfish, the very foundation of Coach Wooden's program.

Stop and think about it. We won the NCAA championship using Coach Wooden's offensive principles. Bobby Knight has won three NCAA titles at Indiana using Pete Newell's defensive principles. I think it's safe to say that what those two gentlemen taught has more than stood the test of time.

In 1970, Billy Ingram, one of the best players I ever coached, was being heavily recruited by San Diego State. One day I got a call from a San Diego guy named Max Shapiro, who ran a series of California sports camps. Max told me that he wanted to have a summer basketball camp in L.A. and that Dick Davis, the San Diego State coach, had recommended me to help run it. He wanted to know if I'd be interested in being one of the camp directors. I said sure, why not. Coaches are always looking for ways to make a few extra dollars in the summer. It was a nickel-and-dime operation, nothing big or impressive, certainly nothing like the sophisticated, expensive camps you see these days. I worked the camp for him and it turned out fine. Anyway, the next summer he calls and asks me if I'd like to do it again. I told him that I'd be glad to. Then he says, "By the way, this year it's going to be the John Wooden Basketball Camp." That's when I began my personal relationship with Coach Wooden.

One year I worked Coach Wooden's camp for six weeks. That's a lot of work, taking care of 200 to 300 kids each week. It was during that time that I got to know Coach Wooden really well. The camp directors would gather around him during lunch or dinner (actually, we would jockey for the seats closest to him) and talk basketball for hours. Well, mainly, we just listened. We'd ask him hundreds and hundreds of questions, and he was always gracious enough to answer each and every one.

It was during this time that I became obsessed with organization. With planning and preparing. With leaving no stone unturned. That goes back to my roots as a seventh-grade teacher, when I was responsible for every aspect of the kids' education. At Morningside I would fill out an index card with that day's practice schedule on it. That's a habit I've continued every day since I became a head coach. Ask me what we did on such-and-such day and it'll take me about two minutes to tell you. All I'd have to do is locate the card. I've kept every card I ever filled out. There are thousands of them, all over the place. I'm a collector, I guess. I never throw anything away. Drives my wife nuts, but that's just me. My three sons are the same way. They all carry a Franklin planner with them everywhere they go. Sally's convinced we're all crazy.

From the very beginning of my coaching career, I always felt comfortable on the basketball floor. Working with young people, relating to them, helping them . . . that came as second nature to me. I genuinely enjoy being around young people. They keep me young and energized.

I would say the huge majority of players I've coached over the years would say positive things about me. I'd say most liked me, which is nice but not essential. It's icing on the cake. But from my perspective as a leader, being liked will never be as important as being respected. Players may not agree with me, they may not like what I'm trying to get them to do, but as long as they respect me things will work out. Remember, a coach has to be extremely demanding. He has to demand of his players things they aren't inclined to want to do. The dynamics of the coach-player relationship is one that's ripe for disagreement and dissatisfaction. But when push comes to shove, I hold the trump card — I'm the one who dishes out playing time. Athletes aren't stupid; they understand that it's better for them if they stay on my good side.

The secret to dealing with athletes — with people in general, for that matter — is honesty. Be honest, fair and up-front with them. *All* the time. If you don't, the situation will backfire. You'll lose their respect, and once that happens you can forget about it. My philosophy is, you can con a con, you can fool a fool, but you can never kid a kid. Because I always followed that philosophy, even when they disagreed with me or when I jumped their case, they got to know me. *Really* know me. When they did, trust quickly followed.

Don't forget, this was the '60s, perhaps the most turbulent decade in our country's history. Everything was starting to happen — the war in Vietnam, civil rights unrest, the women's movement, gay rights, drugs, hippies, protesters on both sides of the fence. There were times when I thought this country was going to explode, when I was certain we were tearing ourselves apart. Everywhere you looked, there was violence and confrontation. It was a nasty, angry period in our history, a time of immense change.

Being in a position of authority made me a natural target for mistrust. I was viewed as a member of the establishment, and as we all know, "establishment" figures were the most mistrusted, despised people of the era. In those days it was cool for young people to rebel against the establishment, whether they had a legitimate reason to or not. Fortunately, I never had any problems in that regard, either as a coach or as a teacher. I'm convinced the reason is because I took time to get to know my players and to allow them to get to know the real Jim Harrick. I made it a point to develop one-on-one relationships, to see them as human beings and not just students or athletes.

We had a lot of success during my four years as head coach at Morningside, winning 87 percent of our games, averaging 26 wins a year and never losing more than six. Three of those four years we won the Sky League title. The 1973 team, which finished with a 28-1 record, was voted the best high school team in the country by *Basketball Weekly*. That team was undefeated during the regular season, but was upset in the playoffs. I later learned that three of our players smoked dope prior to the game we lost. That remains one of the most disappointing things that ever happened to me.

I had several outstanding players at Morningside, but without question the two best were Jackie Robinson (no relation to the great Dodger) and Billy Ingram, who's now pastor at one of the largest churches in the Los Angeles area. Billy was the captain of my first Morningside team, which lost in the playoffs to Jamaal Wilkes' team, even though we led them for 31 minutes. Billy is now a close friend of mine, as are many of the players I coached. When the Los Angeles Headquarters Association presented me with the 1995 Spirit of Los Angeles Award, I chose Billy to come and say the prayer.

The next three years, Jackie was our star player, our go-to guy. He had some huge games for us, just monster games. Jackie and Billy were big-time players and outstanding young men. Jackie went on to play for UNLV, Billy played at Oregon and Biola. Any time I'm asked who was my best high school player, I always say it's a tie between those two.

One of the greatest joys for a coach is seeing his players become successful adults, then have them come back and become friends with you. Many times it's not until then that you learn how great an impact you've made in their lives. I know how much it means to Coach Wooden to have so many players — many of whom didn't get along with him that well while playing for him — stay in close contact now. I feel the same way. As far as I'm concerned, that's what coaching is all about. I've been fortunate that way. I also consider myself fortunate to have never lost any of my players in the Vietnam war. Sadly, a lot of my fellow coaches can't say that.

*   *   *

During my nine years at Morningside, the racial make-up of the student body changed from mostly white to mostly minorities. And that was the single greatest learning experience I've ever had. I learned more about life and people in those nine years than I had in all the years before. It was a great awakening.

Most Caucasians grow up never knowing what it's like to be in the minority. Because we are born white, we've seldom been in that situation. It's difficult for us to relate. (That's not necessarily true for college basketball coaches, however. In fact, many times it's the norm. Recruiting, we often go into gyms where there may not be a dozen white people. That's why I think college coaches have a better grasp of the racial situation than do many of our fellow citizens. We can relate to being in the minority.)

My first year in college I roomed with a black player. I never gave it a second thought. He was just a guy, same as me. His color wasn't important. I hadn't gone to high school with blacks, but I had known many through the pick-up games we played over the years. I'd been exposed to blacks, at least on a superficial level, so it was no big deal to me that a black guy was my roommate. I am very proud of the fact that the evil bird of racism never came to rest on my shoulders. Maybe that's because being Lebanese in Charleston put me in a minority group. Taking it one step further, even within the Lebanese community I was in the minority. Remember, I was Catholic; most Lebanese weren't. That gave me a sensitivity to minorities that many people don't have.

During my years at Morningside, I was fortunate enough

That's me as a two year old. I had a wonderful childhood in a great city, Charleston, West Virginia.

As an eighth-grader at Lincoln Junior High during the 1951-52 season. We went undefeated that year, winning the conference championship. We won it again a year later.

My Stonewall Jackson High senior picture in 1956. I don't remember being quite as serious as I am in this photo.

Check out the form on this jumper. We were good my senior year at Stonewall Jackson High, but our season came to an end when we ran into a guy named Jerry West.

The nine years I spent at Morningside High School was the single greatest learning experience of my life. This is during the 1972-73 season, my last before moving up to the college ranks.

Offering advice to my Morningside team (upper right and right). In my four years as head coach we averaged 26 wins a year and won the Sky Conference title three times.

Larry Farmer and I were Gary Cunningham's assistants during his two years at UCLA. Had Gary remained as head coach, many of the problems that happened during the 1980s would never have occurred.

What can I say about this man that hasn't already been said? Coach
Wooden is the greatest man I've ever met and a truly wonderful human
being. He's also been the biggest influence in my life, as a man and
as a coach.

The reporters had a million questions for me at the press conference at
which it was announced that I was to be UCLA's coach.

Pooh Richardson (24) makes a point during a tense moment. Pooh is one of the toughest players I've ever seen. I called him a "hardballer."

Talking with Don MacLean before practice. Signing Don was a critical step in bringing some consistency to the UCLA program.

Tracy Murray makes a statement during the 1991-92 season. Tracy is another player who helped turn the UCLA program around.

The 1992 team finished with a 28-5 overall record, but a West Regional final loss to Indiana in the NCAA Tournament was all my critics cared to remember.

I have always considered myself a teacher. The only difference now is that the gym is my classroom and basketball is my subject.

Rod Baker, Reggie Minton, Bob Huggins and I coached the U.S. team during the 1993 World University Games in Buffalo.

Ed O'Bannon was a member of that gold medal-winning U.S. World University Games team.

Meeting the media at the 1995 Final Four in the Kingdome. I think semifinal Saturday is the greatest day in college sports.

Alone with my thoughts prior to our semifinal game against Oklahoma State. At this stage of the tournament, surviving one game at a time was the only thing on my mind.

omm'A Givens, Kris Johnson, and Charles O'Bannon try to relax during those long minutes before the final game against Arkansas.

Giving some last-minute instructions to Toby Bailey prior to facing the Razorbacks. Toby responded with a 26-point effort and a monster dunk that electrified the crowd, me included.

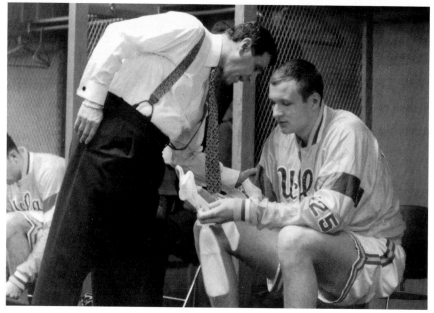

Sharing a quiet moment with George Zidek before the championship game. George's great post defense on Corliss Williamson was one of the reasons for our win.

Addressing the team during halftime of our semifinal game against Oklahoma State. The Cowboys were known for their great defense, but I thought ours was better.

The keys to victory against Arkansas are on the chalkboard behind me. I asked my players to play the game of their lives, and that's exactly what they did.

Making a point to Charles O'Bannon. Once Charles eliminated some flaws in his game, he became one of our most solid and consistent players. He has a chance to be a great one.

For my money, until he was injured, Tyus Edney was the best player in the NCAA Tournament. I honestly didn't think we could beat Arkansas without him.

This is every coach's dream — cutting down the nets after winning the national championship.

Sharing in the locker room celebration with my players just moments after winning the championship.

This is what it's all about — celebrating with the players after achieving the ultimate.

Holding the hardware with my assistants Steve Lavin, Mark Gottfried, and Lorenzo Romar. They deserve much of the credit for our success.

A post-championship family gathering after winning it all. Sitting, from left to right, are Jim Jr., me holding granddaughter Morgan, Sally, and Glenn. In the back are Monte and Melanie. This was a special moment for all of us.

Coach Wooden was on hand as Ed O'Bannon and I were honored by the Los Angeles Athletic Club. When Coach addressed the audience, he looked at me and said what he always says, "Jim, we the alumni expect you to win it next year." Ed then stood up, looked at me and said, "Jim, we the alumni expect you to win another one yesterday."

A huge crowd was on hand at LAX to greet the team when we arrived back in Los Angeles. Our win ended years of frustration and disappointment for the Bruin faithful.

Mickey Mouse and I together at the parade given us by the wonderful folks at Disneyland.

Wounded warrior Tyus Edney waves to the crowd. Tyus is one of the finest young men I've ever been associated with. I'm going to miss him.

Sally and I with President Clinton in the White House. He's a big Arkansas fan, but said we had deserved to win.

Ed O'Bannon and I present a UCLA jersey to President Clinton.

Sharing the spotlight with Jay Leno on "The Tonight Show." We didn't let Jay forget the joke he made about us after we lost to Tulsa in 1994.

"BRUINS!"

to learn from my players, and them from me. We were able to appreciate our differences, but, perhaps more significantly, we were able to recognize our many similarities. I think it goes back to the fact that my players really knew me and trusted me. They'd been to my house, eaten dinner with us, played with my kids, so they knew me as a person and not just as their coach or some big authority figure. They knew that once a bond of trust had been established, I would go to the wall with them. Also, I think being a coach helped. There's something about athletics that almost forces people to come together, even if they aren't consciously aware that it's happening. Those kids saw me in a different light than they saw any other teacher. They'd see me without a shirt and tie, in shorts and tennis shoes, with a whistle around my neck, sweating just like they were. I'm sure that made it easier for them to relate to me.

I never had a player, black or white, who refused to accept the discipline I meted out. That's because I never disciplined a "black" player or a "white" player. I just disciplined players. I never for a moment considered color. To me, every player is an individual, a human being to be dealt with fairly and honestly. And that's how I treated them.

*   *   *

Jumping from high school coaching to the college ranks wasn't something I planned. It sort of came out of nowhere. I was content with my situation at Morningside, and would have been happy finishing my career there. I had no reason to make a move. I did go after one job, but when I failed to get it, I dismissed the idea of coaching at the next level. As it turned out, however, college coaching came looking for me.

The job I tried for and didn't get was at Loyola University here in California. I knew a judge in town, Burch Donahue, who had played football at Loyola many years earlier. When I was coaching the American Legion baseball team, he approached me one day and asked if his son could try out. I let the kid come out, and he ended up playing some pretty good ball for us. Throughout the summer, the Judge, despite being confined to a wheelchair, came to all the games, and we got to be pretty good buddies.

When the Loyola job opened up a year or so later, I thought my friendship with Judge Donahue might give me the inside connection that's so often needed. I made a big, big push for that job. In the end, it came down to two guys and I was one of them. The Loyola people sought out Pete Newell and asked him what he thought. Pete said, "I don't think a guy can go from high school to college." So they hired Dave Benaderet.

I was devastated. A few days later, after a game we lost, Dave came down to the locker room and said, "Jim, I'd like you to be my assistant. I can pay you $12,000 a year." Well, I'm making $23,500 at the time. I have a wife, three kids, two cars, a dog and a mortgage that would eat a horse. I go back and talk to Sally about it. It didn't take us long to decide that there was no way we could live in Los Angeles on 12 grand a year.

In the interim, Frank Arnold, an assistant coach at Oregon, was recruiting Billy Ingram. Frank had recruited Stan Love out of Morningside while I was the JV coach a few years earlier, so we knew each other a little. But we became good friends while he was recruiting Billy. Not long after that, the head coach at Oregon retired and Frank was certain he'd get the job. But they hired Dick Harter instead. Ten days later, Coach Wooden hired Frank as an assistant coach at UCLA. Now that he's in L.A., our relationship grows even more. Frank and his wife, Bea, and Sally and I socialized together a lot in those days.

One evening at dinner Frank said, "Jim, I'm going to get a head coaching job sometime, and when I do, Bea and I would love it if you and Sally came with us. I'd want you as one of my assistants." I said OK, even though I really didn't give it much thought. In this business, it doesn't pay to get overly excited about a real job possibility, much less one that may or may not ever materialize.

Two years later the Utah State job opened and Frank went after it. He got close, but in the end they hired Dutch Belnap, one of the assistants there at the time. Frank called to congratulate him, and during the course of their talk, Frank asked what route

Dutch was going to take regarding assistants. Dutch said, "I'd like to hire a guy from L.A. who can recruit." When Frank heard that, he immediately said, "Well, I've got a guy for you. Name's Jim Harrick."

Dutch contacted me and we talked and talked. He even came down and spent a few days at our house. While he's here, he borrows my car so he could go interview Mike Montgomery, who was just getting out of the army at the time. He's chasing around town talking to my competition — and in my car, no less! Finally, he offers me the job. For $12,000 a year. I told him Sally and I needed to see the place before we made a decision. Dutch said, "Well, you can come up, but I can't pay for Sally's ticket."

The next day we caught a flight to Salt Lake City (I paid Sally's way), then drove the 84 miles to Logan. Neither of us had been to Utah before, and our first experience didn't do much to sell us on the place. There was rain, snow, sleet and sunshine in the hour and a half it took to make the drive. We'd never seen weather quite that bizarre.

Logan is a small town of about 25,000. Our first impression was that it's a cozy little place, scenic, low-key and rather slow moving. Certainly it was a far cry from what we were used to. I don't think either of us was particularly overwhelmed at first. But then Dutch took us to the Spectrum, walked us up to the press box and turned on the lights. Once he flipped that switch, I saw one of the most beautiful, magnificent arenas I've ever seen. It was breathtaking.

My instincts were telling me to take the job. So was my heart. But I didn't want to make a decision based purely on emotion or intuition, so I told Dutch that I wanted to go back and think about it. There were things to be considered — uprooting my family, salary, and the prospect of long hours on the road recruiting. This was one of those crossroad moments. It deserved some serious thought.

Answers to many of our most important questions often come in unforeseen ways, from the most unexpected sources. Bolts of lightning, out of the dark. That's what happened this time — in a manner that was not only strange but somewhat sad.

At Morningside, one of the things teachers would do at lunch was play bridge. We'd take our food to the lounge, eat and play cards. One day I was playing with the guy who had taught English and Latin at Morningside for more than 20 years. Charles Oleckno. I'll never forget his name. Charles was one of the teachers who couldn't handle the changing times, with students who more openly challenged authority. He came from an era when students were totally submissive, when being rebellious or outspoken simply wasn't tolerated. He couldn't deal with this newer breed of students. They were killing the guy, just killing him. He was old, walked with a cane — and he was turning into a truly sour, pathetic man.

When the bell rang we got up and started walking down the hall. I turned to him and said, "I have an opportunity to take a college coaching job, but it would mean an $11,500 cut in pay." He looked at me and said, "You know, I had the chance to go to a junior college once, but it was for $2,000 less than I was making at the time. I didn't think I could do it."

Right then I stopped dead in my tracks and watched him walk away, aided by his cane. And I thought to myself, "Holy mackerel, there I go 20 years from now if I stay in this place! No way I'm going to let that happen. That's not going to be me shuffling down the hall, filled with bitterness and remorse, wondering what might have been."

I turned around, went straight to the principal's office, called Dutch and told him I'd take the Utah State job. I didn't know how we would survive on that salary, but I made up my mind that I would never take or reject any job because of money. The sad example of Charles Oleckno taught me that.

It was the defining moment of my life.

CONDITION: CRITICAL

7

We'd not only survived, but thrived, in our desert excursion. And we'd regrouped from our home-court loss to Cal with four straight wins. But all of it was merely a prelude to the most critical part of our schedule: the "mini-tournament" — five games compressed into a 10-day span, none of them easy, all of them designed to test our willpower as much as our talent. To win the NCAA Tournament you have to win six straight games, but at least they're spread over a three-week period. We'd have to win these five with little rest, and against major opposition: Arizona State and Arizona at home, followed by road games against a good Stanford team and a rematch with our nemesis, Cal; then ending with a nationally-televised home game against none other than Duke, which had been struggling, but which nevertheless represented the most successful program in the nation over the past decade.

In the back of my mind I couldn't help but hear the echoes of my past seasons, faint reminders of the accusations that UCLA would always fold in the second half of the year, would always be the patient that couldn't survive once the condition turned critical.

And that's what this would be. Critical. If we responded to the "mini-tournament" in convincing fashion, it would tell me a lot about this team's character — not to mention its chances once the real tournament cranked up. That was on my mind when I talked to my team.

"Don't snivel to me and complain!" I started. "Other schools have a conference tournament. Well, this is ours. We've got to play these five games, so let's just go play. It's better than having to practice, anyway."

Or so I hoped. Here are some snapshots of what happened:

February 16, 1995 — Arizona State at UCLA.

Taken out of their game at home, Arizona State is not letting it happen this time. They've slowed the tempo, and Mario Bennett (21 points) is having maybe the best game he's ever had against us. Ron Riley (23 points) is also shooting holes in us.

But, oh my, Ed O'Bannon has turned it up. He's everywhere and now it's do-or-die time. We're trailing 66-63 with only 1:29 to go. Ed posts up, gets the ball and makes a spin move. It's not there, but Charles is. Ed dishes to him in the lane and Charles goes up — TWEET! — and hits the shot while getting hacked. He nails the free throw and suddenly we're tied, 52 seconds remaining.

Spectacular shot! Now, defense! Give 'em nothing!

We don't, and when an Arizona State shot misses, Ed goes high to get the ball, but he's off balance and falling out of bounds.

Naw, not that! They're going to get the ball back.

But wait, as his momentum takes him through the air but before his feet land him out of bounds, Ed screams. "Time out!" The refs signal it. He's saved us. We'll get a last shot at the basket. Arizona State won't.

Heady play. Just brilliant!

There's five or six seconds left, a lot of time. We come

down, but we're in a rush and Arizona State has its defense set. They knock it out of bounds with a second to go. They call time-out. We run a play and get a rushed shot out of the corner that doesn't go. Overtime.

It stays close in overtime, but we get up two with about three minutes left. We keep holding them with great stops defensively. Just over two minutes left now, still up by two, and we call time out. In the huddle I call a play designed for Ed. We don't shoot many threes, but I sense that Ed is hungry to bust this thing open.

He's in a whole different zone now, Jim. That timeout call was unbelievable. He deserves a chance here. Let him step up.

We've got the ball under our basket. The play I want is one we haven't run a lot, a new one for this kind of situation. But we've been working on it in practice. I want the second option off it, which means it will go to Ed. He'll come off a double screen that should free him for an open three. Huddle breaks, we line up, Ed slashes by the screen, flashes open and gets the ball. Boom. He nails it. A three. We're up five and that's how the margin stays. We win, 82- 77.

Ed has 23 points and Charles has 22, plus 11 rebounds. Tyus scores 10 but also has 12 — count 'em, 12! — assists. Have we just dodged a bullet, or made a very important statement? Maybe both.

*   *   *

In retrospect, from that moment on, I thought Ed O'Bannon became the best basketball player in America. Finally, after nearly five years, he was back in every way: mentally, physically and emotionally. Ed just wasn't going to let anything stop him, or his team. And make no mistake, in many important ways it was his team. Just as I'd wanted it to be for quite some time. His incredible play when he called timeout while falling out of bounds, and that deadeye three that put the game out of reach in overtime, set the stage for all the brilliance he would show — game in, game out —straight through to Seattle. He was no

longer just a real good player. He'd ascended to a whole different level. He was thoroughly dominating games.

February 19, 1995 — Arizona at UCLA.
        Tyus is bothered by tendinitis in his knee, and it's hurting
his ability to do another defensive number on Stoudamire —
who hits a couple of bombs.
        Try Toby.
        I do. I decide to bring Bailey off the bench for Edney. And
he's doing a great job on Stoudamire. I just can't imagine a freshman doing this. He's staying in front of him, refusing to let him
penetrate, and always getting a hand in his face when he shoots.
        Arizona is up eight at one stage, but we come back.
They're trying everything on Ed. Box-and-chaser. Zone. But he's
brilliant again. (He'll finish with 31 points and 11 rebounds.) We
begin to take control, never that far ahead, but refusing to let our
lead wither.
        And then it happens.
        We're up four late and they've got the ball. It kicks loose,
there's a scramble for the ball, and George slaps it out of a crowd
and the ball kicks toward midcourt — toward Bailey, who
scoops it up on the run and is flying, just flying, downcourt. But
there's an Arizona player, coming in hard and fast at an angle to
cut him off, and there's Toby . . .
        YOW! DO-IT-DO-IT!
        . . . taking the ball left-handed behind his back, on the
dead run, as the defender cuts across his bow, and there he goes,
not slowing a lick, up, up and away, with a huge, huge two-
handed slam. Just a monster! Stoudamire tries to get them back
in the game with a three, but Ed makes a strong move, is fouled,
and drains both free throws. We've shut them down. The final is
72-70, but we were up 72-67 with 11 seconds left. Reggie Geary
hits a three to cut it to two with three seconds left, but we're able
to in-bound the ball and run out the clock.

                    *   *   *

Arizona was the program I pointed to when I took this job. Lute Olson is a terrific coach. When you play his teams, you know you're in a ball game — because they do everything well. Everything. I knew when I came to UCLA that Arizona would be the program we needed to catch. Well, we've played them 15 times now. They're still ahead, 9-6, but they got out to a 6-1 lead in wins on us. The last four years, we're 5-3 against them.

I like what one of my assistants, Mark Gottfried, said about those two wins over the Arizona schools. "The Arizona weekend at home was the beginning of a point where our team began to believe they were good enough to win the national championship," Mark said.

Besides the boost in confidence, the most significant thing to come out of the Arizona game was the play of Toby Bailey. He'd replaced Tyus and played great D. He'd had another big performance in a big game. And that dunk just solidified everything in my mind. With Edney out, Ed and Toby were our only double-figure scorers in that game (Toby had 19). Toby gave us more of a three-point threat. He also gave us incredible quickness defensively, and when you combined that with his size (6-5) it meant he could be hell on quick, but smaller, guards. And he gave us a balance. We could guard big guards, little guards, big forwards, little forwards. It would give us better inside play, because J.R. — instead of playing wing — could spell George Zidek, so we could go with quickness inside or strength inside. And we could also move J.R. out to the wing defensively and put all his size (remember, he's 6-9) on anybody we wanted. Our break would be better because Toby could get out on it. Our three-point attack was better. And there was that big-game intangible of his. Toby was the guy. Toby had earned something.

When he made that incredible move and dunk, I made up my mind right then and there. Toby Bailey would start our next game. It proved to be the last missing piece to the puzzle.

*   *   *

February 21, 1995 — UCLA at Stanford.

We've risen to the number two national ranking. J.R. has started 13 straight games, but now I'm replacing him — going to another freshman — in the starting lineup. In our shoot-around the day of the game, I walk up to him. "J.R., I'm going to tell you something. I'm going to start Toby tonight. But you're still a starter in my mind. We just aren't going to announce you as one." This is always a touchy situation, with any player, but especially a freshman. You run the risk of upsetting their ego, which can be fragile. But J.R. takes it like a man. And once the game starts and I bring him off the bench, he plays like one.

We're trailing 47-44 at halftime, giving up way too many shots.

Remember what the films said. A zone might work here.

Indeed, so I decide to go to the zone in the second half. We're everywhere with the zone, very aggressive and quick, and Stanford scores only 30 second-half points. We win, 89-77. The new lineup is humming: We have five scoring in double figures — led by another great game from Ed, who has 22 points, nine rebounds, five assists, three steals, and five blocked shots; and J.R. has been great, scoring 19 in his new sixth-man role. I like what's happening with this team.

$$*\qquad*\qquad*$$

We work on our man-to-man defense probably 95 percent of the time in practice, but I was beginning to see that the talent on this team begged for more. You know, this year just about every button I pushed, things worked — be it man or zone, press or not, fast break or half-court game. Other years, those things don't happen. This season, they happened like a nuclear bomb happens. And the zone, in particular, was developing into a surprising, potent weapon. It worked at Stanford, and it would work against Duke. And it would help us later, particularly against Oklahoma State in the national semifinals.

I'll tell you what that zone was. It was a very, very quick zone — maybe quicker than any I'd ever seen. We could cover ground. You really had to run some things to get a good shot off it. Toby could tower over smaller guards, not to mention get to them quickly, outside. And if I put in J.R. for George, we were quick at every spot with the zone. Quick, and with long arms to boot. It made our zone something fearsome.

*   *   *

February 23, 1995 — UCLA at California.

Payback time. We are simply awesome now, hitting every mark. We've extended Cal's defense, opened up the court, and Tyus is picking them apart. Penetrating and finding George all the time. Which shows another of our strengths. George, who'd sat much of the time at Stanford, scores 25 points. All our starters score in double figures. We set a school record for field goal percentage (40 of 60, 66.7 percent). We set a school record for assists (32). And Ed, still white hot, ties the school record for threes. He makes seven (of nine attempts) and scores 27 points.

We win, 104-88. In the post-game press conference, Todd Bozeman says: "Tonight, UCLA could have beaten the Lakers." It was a nice compliment. We shook hands after the game, the "controversy" when they'd come to our place long since forgotten. We hadn't changed much strategy-wise this time around, we just went in hoping to play better defense. The first time we played them, Cal was just on fire. Sometimes you run into teams like that and there's not much you can do about it. This turnaround is a clear demonstration that my team is starting to generate its own heat.

"We're just different players out there now."

It's a pleasant thought.

February 26, 1995 — Duke at UCLA.

In the locker room, I hold up my hands, thumbs and forefingers together, like I'm pulling a string or something. I look at my players.

"Fellas, do you see this line?" I say. "See it? This is a fine line. It's the fine line between winning and losing. I'm going to tell you why I'm doing this — it's because I tried to recruit half of the players on Duke's team. And I KNOW that they're very, very talented. They could play in our program. What their problems are, I don't know. Don't have any idea. But I know they're like this line right here, this fine line between winning and losing."

I think they understand. Duke has fallen on some hard times. Mike Krzyzewski has given up the helm temporarily — suffering from back problems and, well, nervous exhaustion; which ought to tell me just what the stress can do to you as a coach, even one as brilliant and successful as Mike. At any rate, Duke has had its problems, never really in sync, but I know they might break out of that at any time, and national television just might be the catalyst they need. Duke needs a big win like this to maybe get into the tournament. As strong as we're playing, we don't want to stumble now. It's been a quick, but grinding, stretch — physically and emotionally. We can't let Duke undo all the progress we've made.

Well, Duke is doing its best to bring it about. They just won't fade. Eight or so minutes to play, and they're still within striking distance. I decide it's time to zone again. It works. My, how it works. We just paralyze 'em. Led by Ed (of course), we begin to leave them them in our tracks. The final is 100-77. Ed has a career-high 37 points. Cherokee Parks — one of the Southern California guys who got away from me, back when they were saying I couldn't recruit — scores 21 for Duke. But it's Ed who's the dominant player now, and I remember how I've been telling Dick Vitale for some time that Ed is being overlooked, that he might not have been the best player in the nation earlier but that he's stepped up. And in the closing minutes, after Ed has done everything but hang new nets, I look over at Dick, who's calling the game for ABC. Ed has just hit another shot, and I'm standing there, looking at Dick, and I just point a finger at him. Vitale breaks up. I can see him laughing as he talks into his mike.

*   *   *

We'd done it. Won all five. We would get the number-one ranking after the Duke blowout. Ed O'Bannon? In those five games he averaged 27.5 points, 9 rebounds, 2.9 assists, 1.8 blocked shots and two steals. He hit 58.5 percent of his floor shots and 16 of 25 threes, an amazing 64 percent. In the toughest stretch of the season, he'd been the toughest player in the nation. Bring your attitude? Ed had branded his attitude — on anybody who'd dared to get in his way. Ed was a 23-year-old, fifth-year senior who was hungry, focused and a veteran of the wars. He'd seen adversity. Now he was inflicting it.

We'd settled on a seven-man rotation — J.R. and Cameron Dollar off the bench — and we could go to multiple defenses with guys who could take on multiple roles. I think our players just marveled at what Ed was doing, but we were also getting exceptional leadership from Tyus and George as well. They'd just taken over. A couple of times in a game I'd say, "We're going to do this," and one of them would pipe up, "No, Coach, let's do this." Know what? There were times when I'd say OK to that. Because I knew what was happening here, and I trusted their ability and their insight. A coach has to be the strategist and tactician, but when a coach senses his players have the right stuff, he would be a fool not to listen and consider their suggestions. It's not just that. If there's no conflict in what I want done, it's good to say OK. It gives them a chance to lead, and in the heat of battle you want that kind of confidence instilled in them. And so there were times when I'd do it. Even off the court. We had a rule that required them to wear coats and ties on the airplane, at all times. But when we went to some places — like Oregon and Washington, where it was rainy — Ed stepped up and said the team wanted to dress a little more casually. Well, I let them. Coach Wooden always said that you probably learn more from your players than you ever realize. It's important to listen to them.

These guys had earned the right to loosen their ties. They'd been on a long, hard journey — and they were showing the ability to take control of their own destinies. Which, though I often wondered at the time, is what I had done in preparing for and finally getting the UCLA job some seven years earlier. Fate played a role, of course, because there were other jobs that popped open and others I looked into while at Pepperdine. None of them panned out, which proved fortunate — because the one I'd always been waiting for was at UCLA, and I was ready when the chance finally came.

*   *   *

When the phone rang at seven o'clock on the morning of April 12, 1988, I had no idea it would be the most important call of my life. I figured it was probably from Sally, who was visiting her mother in West Virginia, or one of my sons, Glenn, who was away from home at the time. Maybe it was from one of my golfing buddies asking me to hit the links with him later that afternoon. Or perhaps it was one of Monte's or Jim Jr.'s friends calling.

I was wrong on all counts. The call was from Pete Dalis.

"Jim, are you ready to come over and take the toughest basketball coaching job in America?" Pete asked.

I didn't hesitate.

"Pete, I've been waiting 28 years for this opportunity," I said. "Yes, I'll take the job, and I won't let you down."

I called Sally and told her about it. I think she was more surprised than excited. In her heart, I really don't think she believed that I'd ever get the UCLA job. I have to confess that there were plenty of times when I tended to agree with her. To say a longshot won the race is putting it mildly.

As I put the phone down, I heard footsteps bounding up the stairs. It was my son Jim coming toward me, a grin about a mile wide covering his face. "YEAH!!!" he yelled, hugging me. He'd been listening on the downstairs phone.

Then I called Tom Asbury, my longtime assistant at Pepperdine. I told him that I would love to have him come join me at UCLA, but that if he chose to stay at Pepperdine, I would understand and help him any way I could. He congratulated me, then said he'd like to try for the head coaching job there. I understood completely. He wanted to be his own man. Nothing wrong with that.

Later that morning, UCLA held a press conference announcing that Jim Harrick was their new coach. Sitting there, flanked by Pete and Chancellor Charles Young, facing a battalion of reporters and a battery of television cameras, I'm pretty certain I experienced every possible human emotion — excitement, joy, fear, relief, disbelief . . . you name it, I felt it. I even felt a sense of sadness at having to leave such a great place as Pepperdine.

As I listened to Pete give his opening remarks, I kept remembering something Tommy Lasorda once said: "How can a third-string pitcher from Norristown, Pennsylvania, turn out to be the manager of the best baseball organization in the world?" At that moment, I knew exactly what Tommy meant.

Fate. I always keep coming back to that fate thing, don't I? But how else can I explain it? How can a second-team player at Morris Harvey College get in his car, drive to Los Angeles, begin a career as a seventh-grade teacher, then 28 years later end up as the head coach at the greatest basketball school in the country? That's more unbelievable than the wildest piece of fiction. If that's not fate, what is it?

As I waited to answer the barrage of reporters' questions, it wasn't lost on me that I was the sixth man to sit in this chair since Coach Wooden retired in 1975. Five coaches had come and gone in this 13-year span, excellent coaches who won better than 73 percent of their games at UCLA. Four chose to leave, one was fired. Despite having records that were consistently outstanding, none of these men ever satisfied the hungry wolves. As a result, UCLA, once the very model of consistency and calm, had become a graveyard for coaches.

One of the quotations I hold onto belongs to Winston Churchill. It says: "To every man there comes in his lifetime that special moment when he is figuratively tapped on the shoulder and offered that chance to do a very special thing unique to him and fitted to his talents. What a tragedy if that moment finds him unprepared or unqualified for that work."

I was about to find out if I was prepared to grab hold of the flame and handle the heat. And I was going to do it in "the toughest basketball coaching job in America."

Be careful what you ask for, it might come true.

But I'm getting ahead of myself. Between the time a high school Latin teacher made an offhand remark that jump-started me to make the leap to coaching in the college ranks and Pete Dalis' phone call, there were many dues to be paid. UCLA is at the top of the ladder, and no one gets to the top without paying a huge price. I'm no exception. The top of the ladder was still a long way off.

Next stop on the road to Westwood: Logan, Utah.

*   *   *

Our four years at Utah State were probably the most enjoyable of our life. We made as many friends in Logan as we have in all our years in Los Angeles. It was a wonderful place to live. Our sons were in fifth grade, in third grade and four years old when we moved there, and they still remember it with great fondness.

I spent most of that first summer alone. Sally and the boys stayed in Los Angeles until the house was sold. During my free time, I would drive around and look at houses. One day, I found one I liked — and felt we could afford — so I agreed to buy it. That's the only time I ever stepped over into Sally's territory and made such a big decision without her input. Fortunately, she loved the house.

From a coaching perspective, Utah State was a different experience from any I'd had. At Morningside High, I was coach, teacher, athletics director and driver's ed instructor. I was all over the place. But at Utah State, it wasn't that way. I was free to concentrate totally on basketball. All my energies were focused in that direction. I organized my basketball life at Utah State.

Dutch Belnap had lived his whole life in Utah. So had Rod Tueller, another assistant. They had their own circle of friends, people they'd known for years. Since I was new and didn't really know anybody, I was kind of a loner. I would spend day after day alone in my office, putting together different plans, plotting various strategies. I must have had 10 different offenses, and at least that many defenses, presses and press offenses. I organized everything into files, of course. This was an important time for me, a period when I really learned the sport. I had the time to break down every phase of the game to its most minute detail and analyze it like never before.

My chief responsibilities at Utah State were threefold: recruiting, scouting and defense. It was a hard, hard job, especially the recruiting. I was the only coach on our staff who recruited out of state, so I was on the go all the time. I practically lived in hotels and airports. Once I was gone for 17 straight days. That's tough. Ask any college recruiter and he'll tell you the same thing. Your family becomes almost like strangers to you.

We were 85 miles from the nearest airport, which didn't make it any easier. Also, Utah State is an independent trying to recruit against WAC schools like Brigham Young and Utah. That's another strike against you. But the basketball was tremendous. Utah State is only 40 or so miles away from three other schools: Utah, Weber State and BYU — and since we all played each other twice, the rivalries were just ferocious. Standing-room-only crowds. Great competition. It was wild.

Without question, the biggest adjustment between high school coaching and college coaching is learning how to recruit. Recruiting is the lifeblood of every program, and if you can't recruit successfully, you're going to lose more games than you win. That goes for every program, whether it's North Carolina or Podunk U. No coach can win consistently unless he has talented players. A great coach with bad players usually gets beat by a bad coach with good players. Simple as that.

Although I had to learn recruiting in a trial-by-fire way, I think I got to be pretty good at it. I know I really worked hard at becoming an excellent salesman, which is what a recruiter is. I had to sell the school, the community and the head coach to the recruit and his family. Of course, first I had to sell myself. If I failed to do that, they weren't going to listen to the rest of my pitch. I had notebooks filled with pictures, graphs, charts . . .

anything that might help give me an edge. Or at least help me get their interest.

The recruiting trail is where you find some of the seediest, sorriest things happening in college sports. It's been documented countless times already, so there's no need for me to go into it in any great detail here. I will say that I don't think it's nearly as bad now as it was when I first hit the recruiting trail. I hope not, anyway. There's no place for cheating in college athletics — there's no place for cheating anywhere, for that matter — and it just makes me sick when I see it happen. I have no sympathy for those who get caught. I have tried never to do anything to break the rules, and I expect my fellow coaches to do the same. All I want is a level playing field. Just give me that and I'm happy. My feeling is that if a coach has to resort to breaking the rules in order to be competitive, he's in the wrong business and he needs to get out. My bosses at Utah State, Pepperdine and UCLA would not have tolerated cheating. Nor should they. And it cuts both ways for me. I don't want to work for an administration that looks the other way while rules are being broken.

Being an assistant coach at the college level is one of the most thankless jobs imaginable. You do an incredible amount of work, there are high expectations, and yet there's not much glory. You're always in the background. The head coach knows what you're doing, and he appreciates it, but not many others do. And talk about being anonymous. I've always said that assistant coaches aren't included in the census. That's a joke, but it's not far from the truth. It's a lot of hours, a lot of sweat and not much else. Assistant coaches have two jobs — recruit and recruit relentlessly, and they are obsessed with four things — recruiting, recruiting, recruiting, and looking for a head coaching job. That never changes.

We were 66-40 during my four years at Utah State. That's not bad. We finished 21-6 in 1975 and made it to the NCAA Tournament. After my second year there, Frank Arnold called to inform me that he was taking the BYU job and wanted me to go along as his assistant. I said, "I'm not going, Frank. I just moved here and I've busted my tail for the past two years. I'm staying here."

So I did. I stayed two more years at Utah State, working, organizing, learning. Then, after my fourth year there, something happened that changed everything. That fate thing stepped in again.

*   *   *

Poor Gene Bartow. All he did was win 52 games and lose just nine during two years at UCLA, yet it wasn't good enough. He didn't win a national championship. UCLA fans, accustomed to watching championship banners rise with the regularity of the morning sun, weren't about to stand for such abysmal failure. Fifty-two and nine? An 85-percent winning percentage? You gotta be kidding. Such mediocrity. We can't put up with this nonsense.

Gene Bartow did a helluva coaching job at UCLA. A great job in every respect. I think any reasonable person would say the same thing. How could you possibly disagree? To win 52 out of 61 games at any school is outstanding. Virtually every school in this country would kill to have that record. His teams won the Pacific-8 title both years, losing just four conference games along the way. He won, and he did so by playing within the rules. And yet, Gene couldn't get out of Los Angeles fast enough.

You see, Gene made one fatal mistake: he followed John Wooden. He tried to fill the shoes of a legend, a coach who had just won 10 of the last 12 NCAA championships. It was an impossible task. The only man who might have done it is Denny Crum, but even for him, it would have been no picnic. Coach Wooden had set standards so high that any coach was almost certain to come up short.

It was no laughing matter for Gene, who, by the time he resigned, had lost 15 pounds and was taking medication for stomach problems. He'd had enough, figuring nothing he could do was going to be good enough. So, after two seasons of dealing with the fans' intense criticism, he called it quits, starting his own program at the University of Alabama-Birmingham, where he has continued his winning ways.

In April of 1977, while Gene was mulling over what course of action he wanted to take, a job came open at a great junior college, the College of Southern Idaho, that I was interested in. It had been a breeding ground for coaches — Eddie Sutton, Boyd Grant and Jerry Hale all got their starts there — so I decided to go after the job. With the help of our athletics director, Ladell Anderson, I managed to get an interview. Sally and I drove to Twin Falls, Idaho, to meet with the school president. We spent about five hours touring the school, checking out the facilities, looking at houses. At the interview, the president had a yellow legal pad with 415 names on it. Those were the people who had applied for the job. Then he said to me, "I'm only interviewing two people." Turns out the two were me and Mike Mitchell, who had just won a national title at a junior college in Texas. Mike got the job.

Four months later, I'm the assistant coach at UCLA. Tell me that's not fate.

*   *   *

About the time when the heat was becoming unbearable for Gene at UCLA, I was preparing to leave with the Utah State team for a 30-day tour of Australia. A day or so before we left, a friend of mine in L.A. called to let me know that there was a good chance Gene might leave. He wasn't for sure, but he had a gut feeling that Gene had had enough.

I was leaving for Australia on a Sunday morning, going alone because I couldn't afford to take Sally and the boys. On Saturday night, while we were eating dinner, the phone rang. I had just instituted a house rule that no one could take a phone call while we were eating. It's one of those rules I put in that doesn't last very long. After about a week of hearing my sons fuss, I usually throw up my hands and give in. Anyway, one of my sons answered the call, then said, "Dad, it's for you, but you can't take it." I took the phone from him, thus breaking my own rule.

It was Gary Cunningham. He said, "I think Coach Bartow is going to resign tomorrow. If he does, I'm going to apply for the job. If I get it, I want to talk to you." I said, "Jeez, Gary, this couldn't have come at a worse time. I'm leaving tomorrow for Australia."

It didn't surprise me that Gary called. He'd done it before, when he interviewed for the job at Colorado. He told me then that if he got hired, he wanted me as an assistant. We had stayed in touch over the years, so I knew I was in good shape with him. Gary, who had been a star player for Coach Wooden and later a UCLA assistant, was working in the UCLA Alumni Office at the time Gene resigned. He hadn't been thinking about a return to coaching, but he said this opportunity was too good to pass over.

Gene resigned from UCLA on the day I left for Australia. In fact, our plane had a three-hour layover in L.A., so I watched it on TV. Then it was off to what I thought was the end of the world. In those days, Australia was out of touch with the outside world. There was no *USA Today*, no CNN, no news from the United States at all. I was 8,000 miles away with no clue about what was happening back home. I could take the suspense only so long, so after 20 days, I finally broke down and called a buddy back in L.A. He said nothing had happened yet. Then I called Cunningham. Remember, that's about a $20 phone call, a lot of money to a guy making 14 grand a year. Gary said, "Yeah, I think I'm going to get the job, but we've got to wait on affirmative action."

Five days later, I called Sally and she told me that Gary had been hired. I hung up and immediately called Gary. He said, "Jim, I'll save you an interview." On the way back to the U.S., we were scheduled to spend a day in Hawaii. I didn't. Instead, I hopped on a plane and flew to L.A. I had no coat, no tie, nothing decent enough to wear to a job interview, so I had to buy a suit and tie.

I could not sleep the night before my interview with Gary. Not a wink. I was at the crossroads of my career and I knew it. The pressure I felt that night weighed heavier on me than a ton of steel.

Gary and I talked all morning. It was a nice, easy chat between two friends who had been away from each other for several years. We talked about basketball philosophy, sure, but mainly we got reacquainted with each other. After Gary and I finished, I went in and talked with J.D. Morgan, the A.D. It was just the two of us. Then I went into one of the outside offices while Gary and J.D. got together to make a decision. By this time I felt good about my chances. Things had gone well. I was confident, but far from cocky. In this business, it doesn't pay to get cocky. A few minutes later, Gary walked out, shook my hand, and said, "Congratulations, I want to offer you the job." I was now a member of the UCLA coaching staff.

While I was still in the UCLA offices, I called Sally, whom I had not seen in 33 days, and told her. She said she'd lost about 15 pounds during the ordeal of waiting and worrying. Then I called my parents in Charleston. They were ecstatic. That evening I caught a flight to Salt Lake City, arriving just a little before midnight. Sally was there, waiting for me. I can't begin to tell you how happy I was to see her. We drove to Logan, getting home at two in the morning.

The weather was perfect.

*   *   *

I said earlier that it's my contention that Denny Crum is the one coach who could have successfully followed Coach Wooden. I say that for several reasons. First, Denny is a terrific coach, which he proved by winning two NCAA titles at Louisville. Second, he played for Coach Wooden, then later served as Coach's assistant for several years. Third, Denny is part of the UCLA "family," a factor that shouldn't be taken lightly. Being in the family means you don't get scrutinized to the nth degree the way an outsider like Gene was.

Looking back, I don't think I'd be far off base if I said that Gary Cunningham also stood an excellent chance of surviving the fierce pressure and expectation that drove Gene Bartow out of Westwood. And for the very same reasons I alluded to concerning Denny. Gary played for Coach Wooden, later was an assistant, and is a member of the UCLA family. And also like Denny, Gary is a superb basketball coach.

In the two years Gary was the head coach at UCLA, we had a record of 50-8. We were 29-3 in conference play, including

14-0 in 1977-78, and we were ranked number one in the country for much of the '78-79 season. That year we went to South Bend and beat a Notre Dame team that had five or six guys who ended up playing pro ball. We came within one game of reaching the Final Four that second year, losing to DePaul 95-91 in Provo, Utah, in the West Regional final. It was a very successful two years. Also, very calm. I don't remember anyone saying or writing a negative word during that two-year period.

Gary proved that he was more than just a favorite son; he proved he could coach with the best of them. Of course, we had a lot of talent. David Greenwood, Kiki Vandeweghe, Roy Hamilton, Brad Holland, James Wilkes, Raymond Townsend — those guys were very good basketball players. But having talent doesn't guarantee success. That's one of the greatest myths in all of sports. A coach has to know what to do with his talent, how to motivate his players, how to blend individuals into a cohesive unit that pulls together. Coaching talented players is far more difficult than coaching mediocre players. It's easy to coach players who aren't especially gifted. They listen better. They have to if they hope to succeed against superior competition. Talented athletes don't always listen and they don't always work hard, because they think they can get by strictly on ability. That's another myth. It can't be done. Talent and potential belong in the same boat — they are worthless unless they are properly developed and utilized.

Red Auerbach, Casey Stengel, Pat Riley, Vince Lombardi — great coaches who seldom received the kind of recognition their coaching ability deserved. Everyone assumed that all those men did was fill out a lineup card, then sit back and watch their team win. Take Riley, for instance. The man won three NBA championships with the Lakers in the 1980s and not once was he named Coach of the Year. People said, "Well, he's got Magic and Kareem and Jamaal and Worthy and blah, blah, blah. He ought to win." Well, I've got news for you. There is no such thing as automatic pilot in this business. You have to get down in the trenches and get the job done. Nothing is ever guaranteed.

For me, jumping from Utah State to UCLA was like going from a VW Beetle to a Bentley. It was a whole new ball game, especially when it came to recruiting. I could no longer be content to sign second-level players; now I had to recruit the top players in the country. I visited the homes of players like Ralph Sampson, Sam Bowie and Greg Kite. Big-time players who could make a good program great or put a struggling program on the map. The pressure to do well in recruiting increased a thousand percent. My gut ached at night worrying about recruiting. Despite the pressure I felt, I loved it all — the hard work, the travel, the demands. I somehow knew I was in the college ranks for good.

During my second year at UCLA, we played Pepperdine in the second round of the NCAA. It was a tough scrap, but we finally put them away, 76-71. After the game, I'm running off the court to see Greg Kite, who was making his official visit to UCLA. Before I get to Greg, I see Wayne Wright, the Pepperdine A.D., off to the side motioning for me to come over. He says, "Jim, we're going to hire a new head coach and you're one of the guys we have in mind."

The next night, Sally and I met Wayne and his wife for dinner. A few days later, I went up to Malibu and visited Wayne for an hour or so. He showed me around the campus, then he gave me a Pepperdine press guide to take home and look through. It was all very nice, but I didn't give it much thought. Foremost on my mind was helping UCLA get ready to play San Francisco in the NCAA Tournament.

We beat San Francisco on Thursday, and on Friday, after we finished practicing, Gary called me up to his room and dropped a bombshell. He was going to resign. I couldn't believe what I was hearing. It came as a complete surprise. I thought Gary would be at UCLA for a long time.

One thing I didn't have to worry about was a job. J.D. Morgan had already told Larry Farmer and me that if anything happened, we would be taken care of. That's always nice to know. At least I wouldn't be out on the breadlines looking for a meal.

Knowing Gary like I do, it shouldn't have come as such a big surprise when he decided to get out of coaching. Gary's a real intellectual, a Ph.D. in botany, and if ever a man was cut out for athletic administration, it's him. He's now the A.D. at Cal-Santa Barbara. He's been the president of the Athletic Directors of America, and he was on the Division I Basketball Committee, which is one of the most prestigious positions in the NCAA. So, he's been a real commodity as an athletic director.

Anyway, I had breakfast with Coach Wooden the following Monday morning and I asked him if he thought I had a chance at getting the UCLA job. He said I didn't. His advice was, take the Pepperdine job if it's offered, and if it's not, stay at UCLA as an assistant until something better comes along.

Still, I wasn't going to be satisfied until I found out for myself. So the next day I went in to see J.D. Morgan. I asked him if I had a shot. He shook his head and said, in that deep, rumbling voice of his, "Jim, my ass is on the line here." He didn't have to say another word — I understood exactly what he meant. There was no way he could hire a no-name like Jim Harrick at UCLA.

Looking back, I realize that not getting hired was a blessing. It would have been a disaster, for me and for UCLA. I was not ready for the UCLA head coaching job. My knowledge of the game wasn't nearly as strong as it needed to be, my discipline of high-quality players wouldn't have been demanding enough, and my experience as a bench coach, particularly in the tournament, was not there.

I'm often asked if I think a good college assistant coach or a good high school coach can go straight from those jobs to the head coaching position at one of the high-pressure schools like UCLA, Kentucky, Indiana, North Carolina, Duke, Kansas . . . schools where basketball is more than a sport and the demand for winning never ends. My answer: Very rarely. It is very difficult for a college assistant or high school coach to step in and succeed in that kind of situation.

When you go from the assistant's chair to the head coach's chair, it's a move of about 18 inches. But it might as well be 18 miles. Move those 18 inches and you suddenly go from being a suggestion-maker to being a decision-maker. Organization of the entire program falls into your lap, everything from the study table to the cafeteria to the dormitories to travel to scheduling to discipline to taking care of players, assistant coaches, managers and trainers. The end result is that the buck always comes back to you.

Every young coach, no matter how good, needs a place where he can learn to deal with the wide range of responsibilities that go with being the guy in charge. Ideally, it would be at a school where the pressure to win isn't the end-all and be-all, a place where you can experiment, where you can try new and different approaches, where you aren't a prisoner of the fear of failure.

A place like Pepperdine.

Word was getting around that I was about to be offered the Pepperdine job. I knew that if it did happen, I'd have to give it serious consideration, if for no other reason than money. I was making $23,500 as a high school coach; now, at age 40, I was making $25,000. Part of me wanted to stay and see what happened at UCLA, while another part wanted to make life easier for my family. Finally, I said to Sally, "If they offer me $25,000, I'm not going. If it's $30,000, I'll think about it. But if it's $35,000, we got to go."

Wayne Wright called and offered me the job. The salary was $35,000. I accepted.

It was my turn to make that 18-inch move.

＊　　　＊　　　＊

While I was waiting to hear from Pepperdine, several of my closest friends advised me against taking the job if it was offered. Wait, they said, hold out for a job of a little more magnitude. I told them they were crazy. From my point of view, the Pepperdine job was perfect in every way. It was a place where I could coach without constantly being put under the microscope, it was an excellent school with high academic standards and principles, and it was located in a setting — on a rolling hill in Malibu — that can only be described as poetic. (How many coaches can sit at their desk and look out the window at the Pacific Ocean?)

Plus, coaching at Pepperdine kept me in the Los Angeles area. I have been a teacher, junior high coach, high school head coach and assistant coach in college, and with the exception of those four years at Utah State, I've spent my entire career in Southern California. Thirty-one out of 35 years in one place. That's a real rarity in the coaching profession. I know it made growing up much easier for our three boys. They were fortunate to have a stability that most children of coaches never have.

I gladly took the Pepperdine job, and once I did, I jumped in with both barrels blazing. It was tough at first, just like I knew it would be. But I was very lucky and very fortunate. For one thing, I brought a strong recruiting mentality to Pepperdine, and even though I often had to settle for those second-level players that weren't acceptable at UCLA, I never stopped going after the best.

However, without a doubt, my biggest piece of luck came when I hired Tom Asbury as my assistant. Tom is a giant, a terrific coach, an unbelievable recruiter and a great human being. He was with me all nine years, and together we turned the Pepperdine program around and made it more than respectable. In fact, one year we were the only California school to make it to the NCAA Tournament. In the nine years I was at Pepperdine, we went to the NCAA tourney four times, the NIT twice, won 20 or more games four times and won the conference title five times. In the 1985-86 season — our best — we were 25-5 and won all of our home games. We had a 15-game winning streak, the longest in the nation that season. Twice we were ranked in the Top 20. It was fun, exciting and rewarding for all of us.

But not at first. We got off to a rocky start at Pepperdine, losing three of our first four games. Our schedule, which we inherited from my predecessor, was a killer. Almost all road games. As a result, we got our brains beat out. But after that slow start, we began to turn things around. We won seven straight, including wins over Oklahoma and Kansas. After the win over Kansas, my A.D. came to see me and said I was making him look good. Then my best player, Ricardo Brown, gets hurt and we lose five of our first six conference games. I remember walking around saying to myself, "It's great to be alive, even though you're one and five." Still, we finished 17-10 that year and got invited to the NIT. A nice start.

Our first trip to the NCAA Tournament came during my third year, the 1981-82 season. We were 22-6 in the regular season and the league champs. We beat Pittsburgh in the first round, then lost to an Oregon State club that had Lester Connor, A.C. Green and Charlie Sitton. They were a powerful team, ranked fourth in the country at the time.

The next year, we suffered a loss that still haunts me. It's one of those games that I keep playing over and over in my mind. We were playing N.C. State in the NCAA tourney up in Corvallis, Oregon, and we have a six-point lead and the ball with one minute left in overtime. Twice they foul us, with 29 seconds left and with 20 seconds left, and both times, Dane Suttle, an 85 percent free throw shooter over his career, goes to the line and misses the front end of the bonus. With nine seconds to go, we're up by two and they have the ball. We foul Dereck Whittenburg. He steps up to the line for a one-and-one, and misses. But Cozell McQueen, who had gone 44 minutes and 51 seconds without scoring a single point, grabs the rebound and banks one in to tie the score. We get beat in the second overtime. So what happens? N.C. State goes on and wins the whole damn thing. Jimmy Valvano gets a championship ring, I get a nightmare that won't go away. Games like that you never forget.

I think I did some of my best coaching while I was at Pepperdine. I've always felt that the year we went 15-13, I may have done the very best coaching of my career. The thing is, we were consistent, and that's what every coach and every player strives for more than anything else, to be consistently successful. Pepperdine is one of those schools that always lives on the edge. Failure and success are never very far apart. I know it's that way everywhere, but, hey, let's be real — at Pepperdine I don't get Don MacLean and Ed O'Bannon and Tyus Edney and Charles O'Bannon, franchise players who ensure that if you do happen to slip a notch or two, you have the potential to bounce back the next year. Recruiting becomes contagious, too, when you sign players of that caliber. They become magnets that draw other talented players to your program.

But that's not the case at Pepperdine. I was lucky if I could get a player like Don MacLean to even make a visit. And if they did, it was usually just as a courtesy to me. At Pepperdine, we had to work our butts off, especially at first when we were trying to get things going. Over the years it got a little easier, but even then it was a struggle. I never had an Ed O'Bannon at Pepperdine. In fact, in my nine years there, I had maybe three or four guys who could have played at UCLA.

In 1986-87, I had my one and only losing season. Ever. As a player, assistant coach or head coach, I'd never been associated with a team that had a losing record. We were 12-18 that season, and, boy, that was tough to deal with. But the truth is, we weren't very good. We were young and inexperienced in the backcourt, and we didn't have a post player. Our one strength was at forward. We had two pretty good players at those positions. But that team, weak as it was, came within one win of making it to the NCAA Tournament. We won our first two conference tournament games, then lost in the final. I know this may sound strange, but I was relieved when we lost. I really didn't want to go to the NCAA tourney with that team.

One thing did make that losing season bearable — my son Jim was on the team. He got 16 starts at guard, and did a respectable job for us. He had the opportunity to play Division I basketball, something I know he's very proud of. I could do that at Pepperdine and get away with it. At UCLA, I would've been run out of town.

*   *   *

When I said that it would have been a disaster if I had gotten the UCLA job when Gary Cunningham left, I wasn't kidding. Not only was I ill-prepared from a coaching standpoint, I wasn't ready on an emotional level. I lacked maturity. In my nine years at Pepperdine, I grew far more as a man than as a coach. The coaching ability was always there — it just needed refining and polishing — but if I hadn't grown as a person, it wouldn't have mattered. No one would have wanted to hire me.

I was a wild man those first years at Pepperdine. Out of control. Once or twice a year, I'd do something to embarrass myself and the school, like the time I almost came to blows with an opposing coach. Every time I'd act up, Howard White, the president, or Wayne Wright would call me on the carpet and tell me to control myself. That happens enough times and you start to get the message.

And I said things I shouldn't have said. Two incidents come to mind where I behaved in an immature and unprofessional manner. One involved a conference playoff game with San Francisco. I thought the game should have been played at a neutral area, but the conference officials decided to play it up in the Bay area, at Santa Clara, 30 minutes from San Francisco. The place was packed with their fans. We didn't have anybody there. I called the commissioner and asked him how he made his decision. He said, "Well, we flipped a coin and you lost." I thought we got a bad deal, and I really showed my anger. I was upset — I still think I should have attended the coin flip to make sure everything was fair and square — but I'm disappointed at the way I acted.

The second incident, one I'm even more embarrassed by, occurred after we lost that NCAA Tournament game to Oregon State. They beat us 70-51, which I could have handled. They had superior talent — they should have won. But what stuck in my craw was the fact that they played slow-down ball in the second half. I just didn't think they had to do that. I know if I had Connor, Sitton and Green, I wouldn't have slowed it down.

At the post-game press conference, I made a remark about Oregon State coach Ralph Miller that was shameful. It's easily the worst thing I've ever said about a fellow coach. I said, "I'm sure when he roomed with Dr. Naismith, he learned that this isn't the way to play basketball." Ralph was in his 60s at the time, and in his 38th and last year as a Division I coach. He didn't deserve to hear something like that. What he did deserve was respect for his contributions to college basketball. So what if his style was different from mine? That didn't give me the right to badmouth him in public. I was angry because we lost, and I handled myself in a poor and immature way. There have been numerous times over the years when I needed an operation to get my foot out of my mouth, but never more so than when I made that terrible remark about Ralph. It was inexcusable.

It was during these times at Pepperdine that a friend gave me a plaque with The Serenity Prayer on it. You probably know it: "God grant me the serenity to accept the things I cannot change, the courage to change the things I can, and the wisdom to know the difference." Well, it was something I needed to learn. And something I still remind myself of. If you come into my office at UCLA, you'll see that the plaque is still with me, right there on the wall.

*   *   *

The term I always use to describe my nine years at Pepperdine is "vanilla life." That's precisely what it was, too, smooth and perfect. Nobody bothered me, the administration treated me with great fairness, and the fans appreciated what we accomplished on the court. And, of course, there was that scenic view of the Pacific. Anytime I'd start feeling the blues coming on, I'd just look out at those beautiful waves rolling in. If that couldn't cure me, nothing could.

With so much going on in Southern California — the Lakers, Dodgers, UCLA, USC, Rams, Raiders, Clippers, Kings — we never received much in the way of publicity. We were pretty low on the totem poll. Even when we had those really good years, we seldom rated more than a paragraph or two in the local newspapers. And I can't recall if we ever had a sportswriter who travelled regularly with the team. The TV stations hardly ever did much more than mention our score. We were the stepchild of the Southern California sports scene.

But what we were achieving in Malibu wasn't going unnoticed by everyone — the athletics directors around the country were paying attention. And it wasn't long before I began to hear from them. I wasn't looking to leave Pepperdine, but I felt I owed it to myself and my family to listen. If a good job in a top conference came along, I'd be foolish not to at least give them an ear.

My first nibble for a head coaching job came from Arizona State. This was after my third season at Pepperdine, the year we went 22-7 and made it to the NCAA Tournament for the first time. Dick Tamburo, their A.D., called and said he wanted me to come over for an interview. He said, "We have to keep this under the rug, so I'm going to check you in under an assumed name — Gertrude."

So I get to the hotel, walk up to the desk and ask if they have a reservation for Gertrude. The guy at the desk handed me my room key, but not before giving me a rather strange look. I go to my room, hang around for a few minutes, then decide that I want to buy a newspaper. I pick it up and the headline said, "HARRICK AT ASU TO INTERVIEW FOR COACHING JOB." So much for secrecy. Right then I learned you can't hide anything from the press.

I had a great interview, and when it was over, the A.D. said, "I have five candidates in mind, but we think we're probably going to hire you. I'll call you at nine on Tuesday morning, and we'll get you over here for a press conference."

On Tuesday, I get to my office at seven-thirty. I'm sweating bullets, because I'm going to take the job and that's a big decision, a big move for me and my family. So I sit in my office from nine until three waiting for the phone to ring. Nothing, not even a wrong number. Finally, Asbury, who's a very humorous guy, comes into my office and says, "Let's go play racquetball. You're not getting *that* job." At three-thirty, my secretary comes down to the racquetball court and tells me I have a phone call. I run up to my office, all sweaty, and it's the Arizona State A.D. on the phone. He says, "Jim, we've hired Bob Weinhauer." That was my first taste of being rejected for a job I really wanted. It wouldn't be my last.

I was disillusioned after that experience, but only for a brief time. Coach Wooden always says, "If you have peace of mind, and if you're not frustrated, then there's no reason to leave." Pepperdine was ideal in every respect, so I had no reason to be down or dejected. Besides, a school has the right to hire whomever they want. You can be disappointed, but you can't be angry.

Over the next few years I had several more job-hunting adventures. Ohio State, Southern Cal, Nebraska, Wichita State, Colorado and Houston are a few of the big name schools I had contact with. Some I was very serious about, others less so. By the same token, some were extremely interested in me, others not so interested.

Funny how that works, how there are certain jobs you'd kill to have and others you want to avoid like the plague. And it's all very arbitrary, very subjective. For example, I really wanted the Ohio State job, but I was fairly indifferent to the Nebraska job. Why? Both are wonderful schools in competitive conferences. Any coach would be overjoyed at the prospect of coaching at either of those places. So, on what basis was I hot for one and cool for the other? Perception? Location? Family considerations? I really can't say for sure.

I had the best interview of my life when I talked to the Ohio State people. I mean, I was prepared. And I knocked them dead, too. Rick Bay, the athletics director, was in on the meeting, along with Jimmy Jones, another assistant A.D., and two faculty representatives. Even though I gave a great presentation, I knew I wasn't going to get that job. I had no chance at it. Ninety percent of the Ohio State boosters never heard of Pepperdine. Couldn't begin to tell you where it is. They're not going to hire me. Are you kidding? You have to be real in this thing.

The USC job I wanted for obvious reasons — a great school located in Southern California. I don't even have to move if I get that job. Mike McGee, the A.D., agreed to give me an interview, saying he'd meet me at the LAX Hilton. Now, I'd never laid eyes on him before and he'd never laid eyes on me, yet as soon as we saw each other in the lobby, I knew who he was and he knew me.

We got a room, then began talking. We must've talked for four hours and not once did the subject of basketball come up. He never mentioned it. So I'm saying to myself, "Well, he's not interested in me." Then Mike suggests that we order a six-pack from room service. He drinks five, I drink one. We're talking about everything but basketball. Mainly, he kept asking about Sam Gilbert, the former UCLA booster everybody has heard about. Then Mike says, "Well, let's eat." I order a chicken dinner, fries, salad, dessert, the works. We eat and talk some more. We're just having a helluva good time. Finally, when we're through eating, Mike says it's time for him to go. He leaves and I get stuck with the check. I knew right then and there that I wasn't getting that job. Not long after that, he called Sally and told her that USC had decided to hire George Raveling.

The Nebraska job situation was another interesting experience for me. It's just that the timing couldn't have been worse. My mother had just passed away, my father was living with us, we had two sons in college and one still in high school — it just wasn't a good time to think about moving. But I agreed to talk with Bob Devaney, the Nebraska A.D., more out of courtesy to him than a genuine desire for the job.

I spent two days in Lincoln. While I was there, Bob took me to the Elks Club, which was an interesting place. After two days, I flew back to L.A. In my mind, I just knew they were going to offer me a contract. The problem was, I didn't really want them to. Neither did Sally. When Bob called and told us they were going to hire Danny Nee, she jumped up and down, screaming in joy, "Yea! We're not going to Lincoln!"

I had been a busy guy in the summer of 1986, interviewing for four or five high-profile jobs. Finally, Wayne Wright, my A.D. at Pepperdine, said, "Hey, Jim, I'm getting too many calls. That's enough. Here's your contract. Sign it. It's time to stop this madness." So I signed my contract, and when I did I was certain that I'd be at Pepperdine for the remainder of my career. I had a great situation there, I worked for people I liked and respected, my family was happy and we had a thriving basketball program that was only going to keep getting better. In short, I was content in all the areas that really mattered.

I turned my eyes and ears away from all those other jobs. They no longer held any interest for me. Except one, a few miles east of Malibu. There, I kept a close watch on what was going on.

And what I saw wasn't pretty. What I saw made me sad and depressed. The school that had once been the brightest star in the
college basketball firmament had descended into the void.

*   *   *

For nine years I sat on those rolling hills above the Pacific
Ocean and watched with great sorrow as the once-proud, once-
mighty UCLA basketball program sank into the muck of mediocrity. The great tradition that Coach Wooden established was
slowly eroding, fading into memory. No longer did the name
UCLA have the same magic as before. NCAA tourney appear-
ances, Top-10 rankings and nationally televised games, once taken
for granted, had become rare occurrences. The fans were turned
off, the administration was unhappy, and, most important of all,
the good West Coast high school players were leaving in droves to
play elsewhere. It was a sad time for those of us who love UCLA.

As I watched it all unfold, it was clear to me that two factors contributed greatly to UCLA's downward slide — unfair expectations and lack of consistency. It was a double-edged sword,
and in a very real way, one side served to sharpen the other. The
coaches, unable to satisfy the fans' demands, came and went
with increasing regularity; thus, the program never had that
solid rock upon which to build a lasting foundation.

And I'm not blaming anyone, either. It was a complex situation, and unless you've sat in this chair, the one I'm in now,
you can't understand — or imagine — what it's like. UCLA,
maybe more than any other school, is a prisoner of its past, and
any time you go one-on-one with the past, you're invariably
going to lose. Coach Wooden won 10 NCAA championships in
12 years. Think about that. Ten. Seven in a row during one
stretch. It boggles the mind. No one will ever match that. Never.
Nor should anyone expect it to happen.

The five men who followed Coach Wooden were, to vary-
ing degrees, successful. But success is a relative term. It's in the
eye of the beholder. And at UCLA, that eye is tough to please.
Take Walt Hazzard, for instance. He won 62 percent of his

games, which is more than respectable, yet it wasn't good enough at UCLA. He got fired.

Had Gary Cunningham remained at UCLA, I'm convinced the 1980s would have been much different. There wouldn't have been all the turmoil and confusion that led to hard times. He would have provided the stability that was so badly missing. His departure created a void, and out of that void, problems arose.

Larry Brown, Larry Farmer and Walt Hazzard coached at UCLA from 1979 to 1988. Larry Brown's two years (1979-81) were the most successful. His teams won 42 and lost 17. His 1980 club made it to the NCAA title game before losing 59-54 to Louisville, and his 1981 team also advanced to the tournament. But after Larry left for the NBA in 1981, UCLA made only one appearance in the NCAA tourney (1983, under Farmer) until I took over in 1988.

Farmer got off to a good start. His first two teams were 21-6 and 23-6. But things didn't go so well his third year — a 17-11 record, UCLA's worst in 24 years — so when the season ended it was "suggested" to him by the administration that he fire his two assistants and bring in Hazzard and Jack Hirsch as replacements. Farmer agreed, signed a two-year extension, and then, four days later, changed his mind and quit. Within hours, Hazzard was given the job.

Walt's four years were described by one sportswriter as "rocky." His first team (1985), led by Reggie Miller, won the NIT. The next three years, they went 15-14, 25-7 and 16-14. By the end of Walt's fourth year, I know the guys in the media were hitting him with everything they had. Tom Kertes did a piece for *Sport* magazine in which he quoted one UCLA player as saying: "The assistant coaches couldn't break down the fundamentals." Kertes also quoted an NBA scout who claimed that "practices were a circus, total chaos." In an article Kelli Anderson did for *Sports Illustrated*, Hazzard was blamed for the defection of Corey Gaines, Greg Foster and Rod Palmer, all of whom transferred between 1986 and 1988.

I don't know about those things, and I really wouldn't

want to comment on Walt's four years, regardless. All I know is that a few days after UCLA lost to Washington State in the first round of the conference tournament, Walt was fired. I expect that it wasn't an easy decision for Chuck Young, no matter what the problems might have been. Firing people isn't his thing. I guess it just reached the stage where he felt a change needed to be made.

In fairness to Farmer and Hazzard, I think they were put in a position they weren't ready to handle. Neither man had ever been a Division I head coach. Farmer had been a UCLA assistant, Hazzard a junior college and Division II coach. That's a far cry from coaching at UCLA, where every move you make is analyzed and critiqued to death. (In fact, of the five coaches at UCLA between Coach Wooden and me, only Gene Bartow had Division I head coaching experience. Gary Cunningham had been an assistant under Coach Wooden, and Larry Brown had coached in the pros, but never at the college level.) I just don't think Larry and Walt had the experience necessary to deal with a big-time program like UCLA's. What happened to them is exactly what would have happened to me had I been hired when Gary Cunningham resigned. I would have failed, too.

Sally and I were at home on a Wednesday morning, getting ready to go to Kansas City for the Final Four, when the phone rang. It was from this character around town whom I had gotten to know over the years. He used to call me all the time. And he never says, "Hello, Jim, how are you?" He always jumps right in with whatever it is that's on his mind. Anyway, he says, "Jim, Walt got fired last night." I said, "I haven't heard anything about it." He said, "OK, see ya," and hangs up.

We get on the airplane and I look up and see all these L.A. sportswriters. Mike Downey, Frank Burlison, Allan Malamud, Chris Long, Bob Keisser — there must have been a dozen in all. After the plane gets airborne, we all congregate in the back and start shooting the breeze. We must have talked for two hours. And nobody says a word about the UCLA situation. Every few minutes I would look back at Sally, shrug my shoulders and mouth the words "I don't know what's going on."

Because none of the writers mentioned UCLA during the flight, I concluded that the guy had given me false information. Boy, was I wrong. When we checked into our hotel room, I called down to the desk and asked the lady if there were any messages for me. She said there were 22. I just looked at Sally and said, "Uh-oh, I think it did happen."

I knew I wanted the job; the question was, did UCLA want me? There was only one way to find out — ask. So, I went immediately down to the lobby and the first thing I hear is that Jim Valvano is a lock to get the job. Jim's there, along with his entourage, and they're all parading around, acting like it's a done deal, talking about how they were going to L.A. to sign the contract. I have to tell you that I was a little depressed when I saw all that going on.

Jimmy V was their guy. They flew him to L.A., wined and dined him, showed him around town, then offered him a contract. The job was his — all he had to do was say yes. But something happened — I don't know the particulars — and Valvano stepped away. For whatever reason, he said he didn't want the job. He took himself out of the picture. So, the next morning I called Pete Dalis and told him I would like to be considered. Pete said, "Jim, we want a high-profile coach." Well, that made me even more depressed. Personally, I thought they were crazy. To my way of thinking, I was a natural candidate for that job. I had nine years experience at the Division I level, I was familiar with the unique challenges at UCLA, having been an assistant there for two years, and I was a product of the Southern California high school system, which would have given me a great advantage in the recruiting wars. Not many coaches, no matter how high profile they were, had a better resume than I did when it came to the UCLA job. But none of that mattered — UCLA wasn't interested in me.

After Valvano gave a thumbs down on the job, UCLA turned its attention to Mike Krzyzewski. Mike expressed an interest, but since Duke was in the Final Four that year, he wanted to wait until the season was over before beginning any serious talks. Meanwhile, Larry Brown, whose Kansas team is also in the

Final Four, starts making some calls, letting certain people know that he's also interested.

On Monday night, Kansas beat Oklahoma to win the national championship. All that week, Digger Phelps and I were talking and I kept saying, "Larry's got the job, Larry's got the job." And Digger said, "Jim, let me tell you something. He's not going to take the job. I grew up with him in New York. I know Larry Brown. He will not coach at UCLA."

While this is going on, the media, as you can imagine, were in a frenzy. For 13 days, everybody was trying to figure out — or predict — what was going to happen. Newspapers, television, talk radio programs . . . the UCLA situation dominated everything. There were dozens of articles and columns about it. Would it be Brown, Krzyzewski, maybe Denny Crum? And in every column, invariably buried somewhere in the last paragraph, you would see, "And Jim Harrick is also a candidate for the job." I was the also-ran.

Three days after Kansas won the championship, Larry flies to L.A. on UCLA's plane and takes the job. Handshakes and everything. A done deal. Everybody on both sides is ecstatic. Everybody, that is, except me. I was miserable. I was tired of being seen as a second-rate contender. This time, I had wanted the job. Really wanted it. But even though I was disappointed, I couldn't complain all that much. Larry was certainly a better candidate at the moment than I was. His team had just won the national championship — you can't argue with that. He was much higher up on the list than me. He wasn't as natural for the job as I was, but he was much more qualified.

I've known Larry since the mid-'70s when he was with the Denver Nuggets. I directed his camp a couple of times, and we became good friends. I have always felt that he has one of the best basketball minds of anyone in this business. He's a great, great coach. But I felt that he was absolutely the wrong guy for UCLA at that time. What the UCLA program needed more than anything was stability, and as every basketball fan knows, stability isn't something you associate with Larry Brown. He's a basketball gypsy, a guy who likes to move around. Larry's a rebuilder, not a reloader. He likes nothing better than to take over a troubled team, fix the problem, then move on to the next challenge. That's his M.O., his style. And that's exactly what UCLA didn't need in 1988.

Larry told the UCLA people to hold off the announcement that he was taking the job. He wanted to fly back to Kansas, tell the administration and his players, then announce it himself at an afternoon press conference. This was on a Thursday. On Friday, at about two in the afternoon, Asbury and I are sitting in my office, going over the final plans for our team banquet later that night. The phone rings. It's from Gary Jones, a sportswriter I knew from my days at Utah State. He says, "Jim, Larry just turned down the job." I was stunned. "Come on, Gary, don't joke with me. That's not funny."

Then Gary begins reading the press release that had just come across the wire. And it was true. Larry held his press conference right on schedule, four o'clock Kansas time, and made his announcement, just like he said he would. Only, he announced to the world that he was staying at Kansas. As I'm talking to Gary, the other phone rings. My secretary leans around the corner and tells me it's Pete Dalis on the line. I immediately hang up with Gary, boot Asbury out of the office and take Pete's call. Without so much as a hello, Pete said, "Jim, we'd like to talk to you tomorrow."

There it was, suddenly, like a blast of thunder in the night. Through the process of elimination, and thanks to a bizarre series of events, I was back in the hunt. And this time, they were coming to me. I struggled through the banquet that night. My heart just wasn't in it. It was a tough night to get through. All I could think about was the interview. I stayed up until four in the morning, planning and preparing, going over the many notes I'd kept from past interviews, organizing my thoughts, deciding what areas needed to be emphasized, looking for the ideal way to convince the UCLA people that I was the best man for the job. This was, as Churchill called it, that "special moment" in my life. Fate had tapped me on the shoulder. Now, it was up to me to be prepared well enough to avoid the tragedy of failure.

On Saturday morning, I went over and had a great interview with Pete and assistant chancellor Elvin Svenson. About halfway through, Chuck Young came into the room. He was steaming, absolutely livid. Boy, was he upset. Larry Brown had not only turned them down and left them hanging, he hadn't even called to personally inform UCLA of his decision. Chuck, like everyone else, had heard about it through the media. At one point during my interview, Chuck jumped up, slapped the table and said he couldn't believe Larry had treated UCLA in such a shabby way. Pete kept telling Chuck to settle down, that it was over and that it was time to move on. Chuck finally did calm down, and the interview went well, but I can assure you that he wasn't at all happy with Larry Brown. And he had every right to be unhappy. What Larry did had embarrassed UCLA.

I was home by myself that Saturday night. The boys were out and about, and Sally, figuring I had no chance at getting the job, had gone straight from the Final Four to West Virginia. By now, the media, aware that something was in the wind, had started calling me, wanting to know what was happening. I told them, "Hey, guys, you tell me. I don't know anything." It's one of the few times in my life that I lied outright, but I felt at the time that it was best to act ignorant and keep my mouth shut.

Sunday was a Greek holiday, and since Pete is Greek, he took that day off. I didn't hear from him on Monday either, so I began to get a little nervous, wondering if maybe they had quietly slipped in another candidate for an interview. As crazy as this situation had been, nothing would have surprised me. I called some of my friends over at UCLA, people who were on the inside and knew what was going on, and they told me that no one else was being considered.

On Tuesday morning, the call I'd been waiting for all my life finally came. And when I hung up the phone, I was UCLA's basketball coach.

The hot seat was mine.

Be careful what you ask for, it might come true.

Since the day I was hired, many people, particularly my critics, have pointed out that I wasn't the first choice for the job.

Or the second, or even the third. They ask me if I'm bothered by that. My answer is, no, not at all. Hey, those things happen in this business. That's the nature of the beast. Sometimes the dice roll favorably, sometimes they don't. Most people aren't aware that Coach Wooden was only the third or fourth choice for the UCLA job when he was hired. I know that's almost impossible to believe now, but it's true. So, I certainly felt no disgrace because my place in the pecking order was lower than such outstanding and proven coaches as Larry Brown, Jim Valvano and Mike Krzyzewski. That would be ridiculous.

I look at the situation in a much different light. How many coaches put themselves in a position to even be considered for the UCLA job? Not very many. I did, and I'm awfully proud of that. I'd paid my dues, working my way up the coaching ladder, beginning at the junior high level. I'd mopped floors, washed uniforms, hauled young people all over the country, sharing in their good times and counseling them during bad times. I had literally given my blood, sweat and tears for this crazy profession we call coaching. And now I was reaping the benefit of all those experiences, all that hard work. Third choice, fourth choice, 10th choice . . . it didn't matter. I had nothing to be ashamed of.

Oh, yes. Remember Digger's prediction that Larry Brown wouldn't take the job? I sent him a box of cigars.

HUMANITY 1, WIZARDRY 0

8

If winning the "mini-tournament" made us come of age as a team, the remainder of our schedule showed we could maintain a roll — comfortable on the fast track, humming along without jumping the rails. And we did it right after being ranked number one in the nation for the first time. We beat Southern Cal, Louisville, Oregon State and Oregon, none of them coming closer than 16 points, to finish the regular season with a 13-game winning streak and a 25-2 record. Our average margin of victory over the final six games was 18.5 points. Smokin'. It showed me that this team didn't feel any heat over being top-ranked, but thrived on it instead. As George Zidek put it: "Last season [when our team got off to a 14-0 start] the No. 1 ranking came early and I'm not sure we deserved it. This year it came late. We'd worked hard, and everybody felt comfortable with it."

Toby Bailey was coming into his own as a starter. At home against USC he scored 24 points and added nine rebounds in an 85-66 win. We just kind of went through the motions in the first half and trailed, 39-38, at the break — but, with Toby in particular stepping up, we just dominated the final 20 minutes to clinch the Pac-10 championship. Our other freshman, meanwhile, was again strong off the bench. J.R. scored 14, same as Ed, while Charles fashioned another of those solid, all-around performances we'd been asking of him: 16 points, nine rebounds, six assists, two blocks and one steal. But the real significance was Toby's performance. It further convinced me that starting him was the last missing link in making this team exceptional. Toby was just warming up. In our next game, at Louisville, he notched the first double-double of his career with 17 points and 11 rebounds — and also dished out a career-high seven assists. We won 91-73, but Louisville had tested us late, drawing within 73-69 inside the final three minutes. In retrospect, that was actually a good thing — because it again showed me this team would come out clawing and scratching when cornered. We stole the ball three straight times, and that ignited an 18-4 explosion over the final 2:52. Ed had 25 points, Tyus 20.

By now it was clear I had two freshmen in name only. At home in an 86-67 win over Oregon State, J.R. came off the bench to score 16 points and grab nine rebounds. Meanwhile, Cameron Dollar gave us a sneak preview of his heroics to come by racking up six points, four assists and six steals in only 24 minutes.

That left only one game, and an emotional one. This would be the last time Ed, Tyus and George played at home — and it was a chance to pay back Oregon for the loss. We'd already done the same with Cal, and it was important to these guys to win convincingly against the only other team that had beaten us. The final was 94-78, and it came before the largest crowd — 13,037 — in the history of Pauley Pavilion. Ed and Charles were magnificent: 25 points and 11 rebounds by Charles; 24 and 10 by Ed. Meanwhile, Tyus scored 22 and was, per usual, everywhere on the court: eight assists, seven steals and in-your-face defense on Kenya Wilkins, whom Tyus held scoreless on 0-for-10 shooting while forcing Wilkins into six turnovers. When I pulled Ed near the end, he ran to the center circle, dropped down and kissed the court. He'd been through a lot in his five years at UCLA. It was great to see him go out so happily.

Of these last four games, the trip to Louisville was special. Denny Crum had played for Coach Wooden and was an assistant there in the '60s. Like me, Denny has used much of Coach's system at U of L — and he's won two NCAA titles. The most enjoyable games I've played have been against Louisville. There's just an unbelievable mutual respect. Our games are always very fundamentally sound, and of course the styles are so similar. Both teams execute their offense well and play sound defense, with no trash talking. To me, they're just beautifully played games. And the fans in Louisville — they're the best ones I've ever been around. I've never heard them say a derogatory word to my team. They appreciate good basketball. We've won twice there and they've actually applauded our effort. Never have I been anywhere where you get that kind of reception. A classy, classy audience. I really loved going back to Freedom Hall to play.

It's no accident that the vibes are so good when UCLA and Louisville tip it up — that you can feel a heightened sense of mutual respect. Not at all. Not when you consider the influence Coach Wooden has had on both me and Denny.

*   *   *

Of the many items I keep in my cluttered files, there's one sheet of paper with a quote I'm particularly fond of. "Winning isn't everything," it says, "but making the effort is."

It's from Vince Lombardi.

I know what you're thinking. Didn't he say something a little different? Like: "Winning isn't everything, it's the only thing." Well, it's true that nobody liked to win more than Lombardi — but that quote is wrong. Making the effort is everything. That's what Lombardi believed. And that's what he actually said.

Funny how legends often focus on the myth and lose track of the man. In some respects, that's true of John Wooden. That "Wizard of Westwood" tag? It's a distasteful phrase to him.

We were talking about it once, and he said he didn't want to be put up on a pedestal just because he'd scored more points in a basketball game than somebody else. That is not John Wooden's idea of success.

He taught that success is peace of mind, knowing you've done your best. That's why I never talk about winning and losing with my players. Just doing your best. It's the only way to live, as far as I'm concerned.

John Wooden isn't a wizard. He's a man with an extraordinary sense of humanity, and that's the real magic to the man. Maybe it says a lot about our society that something as natural and sane as Coach's approach to life makes him so special and relatively rare. I see John Wooden tolerate the bad in others with much the same even-handedness he displays in reacting to people's good sides. Coach calls Abraham Lincoln his favorite American, and he likes to use this Lincoln quote: "It's better to trust and be disappointed occasionally than it is to mistrust and be miserable all the time." With Coach Wooden, you can trust. Always.

I suppose most of the public's experience with him involves a sound bite here and there, or maybe a quote they've read, and I wonder if some might suspect that he's a man who just speaks in platitudes — "carved in stone" stuff. That's why I wish everyone could meet him face to face. We live in the world of the quick fix and the flashy, outrageous comment — and Coach's words can get lost in that kind of shallow claptrap. Coach is the genuine article. When those kind come along, you know it. Somewhere deep inside, you know.

We were doing a taping session for an audio-cassette program not long ago and one of the questions our interviewer asked was, "In one word, could you tell us your definition of success?" Coach Wooden didn't skip a beat: "Well, I heard it said once that any philosophy that can be stated in a nutshell belongs in one . . . " I had to chuckle. The man is 85 now, quick as can be and always able to call on a deep reservoir of anecdotes and wisdom. He finds Abraham Lincoln fascinating and often quotes him. He also writes poetry. For every point he makes, he has a zillion anecdotes or examples to illustrate it. You spend time with Coach and the hours fly by. I try to do it a few times every month, usually at a coffee shop called Coco's in the Valley. We've talked about everything — from the O.J. trial to health care to history. In fact, talking hoops is often the thing we devote the least amount of time to.

Oh yes. He did settle on one word to define success.

"Love," he said.

When people first meet him, they're his best friend yesterday. Listen, it's a crazy world, and there seems to be no end to the messes we can get this planet into. But I often think that if John Wooden were President of the United States — or, better, president of the world — we'd have world peace. He'd be the only guy who ever thought you could get that done. (Fact is, if everybody lived like him it *would* get done.) He taught me that you can disagree without being disagreeable — something I surely have been, particularly in my first few years at Pepperdine. In fact, I used to always be a disagreeable guy. But the things I've learned from him over the years have been invaluable. He's a strength. A mountain of a man.

And a pretty darned funny one, too.

That's maybe the most surprising thing people discover when they first meet him. He's got that gleam in his eye. He loves to tease his friends, and is quick with a grin when you toss it back at him. I saw him recently and he just sort of squinted and cocked his head. "Puttin' on a few pounds, Jim?" And, of course, there's his old standby punch line — one that perhaps only UCLA coaches can appreciate fully. Coach knows how the demands of this job can put a severe test on even his patience. Which is why at times he'll call me on the phone and greet me with: "Jim, we the alumni . . . " And it always makes me grin. At the Wooden Award banquet this year, he put another twist on it. Before introducing Ed O'Bannon, who'd been chosen for the Player of the Year Award that bears Coach's name, he turns to me and says: "Now, Jim, we the alumni expect another championship." Well, everybody just roared. Then he introduces Ed, who gives a nice acceptance speech. But after he finishes, Ed just stands there for a moment. I notice he's looking down from the podium, straight at me. "Coach Harrick," Ed says, solemn as all get-out, "we the alumni expect you to do it again yesterday." Well, that really brought the house down. I don't know who loved it more, me or Coach Wooden.

At the press conference for the Wooden Classic, all of us coaches were in mid-season form. In other words, we were poor-mouthing. Rick Pitino gets up and talks about how his team had travelled cross country and they're tired and he doesn't know how they're going to deal with the time change. Roy Williams gets up and says he's got four or five guys injured. John Calipari says how this and that has happened to his team. And I get up and talk about how it's only our second game of the season and I don't know if we're ready. All of a sudden, Coach Wooden leans into his microphone and says: "As bad a shape as these teams are in, it doesn't look to me like any of you are going to win these games."

Remember, it was Coach who had a serious talk with Bill Walton during the period when Bill was being a vocal critic of me. Once we got that patched up, the three of us were on the "Coast-to-Coast" radio talk show with Bob Costas. Bill is asking Coach some questions, and he keeps answering with things like, "Well, Bill, it's just like the time you got on UCLA and Coach Harrick." And we just kept bantering back and forth, everybody taking it as it was meant to be, as good fun. It's a hoot, how Coach Wooden can rib you to no end. But you always know it's done out of friendship.

*   *   *

As inspiring as he's been as a man, he was equally influential on me as a coach. I remember when I was starting out and I read his book, *Practical Modern Basketball*. I just picked everything I could out of it, from cover to cover. He's such a marvelous teacher, and maybe the greatest coaching advice I got from studying him was this: Leave no stone unturned. My team oftentimes gets upset at me because I want their foot to be in the proper position, or their angle set to a screen a certain way. They always want to know why, and I always have to stop and explain. As I do, in the back of my mind I'm saying: "BECAUSE COACH WOODEN DID IT, DARN IT! SHUT UP! HE DID IT AND IT WORKED, SO YOU DO IT AND IT WILL WORK AGAIN!" I don't say that, of course. I'll tell them how the angle this position creates makes a defender come off it a certain way and they'll get a much better look at the basket as a result. That's what I tell them. But it's the other I'm thinking. You betcha.

Not that it's limited to players. Whenever I'd get a new assistant in, there would come the inevitable time when the new guy would see a particular drill we were doing — usually it's "floor length and open up" or "flanker" — and the new guy wouldn't like it. "Why do you do that? Why do you do that?" was always the response. So I'd explain the drill. And they'd just sort of shrug and say: "Oh, I don't know if that's any good or not." Of course, I'd gotten it from Coach. So when I'd take my assistants out to breakfast with him, I'd wait for the right moment and say: "Coach Wooden, tell them why we run floor length and open up." And he'd explain it to the nth degree, just go on and on, and when he was finished all my assistants would say: "Oh yeah, that's a GREAT drill!" It was just hilarious.

As I studied him through the years, I developed the philosophy that, well, he was at UCLA for 28 years — every drill he ran, every offense he used, he'd played with and tinkered with over those years and he'd become a master of it. Why should I change it? And so, our offensive flow at UCLA hasn't changed much at all from what Coach Wooden did. Every time I talk to NBA guys they say they like to draft UCLA players because they're fundamentally sound. Well, that goes back to the system, and I like to call it the "Wooden System." I certainly haven't changed anything I've learned from him. Oh, I've added a few drills and subtracted some others — but I've used his basic framework since high school. In this national championship season, I changed the set of our offense. It's still the balance court offense, it's just not the high post. It's out of a 1-2-2 set. (You would too if you had Tyus Edney and big, quick guys like Toby, J.R., Charles and Ed who could operate out high as easily as inside.)

I've expanded a few things, giving our offense a few other dimensions. I learned much of that during Gary Cunningham's tenure at UCLA. Back then — when Larry Farmer and I were assistants and Craig Impleman was a graduate assistant — the four of us would play with the offense and try some different things. But it was always out of the framework of Coach Wooden's two-guard front set and the high-post offense. Always out of Coach's system.

Of all the things I've learned from Coach's philosophy, probably the most prominent thing is the word *balance*. It's a key word in everything you try or accomplish. Balance in a literal sense means your head is at the midpoint of the line between your two feet — not just in shooting, rebounding, defending and dribbling, but also if you're playing tennis, golf, football, baseball . . . any sport. Having your head at the midpoint is the key to everything. Any time you get the head out of the midpoint, you're off balance. And unbalanced players sit on the bench. But it's more. I learned that balance is essential in all aspects of life. Your life must be balanced physically, mentally, spiritually and emotionally. You eat right with a balanced diet, you balance your waking hours with the proper amount of sleep and you have a moral balance. And with a basketball team, you need to be offensively balanced. You need proper spacing on the floor — a triangle of rebounders on every play, a medium safety and a deep safety so your team is balanced, ready to go for a missed shot but also ready to stop the other team if they get the rebound. Same with defense. You need a balance to guard against every type of situation. And so, I learned that everything that's involved in your life revolves around that word, balance.

What I've always stressed is conditioning, fundamentals and sharing the ball. Those were the foundations of John Wooden's program. My basic philosophy with players is that I want to give you some free rein. I'm going to give you a structure. Here's a set. Here's the play you like to run within the framework of the offense. But you take what the defense gives you. If they give you a shot better than what your offense will get for you, take it — as long as you have somebody rebounding. I always emphasize a philosophy that it's a team game. There's a passer, there's a screener and there's a shooter. And you may be any one of those three. You may be the rebounder on a certain play, but none of it is any less important than the other. Why should you, just because you score, think you're a little better than the guy who set the screen for you? That's why we always praise the passer and the screener more than we praise the scorer, because it builds *esprit de corps* and develops your team.

Before we get out on the floor, we talk about four basic aspects. Number one is sharing the ball. I want my team to shoot 50 to 55 percent from the field and execute 20 to 25 assists. That's the goal. I want to score, or get a great shot or get fouled every time down, because every possession is a mini-battle. I'm having a battle with you, and the more times I can beat you in those little battles, the more we're going to succeed. So, in the framework of the mini-battle, if you can get your scorer out and he gets a great shot every time, you're achieving what you want to do. And the team that makes the extra pass is the team that usually wins.

The second thing is, defensively, we want to hold our opponent under 40 percent from the field. Look at our stats and you'll see we did that an impressive amount of the time. When I look out on the floor, I always want to see my players in a stance on defense. We have three different types: on-the-ball stance, deny stance or "open two passes away from the ball help side" stance. They vary in how you position your body, but they're all stances that prepare you to make something happen on defense. Every time I look out there on the floor, I'd better see you in a stance. Straight-leg players sit on the bench. There's no place in the game for straight-leg players. We have something called a line rule, which involves how your overall defense is positioned in regard to where the ball is at a particular time. We play

straight-up man-to-man defense, or "denying man," or we cover
down — having a second guy slip down inside to double-team
when there's a big, effective opponent posting up near the basket. Third is an emphasis on rebounding. And number four is to
play hard, and in that framework comes the word "compete,"
the cornerstone of my philosophy and what I always emphasize.
I want you to compete to the best of your ability.

So that's it: Share the ball, play great defense, rebound
and play hard. Just the way John Wooden's teams did it. Any
coach, of course, adds some of his own personality and insight to
his approach, but what I do — particularly on offense — is
clearly derived from the Wooden System.

Tom Asbury says that a lot of your success comes because
of a system. As I noted before, Bobby Knight's defensive
strength is derived from the system Pete Newell had — and I've
also patterned a lot of my defense from Pete's philosophy. I think
you'll find that most successful coaches, like Dean Smith, operate out of a system they've developed over the years. I see Roy
Williams, former North Carolina assistant, take much of Dean's
system and thrive at Kansas, and certainly Mike Krzyzewski
runs a part of Knight's system at Duke.

Aside from communicating, Coach Wooden's greatest
strength, I think, was in his extraordinary ability to adapt. The
reason he was successful over the decades — decades of
tremendous change both on and off the court — is because he
knew how to adapt, whether it was to players' attitudes or to
the changing face of the game itself. His ability to change with
the changing times, that was the thread that ran through his
career. It's extraordinary, really, that he could be successful
through the '40s, '50s, '60s and '70s. You don't do that without
a knack for adapting. He's very bright, and he could always
adjust — and communicate those adjustments clearly. He
made mistakes like everybody, but he was smart enough to adjust to them. And the full-court press is the greatest example of
how he adjusted.

It's funny, but a lot of people think the hallmark of his
UCLA teams was the press. Not true. Coach won his first two

national championships that way, but things began to change. Coaches everywhere started to mimic the UCLA press, so everybody was facing it more often, and teams got more accustomed to dealing with it. Also, now you had fourth-graders who were playing against the press, and by the time they grew up and were playing at colleges all over the country . . . well, now there were guys everywhere who could handle the press. Where before there hadn't been very good ball handlers, now there were. As a result, it became very hard to press most kids and get much in the way of results. That's particularly true today.

Coach Wooden began to see the trend early on. And he backed off the press, sometimes to take advantage of his personnel. Back when he had Kareem and later Walton, for instance, he didn't run the high-post offense so much. He'd go with a 1-3-1 offense so they could never press, so they would always be in a half-court situation because he wanted the ball to go inside to an Abdul-Jabbar or a Walton. The '64 and '65 teams were the ones that pressed all the time. In the Alcindor years (you remember when Kareem was Lew, don't you?) he pressed only a little. And with Walton, Patterson and Wicks, the same. Teams they could beat handily, he'd press. But then with Marques Johnson, David Meyers, Richard Washington and Andre McCarter, he didn't press at all — or at least so rarely that it raised eyebrows when it happened.

Coach rarely stood up from the bench, but believe me, he made great adjustments in the heat of a game. He was great at substituting, just unbelievable at having a knack of knowing who to put in and light a fire. And while he didn't play zone a lot, he would front the post and back the post sometimes. I remember the 1970 national title game against Jacksonville when Wicks was fronting Artis Gilmore defensively, and Gilmore was killing him. So Coach turned Wicks around and made him play behind Gilmore — and the result was another championship.

You know, as kind and as wise a man as he is, Coach Wooden was also a fierce competitor. Back in the 1960s, his old friend Press Maravich, the LSU coach, used to call him "St. John." Another nickname coaches gave him was Padre. Well, maybe so, but John Wooden was hardly a creampuff once the ball was tossed up. And, I guarantee you, if you're a coach you're not going to please everybody. Life being what it is, a few players would criticize him — usually, a guy who wasn't getting to play. One player criticized him in public — at a UCLA banquet in, as I recall, the late '60s — and Coach quit having post-season team banquets. UCLA didn't have them for years, not until Larry Brown started them up again in the early '80s. Of course, that was back in an era when authority figures were generally held in disdain by the majority of youth. Needless to say, the overwhelming majority of his players held him in great respect — and did so from every era. They all come back to see him. And they're always calling him on the phone to talk.

John Wooden never swore at his players — and I'm sure if he hadn't won like he did, eventually they would have said he was too easy, too soft, too whatever. But believe me, he wasn't soft. Fair, yes, but not soft. In fact, he was tough when he had to be. He just did it in his own style. Coach Wooden always had rules against excessive hair, and one year, on the October 14th "picture day" that was held the day before the start of official practice, Sidney Wicks and Steve Patterson showed up with muttonchop sideburns. Coach Wooden wouldn't give them their uniforms. Wicks says: "Why?" Coach says: "You know why." Wicks, well aware he was being counted on to help fill the void left by the departure of Lew Alcindor the previous year, tried to use some leverage. "You don't have the big guy this year, Coach," Wicks says. And John Wooden answers: "No, we don't. And we won't have you and Steve, either, unless you get upstairs and get cleaned up in the next 15 minutes." Both of them look at Coach for several seconds. "Make that 14 minutes," Coach says. Boom. They run upstairs and get with Ducky Drake, the equipment manager who also cut some of the players' hair. Off come the sideburns and out come their uniforms. After the team picture was taken, Wicks and Patterson waited for Coach Wooden. "We're sorry, Coach," they said. "That's all right," Coach Wooden told them. "When I was your age, I tested people, too. Now let's forget about this and have a great season."

Would John Wooden ever have picked stuff up and thrown it? Under any circumstance? Well, my first answer to that is no. But as I think about it . . . well, maybe. If he thought it might do some good, maybe. I know he was fully capable of dressing down his players when it was needed. But thinking about it, I'd have to say no to the question. Shoot, I don't recall him ever even getting a technical. What he did get were results, and he knew how to motivate his players to produce them.

*   *   *

I remember the first time I met him. It was 1967 or '68, when I was still a JV coach. I went with Lee Smelser because one of our Morningside players was going to get an award for being named to the Helms Hall of Fame. We heard Coach speak, and got to met him afterward. Of course, it wasn't much more than a handshake and a nod, but I remember. Lee and I also got tickets from Frank Arnold to the West Regional in Corvallis, Oregon, in 1967. This was when Kareem was playing for UCLA, and we watched them beat Wyoming, which had a certain player, none other than my friend-to-be Tom Asbury, who years later would become my assistant coach and then my successor at Pepperdine. You just never know.

I'm sure that my first time to actually see Coach Wooden in person was even earlier, probably in 1964 when I first started coaching. I'm sure I saw him speak at a clinic, because I went to every clinic I could find back then. Six or seven a year. (And those index cards have the key points I scribbled down from every clinic I've ever attended— from Adolph Rupp to Bobby Knight to Jim Valvano to Denny Crum. I review them every year, in the summer.)

After Lee left Morningside and I became head coach, I had my first real exchange with Coach. It was in my first season,

1969-70, and that's when I had Billy Ingram on the squad. We played Notre Dame High in Sherman Oaks, a couple of blocks from where Coach lived at the time. So I'm standing courtside as my team warms up. It's either late December or early January. We haven't played a lot of games, so I've just been a head coach for a month or two. I'm standing there and John Wooden comes walking in. Remember, he's already won national championships in '64, '65, '67 and '68. Holy mackerel! Him watching you work! Well, we won the game. They'd zoned us and I had a player, Doug Greminger, who just stood, putting up one-handed shots. Set shot all night. Killed 'em. After the game, I went over to meet Coach Wooden and he says: "I like your spot-up shooter." I'll never forget my answer. "Well, you know," I say, "he shoots about 150 of those a day. He's supposed to make that shot, Coach. I expect him to make it." And he laughed. I suppose it was just bluster covering my nervousness, but I like to think that John Wooden's presence was already bringing out the coach in me.

It was the next summer that I became one of the directors of the John Wooden Basketball Camp. So now I have three meals a day, sitting right across from him. There were a lot of coaches around that table, and he held court, answering every question we had. It was marvelous. By then I had all three sons. Glenn, our little one, was just a baby. He was born that February. Well, because those camps were hard work — I mean, from 8 a.m. until about 10 at night — I'd be away from home for five days in a row. So one day Sally comes out to see me. She just drove out with all three kids. I introduce her to Coach and I turn around to talk to Sally for a minute. When I turn back, there he was with one of my kids in one arm, one in the other and Monte, our oldest, holding onto him. He had all three of them, and I don't know who was having the better time, the kids or Coach. You can't fool kids. They flocked to him. You get around John Wooden, you just *know*.

That fall, I'm back in my office when a card arrives. It was from Coach, and I remember that the card had a drawing of a man walking along a sandy beach with a little child behind, stepping in his footsteps. I opened the card and saw a poem. It's been almost 30 years, but I can recite it by heart: "A careful man I want to be . . . A little fellow follows me . . . I do not dare to go astray . . . for fear he'll go the self-same way . . . I cannot once escape his eyes . . . what ere he sees me do he tries . . . Like me he says he's going to be . . . the little chap who follows me . . . He thinks that I am good and fine . . . believes in every word of mine . . . The base in me he shall not see . . . the little man who follows me . . . I must remember as I go . . . through summer sun and winter snow . . . I'm building for the years to be . . . the little chap who follows me."

From those camps we began to become friends. Not close friends, but friends. Every year a couple of weeks before our season, I would bring my Morningside team up to Westwood. We'd sit there in Pauley Pavilion and watch UCLA practice. Now, to watch them work out with Wooden . . . well, you gotta be kidding. Remember, it wasn't but a few years earlier that Sally and I would go buy tickets and sit high up in Pauley to watch them play. Now I was spending the pre-season going up there to watch practice almost every day on my own, and then bring the team up for one day. Coach would always walk over and say hello and have something to say. Believe me, for him to know my name was a big thrill.

Of course, it wasn't until I was around him more frequently that we became good friends. And that happened when I came back to UCLA as Gary Cunningham's assistant coach in 1977. I'd be in my office and John Wooden would walk in. I'd take the phone and drop the receiver on the floor. And for the next hour we'd talk and talk and talk. I'll never forget things like the time I was having trouble with David Greenwood. Well, not trouble, really. It was just me, Mr. Intensity, fretting and fussing. I'd look at Coach Wooden and say: "Coach, this player won't work hard, he's kind of lazy in drills and we can't get him to play harder (and blah blah blah — just whining on. Now, the guy was getting 20 points and 10 rebounds every night, but I wanted him to get 25 and 12). So I finally stop, and Coach, who'd stayed silent, said this: "Jiy-ummm . . . would you rather have him or *not* have him?" Game, set, match. Bam. Just like that, he'd cut to the heart of the matter. I just nodded my head, OK, OK.

Those two years as a UCLA assistant were full of moments like that, and I look back at that time as priceless. This was also when Sally and I began to socialize with Coach and Nell. We'd have dinners together at our house or theirs, and Nell was also at the basketball camps and Sally would come around, so she got to know Nell pretty well. Oh, she was something. Nell was a holy terror, dynamic and feisty and quick to tell you what was on her mind. A terrific, terrific woman. I loved her. You just had to love Nell.

In many respects, she was just the opposite of Coach — which is probably one of the reasons they were so good for each other. Where Coach might hold his tongue, even when he had a legitimate beef, Nell wouldn't. She was the one who took UCLA to task for Coach's salary and retirement package (remember, he never made more than $32,500). Not long ago, Coach was reminiscing about an incident involving Nell. Because they didn't have kids in the household anymore, they'd sold their house and moved into a smaller place, a condominium in Encino. Well, Ventura Boulevard, which pretty much runs the length of the Valley, is sort of a line of demarcation in Encino. Just south of the street the mountains rise up, where a lot of fancy homes are perched. (Coach would take his daily five-mile walks and bump into people like Ron Howard, the director. Like everybody else finds themselves doing, Ron Howard wound up having chats on a regular basis. He'd sit with Coach and show him pictures of his kids.)

Anyway, the point is that the "south side" indicated you were big-time. Coach's condo was a block or so north of Ventura. So he and Nell are at some function, and a woman comes up to talk to them. They mention they're living in Encino now. "Oh, I didn't know you lived out there," the woman says. "The south side, I presume." Coach answers that, no, they're on the north side. When they get home, Nell is livid. "Oh, the nerve of that woman! 'The south side, I presume' " and on and on.

Coach tells this story with a little grin on his face. He

loved her spunkiness, her passion for life. Where John Wooden might face injustices — or just smaller, vexing moments like the woman's thoughtless comment — with detached calm, Nell would roll up her sleeves, ready to do battle, if only in the privacy of their home afterward. I think he admired that great ability she had to be up-front and outspoken in her principles, and yet so gregarious in her caring for people. It's that idea of balance again. You know, they went to the Final Four and the coaches convention together for 37 straight years — Nell quick to shoot a disapproving look at any coach who looked like he might have forgotten he had a family back home.

I've often been struck by the notion that their marriage had much the same chemistry as mine and Sally's. They really were a lot like Sally and me — except, of course, that we have the opposite roles. Where Coach was quiet, shy and unassuming, Nell was a dynamo. With us, Sally is the laid-back one and I'm more like Nell. As I've said, sometimes I have to have an operation to get my foot out of my mouth.

After I got the Pepperdine job, we'd continue to see them from time to time. When I found myself considering going after another coaching job, I'd call Coach Wooden for advice. And he'd help me gain perspective. "Jim, if you have peace of mind and you're not frustrated where you are now . . . " He always emphasized that I should make that a major consideration. While at Pepperdine, I remember we went to a UCLA football game once. Picked him up at 10 a.m., went to the game and had dinner afterward. We didn't get back until 10 that night. But through this period of time, Nell was starting to get really sick. We'd go over to his house occasionally to visit, but sometimes we'd be going to the hospital instead. Nell had had some strokes. I remember being in Seattle with Coach at the Final Four in 1984. And Nell was there in a wheelchair. She could still walk, but not very well. It was the last Final Four they attended together. Nell died in 1985. The last time she went into the hospital, at St. Vincent's in downtown L.A., she was there for 100 days, in intensive care. Three or four times Sally and I went down to the hospital and spent an afternoon or evening with

Coach. He was there religiously. Probably slept there. And you could see the toll it was taking on him. They'd had a relationship second to none. It was a rough, rough time.

Finally, Nell passed away. We went to the funeral. She was buried out at Forest Lawn. Right after that, Coach was talking with me and said, "Jim, death does not scare me at all. In fact, I'd like to die — so I could be with Nellie." There was nothing I could say. Sometimes words just don't work. As the months went by, his gloom didn't lift. Coach began to become isolated. His friends and family tried in vain to help him, trying to get him out of the funk he was in. For the longest time nothing seemed to penetrate. John Wooden still had that marvelous intellect and gentle soul, but his heart had left him. All of us feared it would never return.

Thank God it did. The depression finally lifted with the births of some great-grandchildren. That snapped him out of it. The kids brought Coach out of his grief. (*"A little fellow follows me . . . "*) Maybe he saw some of Nell in them, what with all that wide-eyed wonder and excitement for life that kids always have.

Still, Coach didn't go to the Final Four in all the years that followed Nell's death. The Final Four and the convention was one of their special times. I helped organize a special recognition held for him in his native state when the Final Four was played in Indianapolis in 1991 — and most of his family was there, so it was a nice deal — but that's the only one he attended and I don't think he even stayed for the championship game. You know, to this day I keep telling him that we need him at the convention at the Final Four; that he's one of the great foundations of our profession, and all the coaches of America would love to get a chance to visit with him and get to know him and share ideas. I keep hoping he'll do it, because I know how he loves to sit and talk with other coaches. I also know how many coaches would treasure the moment. But I understand if he never brings himself to do it. Coach still keeps Nell's things around, still sleeps on his side of the bed. It is such a relief to see him smile now when he talks of her, to see that he's at peace with losing her. But I also know how some lines aren't meant to be crossed. I understand if he never comes to the convention again.

And that's why the fact he came to see us play Arkansas for the national title meant so much to me. Remember, it was played in Seattle — the same city where he and Nell attended the Final Four and the convention together for the last time. I was glad that our friendship (and, of more importance, his love for the UCLA program) brought him. But I was also glad because it was another step for him, another example of his healing from the grief we once feared might cost him his life.

As the season progressed and our successes mounted, I told Coach that I really wanted him to be there if we made it to the Final Four. He never said no, but he never would give me a yes. Like he always does, he'd say: "Well, Jim . . . I'll think about it, I'll think about it." After we win the West regional, I call him up and leave another message. He calls me back and says, "Jim, I completely forgot about my commitment with McDonald's." For some reason, they shifted the day for the McDonald's All-Star game for high school standouts to the Sunday of the Final Four weekend — not a particularly good idea, if you ask me. And Coach was scheduled to make an appearance at the game, which was being held in St. Louis.

I went to Seattle, resigned to the fact he wasn't going to be there. But after we beat Oklahoma State in the semifinals on Saturday, I tried again. I called for him in St. Louis, but he wasn't in his hotel room. Then I called his daughter Nan and told her we would fly him up. We'd send a private plane to get him, because I had a friend I knew would do it. So I told her to get hold of him and let me know what's going on. Finally, she called back. She said he was going to come, but — typical of Coach — he didn't want me to dispatch a plane to St. Louis. (As it turned out, he'd already made plans. In fact, he sat next to Bill Gates of Microsoft at the game after giving a speech for the Arthur Andersen Group at the Microsoft campus that afternoon. I think maybe he just didn't want to tell me in advance for a reason so typical of him. He's always wanted to stay in the background and not rain on my parade, and he knew that the media would be asking me if I knew whether he was coming or not. Coach, of all people, knows what the pressure has been like for the men who have followed him; and he also didn't want to detract from what the team had already accomplished. That's where the focus needed to be, on the team. That's how he thinks.)

To get to Seattle, Coach had flown back to Los Angeles, not getting home until about 11:30 Sunday night. Then he got up at about 5:30 in the morning to catch a plane for Seattle. He worked all day, delivering his speech and meeting with folks, and then he came to the game. Remember, he was 84 at the time. Remarkable. And I can't begin to tell you how important it was for me that he took the time to come. I never got to speak with him that day, or that night after we'd won, but I saw him there in the stands. It was a special, special moment.

Did I ask him to talk to the team before the game? No. By now you should understand why. If I'd seen him I'd have asked him, but I knew he probably wouldn't. This was my challenge, and my team. He knows he's a powerful figure and carries so much influence, and he just wouldn't want to step in on that, no matter how much I might like him to. And I'm big on that. I had Walton talk to the team before we went to the first round, Mike Warren before the West regional in Oakland, and Marques Johnson before the West title game. And I had Magic Johnson talk to them via phone from Hawaii the week before our trip to Seattle. But I knew that Coach Wooden would want to stay in the shadows, rooting from there.

*   *   *

The story is true about what happened as John Wooden was walking off the court in San Diego following his 10th and last title in 1975. (The previous year, UCLA was beaten by North Carolina State, in double overtime, in the national semifinals.) He'd announced his retirement before the championship game with Kentucky, remember. So now he's won another title, and as he's leaving a UCLA booster rushes up to him and says: "Congratulations, Coach. Great job. You let us down last year, but this makes up up for it!"

("We, the alumni . . . ")

It just never ceases to amaze me. You know, somebody asked me if I thought even a John Wooden could win 10 championships in the current era, with the tournament expanded to 64 teams and the regionals balanced in strength by a nationwide seeding system. He probably couldn't. If anybody could, it would be him — but I don't think there's a coach in America who would think he could do it at this stage, with 13 scholarships available now.

That comment to Coach by that "fan" was a telling moment. If John Wooden were still coaching today, he might be a victim of his own success. Given the climate of criticism and ridiculous expectations, he probably wouldn't have escaped the heat. But he'd have figured out a way to keep going. He's a survivor. He is, after all, a coach.

I learned something from how he went out. Coach Wooden left that floor in San Diego on his own terms, with a smile on his face. And most of the time ever since — not in his personal life for a time there, but at least when it came to his basketball career — he's had that inner smile. It taught me that I'd like to go out like that someday. I'd like to win a national championship in my last year of coaching. Boy, wouldn't that be nice!

That isn't likely, of course. But I'll tell you this. I've had that smile myself ever since that April night in Seattle, and it stayed with me until October 15 of 1995, when the next season began. It's an inner smile, a sense of self-satisfaction. While I know that a new season will put my game face back on me, I also have a feeling of accomplishment that won't fade.

I hope winning the NCAA title gives everybody a different perspective, but I'm not holding my breath. If Tyus hadn't hit that shot against Missouri in the tournament, it would have been a bitter pill to swallow. But the tournament is a bitter experience for a lot of people. It's hard to win a national title. It's hard to get to the Final Four. But it's also hard to get a certain segment of people to understand that. The other day I was watching one of our videotapes and an announcer was talking about coaches and NCAA championships. What he said was this: "Well, Dean Smith has won only two."

Only two? There are only three men in the history of college basketball who have won more than two. That's Wooden, Knight and Rupp. Sometimes you wonder if *anybody* understands that. Sometimes you wonder if the madness of March and the imposing nature of the challenge can be appreciated by anyone other than a coach and his players.

Well, I certainly knew. Heading into the 1995 NCAA Tournament with the nation's number-one ranking and the tournament's number-one seed, I knew that none of that assured us of anything. At that point, I only knew we had one whale of a job awaiting us, and one monstrous load of other people's expectations on our shoulders.

EDNEY'S MIRACLE

9

March 17, 1995 — The NCAA Tournament, first round game: UCLA vs. Florida International.

Tulsa or no Tulsa, I've looked at video of Florida International and I find myself saying, "Well, even I don't think they can beat us." At the press conference the day before, a couple of their players were talking about how thrilling it was just to get a chance to be on the same court with Ed O'Bannon. That means it's going to be a tough game, not to win but to maintain focus and build momentum for the task ahead. And the task ahead looks daunting.

When the pairings for the tournament came out, with us the No. 1 seed overall, I saw us bracketed opposite the winner of Indiana-Missouri, the Nos. 8 and 9 seeds in the West, in the second round and thought, holy mackerel, that's a tough draw. Couldn't believe it, really. I thought we had the toughest second-round matchup of any team in the tournament.

But right now there's Florida International. I never, ever tell a team "We should beat these guys," so I decide on a theme in the locker room. "There's only one thing I want tonight," I tell them. "LEAVE . . . NO . . . DOUBT. Leave no doubt!"

Turns out, there is none. We're up 43-23 by halftime and I start pulling players with 15 or so minutes still to play and us up

30. None of our starters plays more than 25 minutes. J.R. comes off the bench to lead us with 16 points in 23 minutes. The final score is 92-56.

I walk into the post-game press conference. Florida International's players want to have their pictures taken with Ed. Their coach, Bob Weltlich, is wearing a badge that says "I want a job!" 'cause he'd already resigned. Bob had coached at Mississippi and Texas and probably was used to schools that put a lot of effort and money into basketball, so he found it frustrating where he was and quit. The badge makes even me smile.

Thing is, I had noticed out on the bench in the final minutes that all my players were smiling as well. And laughing. And cutting up. I think maybe they're horsing around a little too much. And the feeling I get is an uneasy one.

March 19, 1995 — NCAA second round: UCLA vs. Missouri.

Instead of going away, the feeling has gotten worse. I found out that some of the players stayed up later than usual in the hotel after the Florida International game. And the next night as well. Have we lost our edge? I look at them as I go through our pre-game in the locker room, and they seem focused. But the ominous feeling still follows me around.

Trouble.

Missouri has got the tempo slowed down and they're hitting a ridiculous number of threes (they will hit 12 of 19 in all). We've tried to press, tried to break out, but Missouri keeps controlling the tempo. We just can't get anything generated. We're down eight at the half, 42-34. Still, my players are confident during the break. I can tell they are determined to come back. I can tell they feel they will.

Second half now, and Missouri is having none of it. They still are hitting from everywhere, deep and deeper. I look out and, for the first time this season, I see our guys dropping their heads and their shoulders. They've got that "What are we going to do?" look on their faces.

C'mon, Ed! It's time to take it up, maybe to a notch you've never even thought possible before. Don't let it happen, make it happen.

Sure enough, Ed starts cranking it up. We go on a 15-0 run. We're up six.

OK, breathe a little easier now.

No such luck. Missouri won't cave in. The clock shows 3:49, and Missouri's back ahead, by three. Stretch drive, you go to your thoroughbred: Ed hits a basket, then a couple of free throws and then, on a nice pivot move, he drops an eight-foot bank shot inside the final minute. We're up, 73-72. Missouri gets it back down and is working the ball around, looking for an opening. There is none. We are playing great defense. Beautiful. Crunch time and we're applying the crunch. I stand up. Right in my line of sight, Paul O'Liney comes around and Dollar is trailing him. I can see it clearly. Missouri's Jon Sutherland is standing right there and suddenly he steps right out in Cameron's path. Whistle blows! Yeah! Yeah, baby! Call it!

What's this? Are you kidding me? No, he is NOT calling the foul on Dollar! Is he?

He is. A firestorm erupts in my chest. How could they miss that call? It was one of the easiest ones I've seen all year. A no-brainer.

Hold it in, Jim. A technical now is suicide.

The game clock's at 40 or so seconds. Worse, the shot clock gets reset with the foul, so Missouri won't be rushed to get something off. Mygosh! I look out and see Missouri in a stall, waiting to take one final shot.

Why do it? They miss and they're dead ducks. We'll take this. They run most of the clock down and if they miss they won't have time to foul us and have a chance at getting the ball back for another shot. Big gamble.

We are on them, shutting everything down. Shot clock is melting. Good D, good D. And then . . . It happens so fast. With no time for any other move if this one doesn't work, one of their guards penetrates on the dribble into the lane, then dishes inside to Julian Winfield. With only one second left on their shot clock, he banks one in. We're down, 74-73. I look at the game clock.

There are 4.8 seconds on it. Thank God for the new rule that stops the clock automatically after a basket inside the final minute. It saves us some precious ticks. I call timeout. Back in L.A., the radio call-in lines are probably already jammed with I-told-you-so'ers.

Oh, Lord. Again? To this *team?*

That's all I allow myself. There are 4.8 seconds. There is a game to be won, not emotion to be indulged. I cannot, will not, allow disappointment or fear or whatever gawdawful thing that's crawling inside my gut to take over. It's my job to give us a chance. Some memories rush up — warp factor-like — as the players walk toward me and the bench. The buzz in the air, the pandemonium from Missouri fans on one side of the arena and the murmuring undertow of gloom from ours . . . it is all distant, nearly mute. My mind focuses on those memories, processing them in an instant. And just as quickly . . .

I know what I want done. I will not consider what happens if it doesn't work out.

*   *   *

Two things flashed through my mind at that moment, one of them a memory of something that happened three decades prior. I was at a Lakers playoff game in the Sports Arena, back when the Boston Celtics had Bill Russell and K.C. Jones and Sam Jones and the Lakers had West and Elgin Baylor. The Lakers were down with three seconds to go, and had the ball at the free-throw line extended. They had to go the rest of the floor. They got the ball in to West, and he did it, driving and laying the ball up over the rim right at the buzzer. Well, there was a big controversy over that shot. Could even a Jerry West have done that in so short a time? Did the timer have a slow hand? So some sports-writers went down there later and timed NBA players duplicating what West had done, and they found that it was indeed possible.

This was back when I was a high school coach. So from then on, in practice I'd run a drill where I'd just flip the players the ball and let them go three-quarters of the court with the clock up there. And what it did was make them aware of the time they had and not to panic in that kind of a situation. Later I went to a pro practice and saw a drill where a coach stood underneath the basket with a player standing in the middle of the lane. The coach flipped the ball to the guy and he had to turn and go one-on-one the length of the court in six seconds. That's one of the toughest drills I've ever seen. So I incorporated that drill, and we practice it at UCLA about four times a year.

What we found from that drill was that Tyus Edney was just terrific at it. He was one of the few guys who, the first time we ran it, he could do it. Nobody could stop him, and he'd just be a blur getting down the court. Other guys might try to do an evasion maneuver with a crossover dribble or go between their legs, but they'd lose the ball. Not Tyus. His speed afoot, and his quickness with the ball, was just unrelenting.

The second memory was of a bitter experience, which just goes to show you that things that appear disastrous at the time might prove a blessing someday. In the 1988-89 season, my first as UCLA coach, we were playing Cal-Irvine and Pooh Richardson hit a jumper for us with five seconds left to give us a 90-89 lead. Their team called timeout. We decided to double-team their best player. He broke our double-team and as he charged down the floor, everybody just split and let him go because we didn't want to foul him. So he went in, made a very difficult shot — kind of an underhand flip from the foul line — and Cal-Irvine beat us 91-90. It took a wild shot, but the kid got the chance because we couldn't afford to foul him. That's an experience you never forget, an experience you put in the bank.

And so — in the toughest of situations, facing the most critical coaching decision of my career — it was time to make a withdrawal.

*   *   *

I look at my five players, 94 feet away. They turn to walk toward our bench, 4.8 seconds left. They turn and 10 eyes are riveted on me. Five desperate players, needing and wanting help.

All right, Jim. You've always been such a strong believer in good communication. What's a coach if he can't communicate his thoughts and ideas to his players? Well, you've NEVER faced a bigger communications situation than you face now.

Don't falter. Don't put your head down. Don't show disappointment. Don't let your voice crack. You must be positive. Strong. Decisive. Remember what Hubie Brown said: "The notoriety of the coach is dictated by the team's execution while under pressure." Well, you know EXACTLY what you want to do!

I hear one of my assistants shouting.

"We gotta throw the long pass, gotta make a long pass!"

"No," I hear myself answering. "We're not going to do that."

The players arrive. We huddle.

Show confidence. Don't waver in what you want done.

As soon as they take their seats, I look them in the eye and say: "This is what we're going to do." As I begin to talk, I hear Ed O'Bannon: "We are NOT going to lose this game! We're NOT losing!" I look at Tyus. "Edney, I want you to get the ball. Hopefully, you can get it around the foul line and push it down the floor like you always do . . .

Remember. Remember Cal-Irvine.

". . . and they're NOT going to foul you. Take it to the rim. Take it to the rim! Ed, you spot up on the left side. Toby, you spot up on the right. J.R., you and Charles get in there to tip it in."

The buzzer sounds. The huddle breaks.

Think! What else? What is it? Michigan! Tyus Edney was a sophomore and stole an in-bounds pass seconds before the final buzzer and if he'd shot we'd have upset Michigan in the 1993 NCAAs, but he decided to pass to Ed for what looked like a better shot. But that gave Michigan time to recover, and they stole it. Kept us tied, put the game in overtime, where we lost.

So I find myself walking with Tyus. I have something else to tell him, and even if Norm Stewart and his players and the

Missouri mascot — even if the entire free world knows who the ball is going to, for that matter . . . well, I don't care. I know Tyus. I know magic. I used to worry about him penetrating and trying to go up against a 7-footer or a 6-11 guy, but in four years I almost never saw him get one blocked. That's why I want him to take the shot. So I stand there with him and I lean into his ear and I say this: "Tyus, *you* shoot the ball. Make *sure* you shoot it! It's your ball. Your rock. Your game. Just go on and make it happen."

What happens next is not 4.8 seconds in slow motion, it is eternity. I can only watch it unfold, oblivious to everything else, even the consequences. I am just another spectator now, frozen, glued to the moment.

0:04.8

Tyus gets the ball in the paint. He is in the lane, 10 feet from the Missouri basket, with his back about 84 feet from the one he needs to reach. He spins to his right and begins his dribble with his left hand.

0:04.6

He's travelled five feet, crossing the free-throw line, and his defender is dogging him, about three to four feet away and closing, but warily.

Good! The guy is playing it safe, afraid to foul.

0:03.1

Tyus reaches midcourt. Another defender is closing at an angle, giving them two on a path to cut Tyus off. Tyus sees it developing, begins to pull up, and, as he begins to take evasive action, shifting his feet and adjusting his balance — all of this happening in an instant — I see him maintain his dribble with a pat of his left hand, slapping the ball behind his back — 0:02.9 now — as he stutter-steps right and picks up the dribble with his right hand. He's a couple of feet beyond the midstripe.

Yow! Beautiful move!

0:02.5

The maneuver's complete. Changing his angle of attack, he's got the defenders on his left now and a clear dribble with his right hand. He's still 15 feet from the free-throw line and heading straight toward the top of the key.

0:01.8

Top of the circle now. His foot hits the three-point line. The two guys giving chase can't cut him off, but they're right beside him, applying some pressure. Out on the left wing, Ed O'Bannon is by himself and has both arms raised, calling for the ball. But he's 25 feet from the basket, and there's a defender close enough to jump out and contest any shot by the time a pass got to Ed. If, that is, it could even get to him in time to release a shot. And there's no time.

Keep it, Tyus! Your rock! Your game!

0:01.5

He's at the foul stripe. The two guys to his left are still bunched beside him, on the run. And there's that big man, Derek Grimm, 6-feet-8, with one foot in the paint midway between the goal and the foul line to Tyus' right. The big guy's going to slide into the lane and challenge! I know it!

0:01.2

Liftoff. Tyus is airborne in the lane, and the big man is in there with him, hands high, right in front of Edney's path. But he won't risk putting a body on him by leaving his feet and trying to block it. *(Uh-oh!)* He doesn't have to. He's got the shot angle cut off with those long arms.

0:00.9

On the fly, Tyus is adjusting his shot, hitching, scooping toward the right to avoid those arms.

0:00.8

The ball leaves his hand. I see lightning! No. It's a strobe light from a photographer.

Goin-goin-goin-goin! PLEASE . . . GO . . . IN!

0:00.2

The ball hits the glass, high up on the top right corner of the painted white square.

0:00.1

It's descending, but not yet halfway down from the spot of its carom to the rim.

0:00.0

Buzzer sounds. It's still above the plane of the rim, barely.

And then I see, a blink later, the ball tap the inside front of the rim and fall through the net. Everything stops. It seems like total quiet. Then, an explosion. I watch a wave of sheer, utter joy crash around Tyus Edney. Our players are hopping and slapping and screaming, and a couple of them are lifting up Tyus, like a rag doll. In the midst of this unbelievable moment, this moment beyond words, I see something else. I see Cameron Dollar hugging a Missouri player — Cameron, as concerned for the shock and disappointment in that other kid's face as he was happy for himself. He embraces the guy, who is hugging Cameron too, and pats him on the back as he speaks consolingly in his ear. Sally, meanwhile, has opened her eyes. She'd kept them shut through the entire 4.8 seconds.

I feel for Norm, who has won 600-some games but never a national championship, and I wonder if once, just once, those "fans" who think an NCAA banner is the only way to measure a coach's worth will understand how difficult it is, how there is far more to judging a coach than a championship, a championship that is dependent on so many factors you can't control, like the breathless bounce of a ball that turns one way, then another, your fate consigned to its unpredictable trajectory. Like the one that has just saved me and sunk Norm. I wonder, but not very long. I know what's happened here. I didn't dodge a bullet. I dodged a 50-megaton bomb.

In the locker room, the players are still awash in giddy release from what looked like certain doom, but that other feeling is not far away. And I know it's time to address the significance of what we just experienced.

"Fellas, I'm gonna tell ya, I've been watching basketball a long time and I've never seen a team NOT have to go through that to win it all. I remember Duke going to the Elite Eight twice and Christian Laettner hits buzzer beaters in two Elite Eight games to take Duke to the Final Four. That miracle shot against Kentucky. And I've seen Arkansas do it against Louisville back in the early '80s on a half-court shot. Ulysses S. Reed. From behind half-court on a two-hand, high-lob backspin. Went right through and beat Louisville.

"Sometimes you need luck to go all the way. And we were lucky today. I wanna tell you that. We were lucky. But to do what we've done, you've gotta get some balls bouncin' your way. I don't want us to put ourselves in that position again. Every team is going to come at us like that. We took a shot that was unbelievable today and got out of it."

I pause, letting that sink in, as if it needs far to sink.

"I'm proud of ya, fellas."

I don't mention the lack of focus I'd feared when they were up late at the hotel. But I remember it. And I have something in store for these guys. Not now. But soon.

*   *   *

I've joked since that when Tyus Edney made that shot, I felt like a guy who was facing a firing squad, heard the executioner yell "Fire!" and then all 12 guns failed to go off. Well, there's a whole lot of truth in that. It certainly had that feel.

But you want to know just how that game affected me? I was so petrified from the experience that, from that moment on, the idea of winning the whole thing never crossed my mind. Getting ready for the next game, that's all I thought about. I didn't entertain any fanciful ideas of winning it all. I thought we could go to the Final Four, and I hoped we could win a national championship, but those are just words. Doing it is completely different. And from the Missouri game on, I never thought about the title. That was a desperate time. I was just hanging on by my fingernails after that game, just trying to survive the next day.

Survival. That became my operative word. Prepare, prepare, prepare — then try to survive whomever and whatever jumped up next.

March 20-21, 1995 — Back in L.A., awaiting the West Regional semifinals.

I gave them Monday off. We were supposed to leave for Oakland and the tournament today, Tuesday, but I've postponed it until tomorrow. Two reasons. I just think it better if we can give them another day at home. But the other reason is right here in the locker room at Pauley, where I've arranged a semicircle of chairs.

I have turned the locker room into a classroom, and I am about to deliver a lesson. I make it a point not to get on my team after a loss, and I rarely dress them down unless I feel it's truly called for. I've made them run a few times this season, but I've not really gotten on their case that much. Well, this is the time. Didn't I sit down and take more than an hour rehearsing this speech? You bet I did. It's a lesson plan that includes fire and brimstone. Jim Harrick, teacher — although that's probably not the first descriptive noun that will come to mind from my players once I'm done.

OK. Time for the start of practice has arrived. I need to get onto the court. Out there, I see the guys are sauntering in like they usually do. I get their attention.

"Let's go into the locker room for a minute."

They know something's up. We don't have chairs aligned in that position normally. If we were just watching videotape, they'd simply turn their chairs around from in front of their lockers and watch from there. Nope, this is a meeting of my mind and their behinds. They can tell this isn't going to be a normal session. *Good.*

I launch in. I have rarely raised my voice to the team all season. Maybe an individual here and there, but rarely. And I'm not too much of a screamer or yeller. But now . . . now I am getting on them unbelievably hard. I bring up their Late Night With Hotel act. I tell them we'll be having a security guard on the floor at the hotel in Oakland, and that he'll be on the phone to me quicker than the Presidential hotline if anybody's caught outside his door beyond the appointed hour. I hear my voice, and it's booming. Got their attention now.

I tell them about my Morningside team that let me down. I tell them how they were 22-0 in 1973 and got voted the number-one team in America, went on to go 28-0, get in the playoffs and how I then have some players do some silly, dumb things and we got beat. And that's my theme. I tell them maybe we lost our focus because Florida International was such an easy game, but that was no excuse for the kind of thought patterns they seemed to take from it. I single out each player — not so much the subs, but the seven who played — and I raise cain with each one. I get on Ed O'Bannon hard. And Charles. And George. All of them.

But now I'm looking at Edney.

OK, tough guy. What you gonna say now? This kid just saved your hide, and his teammates' hides. This guy has been such a nice kid for four years, you don't even have anything to get on him about. Gonna have to dig down deep for this one, sport. Gotta come up with something.

"EDNEY!" I holler. "That fourth foul you made in that game was just the stupidest thing you've ever done since you've been here!"

That's all I can think of. Thank goodness it's at least true, that it was an ill-advised foul. I, of course, have turned it from misdemeanor into felony. I have ranted and raved world class. But I know I've made some important points, and it looks like it's registering on their faces. I send them out onto the court. We are going to have a very fierce practice. And what I begin to see is . . . well, beautiful. They are playing crisp, all business, moving with purpose and focused.

And I think of the last thing I told them before we left that locker.

"Fellas, we may go to Oakland and lose. But I guarantee you, if we do we're going to lose right!"

Which is another way of saying we are going to prepare to win. If we lose, it won't be because we've failed to put ourself in the best possible position to win. Mentally, physically, every which way. If we lose, it won't be because we lost our edge or cheated ourselves out of a chance of a lifetime.

March 23, 1995 — NCAA West Regional semifinal game: UCLA vs. Mississippi State.

I think the thing I like most about this regional is that there's four coaches — Gary Williams of Maryland, Jim Calhoun of Connecticut, Richard Williams of Mississippi State and me — who've never made it to the Final Four, and now one of us is going to get to go.

Ours is a dangerous opponent. Mississippi State has quickness and size, and loves to shoot threes, and with Missouri's long bombs fresh in my mind, I know we might have our hands full again. But I also know that my guys have been zeroed in all week, ready to go.

Game starts, and Tyus Edney is a tiger again.

Early on, he gets a steal and drives down and takes it right up the middle, right in front of 6-foot-11 Erick Dampier. Tyus goes up, Dampier fouls him and Tyus, wizard apprentice of Westwood, pulls another rabbit out of the hat. He tosses up a semi-right hand hook and in it goes. He sinks the free throw. Three-point play. Great play.

State is in a man-to-man and Tyus just keeps slicing it up. Now, about five minutes after that attack in the face of Dampier, he's doing it again, driving the left side this time and Dampier fouls him again. He makes it. Two straight adventures into dangerous territory, two magnificent plays.

Because of Edney, State switches to a zone. And Tyus just keeps going. Mark Gottfried played for Alabama in the SEC and he's scouted Mississippi State extensively. Mark sees the zone, and I feel him punch me in the ribs.

"Run wide!" he says.

I call it out. All it is is a screen on the defensive guard at the point. We take both our low post guys up and screen the point. Tyus uses the screen to get free and, boom, nails a three-pointer.

Next time down we run it again, but they've got Tyus double-teamed this time. So he kicks it to Ed in the corner. Three. Good. (*Very* good!)

And we run it again. This time it's Dampier who steps out to cut Tyus off. So he drops it down low to Zidek, and George hits a short jumper. We've gotten eight points off that play in three straight sequences. They've tried man, and that didn't work. They've gone to zone, and that didn't work.

Nail in the coffin!

I really think so. We've set the tone early and just shredded everything State has thrown at us. I can see their frustration, and maybe a little confusion as well. I can also see emotion in our players. Lots of emotion. We are on a high, and we just keep rolling. The halftime horn sounds and I look up at the scoreboard: UCLA 40, MISSISSIPPI STATE 19.

We are too focused, too furious, and too much fueled by Tyus Edney to let this thing slide in the second half. I wind up playing none of our starters more than 31 minutes, and that distinction belongs to one of our freshmen, Bailey. In 25 minutes, Tyus scores 10 points and dishes out eight assists. Ed has 21 points and I wind up getting to let all 12 players see some action. The final score is 86-67.

March 25, 1995 — NCAA West Regional championship game: UCLA vs. Connecticut.

"You ever take a charge, or dive on the floor, this is the time you gotta do it. Playing hard, playing hard all the way. Fellas, I remember us on the track back in May. Running, lifting in the weight room, practicing. Always talking about the Kingdome . . . It's right here . . . right now. Right here, right now.

"We've worked hard. We've had goals, objectives and we've filled them all. And all you gotta do is get on the ball. Right now! Let's have some fun and have a great game, fellas."

It's time to leave the locker room now, and as I finish my speech the players gather and put their hands together skyward as they've always done and I hear Ed: "Here we go. ATTITUDE! We gotta go out and take it to 'em! Right away! First five minutes. Here we go. Bruins on three. One-two-three . . . "

"BRUINS!" they yell in unison, and it's a hearty yell, emotion busting out everywhere.

I've debated starting George. This is going to be an up-and-down game, more helter than even skelter oughta allow. In the press conference yesterday, some of Connecticut's players were talking about how quick they were. Our guys got the impression that they didn't feel anybody in the country could run with them.

Thank you, Oh Great Bulletin Board Clipout Guy in the Sky! For my guys, and for Tyus in particular, this is waving the proverbial red flag in front of the proverbial you-know-what.

You open the court on us and try to press us a little, well that just makes Edney that much more effective. And the LAST thing you want to do is imply that Tyus, of all people, isn't up to it. And, of course, I don't have to tell Edney that one of Connecticut's guards, Kevin Ollie, just happens to be from Los Angeles.

The game starts, and the pace is just as I figured. Only not as Ed planned in the locker. It's Connecticut jumping out in the first five minutes and this Ray Allen . . . my oh my! They're running double staggered screens for him to take three-point shots! He's filling it up (he will score 36).

This guy might be the best we've played against all year long. Well, there's Stoudamire. Of course. But this guy's really something. Be careful, Jim. You're starting to become a big fan of his, and he's doing his best to stay between you and a trip to Seattle.

Holy mackerel, we've got to start switching on those screens!

The Huskies have jumped out early, all right, but now we're right back in it, thriving on this open-court stuff, and we begin to maintain a lead all through the half. Now it's the final seconds of the half, and there goes Allen again. He hits a three. And our lead is down to four. Not good. That's a nice momentum builder for them going into the locker room. We'll just have to forget it and—

WHAT IN THE WORLD???!!!!??? OHMYNO! Charles O'Bannon is signaling for a timeout! There's only three seconds left in the half. You only get three timeouts, and we don't want to waste one here! What in the world is he thinking of out there? We're up four, we'll take that.

Well, it's too late now. The clock's been stopped and here come my players for a huddle. I don't say anything to Charles, but I fix him with a look that says "What the hell are you doing, son?" Well, gotta do somethin' here. Milk's already been spilled.

So I look at — who else? — Edney. "Tyus, just like Missouri, you take it down there. But this time you gotta shoot a 30-footer or something. No time to go all the way. Just run it down and pull up with a long jumper."

Buzzer sounds. Tyus gets the ball, darting, darting . . . pulling up . . . about 28 feet from the basket, two hands in his face . . . releases the ball . . . horn goes off . . . ball goes . . . in?

IN!

Tyus stands frozen, then just drops his arms and stares into the eyes of Cameron Dollar as Cameron rushes up to him, Tyus standing there motionless, as if to say "Well, of course it went in!"

Now we're running into the locker room, riding this big momentum-breaker. We get inside. I'm looking for Charles O'Bannon. I find him. And matter-of-factly, with a straight face, I say this:

"Charles. That was a nice call, son."

Well now, let's see if we can capitalize on this surprising turn of events. Let's open the second half with a set play for Zidek.

Second half opens, and George posts low. There goes that big ol' beautiful hook. Swish. We're up 50-41, just five seconds into the second half. That means that, in a span of eight seconds of game time, we've gone from four up to nine up.

That's a backbreaker!

It starts to look that way. We just never have to break stride. The minutes whiz by and I see us remain in this comfortable, confident rhythm. Connecticut makes stab after stab at us, but theirs is a struggle, and they just can't get all the way back. Finally, it's just a little more than two minutes left. We're up 15.

Hang on, hang on, hang on!

Might sound strange if someone could hear what I'm thinking, but that's the way it is in this business. And it's particularly the way it is when you've dreamed of this chance at making the Final Four for years and years, and put up with so much to get this close. Sure enough, there's reason to worry. Suddenly we're not guarding them. They're fouling us to give two and they're trying to counter with threes, and the strategy is working pretty good.

"Get the ball in Tyus' or Ed's hands every time!" I tell them. I want them at the line. If we're going to go down, we're going down with Edney and O'Bannon missing free throws at the line. Fat chance. They foul Edney, he's going to make them pay.

It never gets to the meltdown crisis stage, thank God. We win 102-96. Our two freshmen, Toby and J.R., just thrived at this kind of pace. They wind up with 44 points between them, Toby getting a career-high 26. Ed has 15 points and six rebounds, and Tyus is just remarkable once again. He not only gets 22 points, he also grabs 10 rebounds. And he plays the full 40 minutes. With one turnover.

I hear the PA announcing him the regional's most valuable player, and I find myself smiling and nodding approval.

What an incredible tournament he's having. Hey. What an incredible tournament we're ALL having.

*   *   *

I look back at the videotape of the late stages of that game, and when the CBS camera pans to my wife in the stands I see in her face the 35 years of coaching, with all the frustration that often accompanied it, all peaking now in this struggle going on before her eyes.

You could see the tension in Sally's face as we held on at the end, the camera zooming in tight as she stood in the crowd, eyes intent on the court, looking as if she wasn't going to draw another breath until the buzzer sounded and this thing was absolutely, positively, finally won. You know, all the criticism about me over the last couple of years probably hurt Sally more than it did me, and to see the person you're closest to in life share that struggle with you . . . words can't do justice to what she's meant to me. And now we could experience this release, this wonderful sense of satisfaction — and yes, maybe a little vindication — together.

One of the most gratifying things to me during this time was a poll that had come out in conjunction with the tournament. Some publication asked a nationwide sample of coaches who they most would like to see win the national championship, and the two names mentioned most were Roy Williams of Kansas and me. That meant a lot. It told me that my peers understood the kind of challenge the UCLA job held. And to have their support was, in some ways, as meaningful to me as getting to the Final Four.

You know, I think I probably have a lot more respect out of California than in it. Some of that's natural, of course. It's that you-can't-see-the-forest-for-the-trees syndrome. And it's also those incredible expectations that cover — and have in the past smothered — the UCLA basketball program.

In the lobster tank, every one of your strengths and every one of your weaknesses are characterized, and the weaknesses tend to get magnified, and a lot of people read or hear those characterizations and form their opinion from them. I understand that. But I also understand that the winning of a game — even this last one — didn't define me as a coach, didn't suddenly elevate me from moron to genius.

But if you think I'm saying I didn't feel as if I'd cleared a very high hurdle, you're wrong. Of course making the Final Four was something I'd coveted, something I hoped would prove a little something, something that — fair or not — seems to be the decisive factor in determining whether or not you've arrived as a college basketball coach. Walking off that court with a trip to the Kingdome secured . . . that was a very, very special moment for me, and for Sally.

Still, there's one other brief moment I need to tell you about. It happened on the flight back to Los Angeles after we'd won the regional.

Sally leaned over to me.

"Really, it doesn't matter now," she said. "We're going to the Final Four."

"Oh yeah? Don't give me that!" I shot back. "I don't want to hear that."

The coach in me was already in high gear again. I wasn't going to let the satisfaction — and yes, relief — of maybe silencing a lot of critics make me lose sight of what this tournament, this team and, indeed, this coach were all about. All these years, it was never about trying to prove myself to doubters. It was always about trying to be the best you can be. The biggest challenge was still in front of us. Which is why, in the post-game locker room celebration, I finally got things quiet and told my players this:

"We're not done yet."

THE FINAL FOUR

![10]

April 1, 1995 — The Final Four, NCAA Semifinal Game: UCLA vs. Oklahoma State.

This is it: college basketball's most exciting day. For me, the Saturday games have always marked the grandest moment of the Final Four weekend. Three teams are going to end their seasons in defeat, but right here, right now, we're all being showcased — and deservedly so. This is the pinnacle, really, of everything you've been working for. A doubleheader for the four best teams.

I'm glad we've got the first game. It's not fun to sit around, anticipating, waiting. If we win, it's going to be a lot easier to concentrate on scouting Arkansas and North Carolina, since you know you'll be playing the winner for the national title. Who wants to focus on that job before you even play, before you know if a scouting report is even necessary?

Personally, yesterday was immensely satisfying. Friday is always reserved for open practice. The arena fills and fans cheer every team, oohing and aahing and chortling at all the dunking and whatnot. It's a lighthearted, celebratory time, perhaps the only one where the participants can leisurely absorb all the attention and atmosphere. Once these workouts end, the pressure and competition that's to come will block out most of the festive feel.

I know how fun those Friday workouts are because I've been coming to them for some 20 years. The National Association of Basketball Coaches convention is always held in conjunction with the Final Four, so I'd been around to see it over and over again. It never seemed boring. I'd sit in the stands on those Fridays, allowing myself to fantasize a little about what it must feel like to stand out there. Yesterday I discovered that the reality is every bit as nice as the fantasy. We did what I term a "short-sharp" practice during our hour. Mostly, what we did was feel the excitement buzzing around the Kingdome, where there were about 35,000 people on hand. If Final Four Saturday is Showcase Day, Friday is Mardis Gras.

Of course, Saturday changes quickly from showcase to showdown. And now it's just about time to crawl into the trenches.

I'm not overstating it by much when I say this Oklahoma State game is going to be war. Ol' Big Country — Bryant Reeves — is 6-feet-11 and 295 rompin', stompin' pounds of imposing pivotman. They're billing the battle between him and Zidek, who is giving away 45 pounds to Reeves, as Big Country vs. Foreign Country. Pretty good line, and we hope to have a few of our satellite nations join the fracas (like Ed or Charles coming in for weakside help; and J.R. spelling George).

I'm worried about Randy Rutherford, too. Tough outside shot. Tough enough, in fact, that during our practices in L.A. we focused on finding Rutherford — because if he slips open away from the ball and then gets it with daylight, he'll drill you to death. All week we simulated their plays, with one of our players donning a red shirt and imitating Rutherford — all the better to get everybody accustomed to where he's going to be coming from.

We've watched no tapes of Arkansas or North Carolina. Just Oklahoma State. You get in the NCAA Tournament, you get in a desperate mode. Particularly after Missouri. The game ahead, that's all I concentrate on. Surviving what's in front of me.

I'm a bit perturbed because the billing for this game is Oklahoma State's defense versus our quickness and high-rev offense. There's no doubting Eddie Sutton's team plays excellent D, but I just can't believe people don't look beyond the surface to see the kind of defense we've been playing all season. Didn't it bring us back in December against Kentucky? Didn't we do a number on Arizona (and Tyus on Stoudamire) with defense? Haven't these observers seen all the blocks and steals and in-your-face-everywhere hustle? How do they think we've held 14 teams under 40 percent accuracy from the field? Wishful thinking?

Part of it is just natural, I guess. If you get it up and down the court as quickly and effectively as we do, it can mask the hard work going on at the defensive end. But it does bother me, knowing it's been overlooked, because I know the effort behind it and the role it's played. I'm going to mention this slight to the guys in my pre-game speech.

Which it's time to do.

"All I've heard ALL WEEK about Oklahoma State," I tell them, "is: 'It's the best defensive team . . . great defense . . . what a defensive team!' Well, we're a defensive team, too. That's how we got where we are."

"In your stance, line rules, cover down and swarm the post. Swarm 'em! Don't let ANYBODY outhustle you out there."

We head onto the court and into the crowd's loud rumble. I look over and watch Reeves warming up. In that black uniform he looks more like 395 pounds than 295. Little wonder that he accidentally shattered one of the glass backboards yesterday while dunking during their workout. Big Country? Big Universe is more like it.

Less than 30 seconds into the game now, and Tyus makes a move on Andre Owens, breaking free for a drive where he's fouled. He hits one of two. Less than a minute later, Tyus makes another move and darts right in for a layup. We're up 3-0.

Remember that one, Jim. The kid can't keep up with Tyus. Anytime you need a bucket, turn him loose.

The game starts to take a shape I don't like. Too open, Rutherford hits a 22-footer. *(Maybe we should have demanded he wear a red jersey.)* I decide to put in Cameron Dollar in place of Bailey. Cameron will get in his face. And George has already picked up a foul on Reeves. It's 9-9 with 16:10 on the clock. I sub J.R. for George. They get a follow shot by Chianti Roberts at 15:25, and we're down 11-9.

We need a run, and Ed starts us out with a three-pointer from the left wing. Boom, suddenly we're up 12-11. *(Good!)* We're starting to give them problems on defense. Get the ball back, and there's Charles hitting a seven-footer. Get it again, and Charles gets fouled, hits one. Get it again, and Ed hits another three-pointer, this one from 22 feet on the right wing. *(Better!)*

Now we've got a fast break, and there goes Tyus, in traffic. Arms and bodies everywhere as Tyus twists in the air, his back to the basket now, sailing for out of bounds . . .

Not this time, son.

. . . but he flips it up anyway, a blind prayer, and — YAGOTTABEKIDDINGME! — it goes in! Guys on the bench are going crazy. Unbelievable shot. Oops. Ref comes over to warn our players.

What's he going to whistle 'em for: Excessive incredulity?

I look up. We're ahead 20-11 with 13:34 to go. We've scored 11 straight points. But now Oklahoma State comes back, scoring six straight, and we're ahead by only three. Reeves keeps owning the inside. He goes into the paint and drops a 14-footer and our lead is down to 24-23, 8:07 left.

But here we come again. Charles hits an 18-footer off a nice pass from Edney, they miss the front end of a bonus at their end, and Charles scores again, this time from 16 feet, again with an assist from Tyus. Now it's Bailey with a driving scoop off a pass from his fellow freshman, J.R. (I've been shuffling J.R. and George in and out because Reeves is proving a handful). Now we get it again and Tyus is fouled driving. He hits one. We've scored seven straight. We're up 31-23 at 4:50.

Maybe this blitz will keep the momentum ours.

Maybe not. Owens drills one from about 22 feet for a three. We get a nice alley-oop reverse layin by Charles off another Edney pass, but they get a 14-footer from Chianti Roberts followed by — not again! — another three, this one by Terry Collins. Suddenly they've outscored us 8-2. Less than a minute and a half after our eight-point lead, it's down to 33-31.

Worse: I see Oklahoma State on a three-on-one breakout and Edney is the one defending. He slides down the block to cut off a guy taking a pass while coming in off the right wing. Both of them go up. In the airborne collision that follows, Tyus is sent flying awkwardly toward the baseline. He lands in a heap, directly on his right hand. Great play. He's drawn a foul out of it. But he's lying prone by the basket support, squeezing his hands into fists, apparently in some pain, trying to move that right wrist some . . . then, finally, he gets up.

Whew! Looked bad for a second there. But he's OK.

It stays tight the rest of the half, and when Reeves hits a pair of free throws with 34 seconds left, we're tied 37-37. It stays that way until the buzzer. Outside the locker room I study the first half boxscore, and it merely confirms the writing I've already seen on the wall. Reeves has 18 points and six rebounds. We've pretty much kept Rutherford in check, but they're 54.5 percent from the field overall and 3 for 5 in threes thanks to those two late ones by guys we didn't think would hurt us. In one of our runs in the first half, we'd stopped them at their end somewhat by shifting to a zone, something we've rarely used all season.

Scouting report said they might be vulnerable to a zone if we could shadow Rutherford decently. Those other guys hitting is probably just an abberation. Make a note of that zone. It might come in handy again.

The good news is, I've at least been able to rest Zidek through much of the half. I'm hoping that Big Country gets tired down the stretch. We'll use George as much as we can these final 20 minutes, but we've got to get him more aggressive on Reeves — without picking up any more fouls. He's got to move a little faster so he can avoid the weight disadvantage.

Tyus.

He's the trump card, all right. If it's a white-knuckler at the end, we'll let Edney take his man every which way. We've taped up his wrist and he isn't complaining, so we're OK on that front. We are also going to turn it up, on all fronts, defensively. Right now. The guys look a little down. "Hey!" I call to them. "You didn't think this was going to be easy, did you?" We go over some things. It's time to get back out there.

Ouch. Second half opens with Oklahoma State nailing us for still another three-pointer, this one by Collins. Worse, George picks up his fourth foul early in the half. We switch to a 2-3 zone, Ed in the middle. We'll stay in it for a fairly long period of time, and Reeves will get only one field goal in the span. Down 40-37, we start to roll again. Our defense is picking up everywhere. We run off 11 straight points, Ed and Charles O'Bannon scoring nine of them and George the other two. We're up 48-40 with 13:46 left.

But now — figures — Rutherford finally breaks free. Our defense on him, led by Dollar, has been superb. He's missed his last eight three-point attempts since the one he dropped in early, but in a 9-0 Oklahoma State rally he finally hits one and Reeves — who'd been bottled up all this half — has five points on a layup, free throw and a 14-footer. Rutherford's bomb gets them within one and Reeves' jumper puts them up, 49-48. I check the clock. It's at 9:33

Is that big fella ever going to tire? He's the best we've faced all season — Reeves, and the Allen kid from Connecticut.

We come right back with an 8-2 spurt (*this ping-pong stuff is nuts!*) as Reeves starts to get roadblocked again and we're up 56-51 at 5:53. But Rutherford counters with another three and our lead is down to two. Ed answers it with a 16-foot, big-time shot, and Sutton calls timeout. It's 58-54 with 4:43 left. I decide to give George a brief rest. He's contained Reeves, but both he and J.R. have four fouls.

We just can't shake 'em. We keep Rutherford in a bottle all afternoon, and now he's hit two straight. It's the gut of the game and he's cranking it up. Sure, we seem to have Reeves contained, but for how much longer? It's time. Tyus has scored only three points this half. Doesn't seem to think about shooting. The wrist? Nah. It's time for the kid to do his thing. Tell him to take over. Tell him to go one-on-one with dribble penetration, every time down.

And I do.

After the timeout, Oklahoma State cuts it to 58-56 on a layup by Roberts. But here comes Edney. "Take him, Tyus! Take him!" — and there he goes, driving for a layup at 3:36 to make it 60-56. Again it's cut to two on a reverse layup by Reeves. "Take him!" I yell again. His teammates are yelling the same thing. Tyus drives once more, is fouled and makes both. It's 62-58.

But there's Rutherford with still another three, a 22-footer from deep in the corner, our lead melting to 62-61. "Take him, Tyus!" There he goes, a waterbug with the flashlight on him, and . . . sailing, hitching, scooping, he hits another shot off a drive. Three straight challenges, three straight Edney answers. We're up 64-61. Oklahoma State calls timeout. Only 2:09 remains. We've switched back to our man-to-man, but . . .

Zone! Go back to the zone now. Slow 'em down a little.

Buzzer sounds and as Oklahoma State brings it up, I see Big Country recognize the zone, and he doesn't like what he sees. He gazes at his bench, raising both arms up to Sutton, as in "What do we do now?" (*Yes! They're a little out of sync. Confused!*) Rutherford gets it in the corner and he rushes up a three-pointer. If it goes, we're tied. Clock's turning just inside two minutes and . . . airball!

How sweet it is!

It continues to snowball. Oklahoma State never scores again after that timeout. We close the game with a 12-0 run, our last 10 — all after the timeout — on free throws. It's the closest 13-point win I could ever imagine, much less witness. Tyus has 21 points and five assists with only two turnovers. Reeves scores 25, but only seven in the second half when he missed six of eight shots, and he adds nine rebounds, but six of those came when he was dominating in the first half. Down the stretch, he was bent over and tugging at his shorts, fatigued. Finally. We didn't have a single three-pointer after the two Ed made early (we were two of seven), but Charles has had a brilliant all-around game — seven-of-nine floor shooting with 19 points and six rebounds — with Ed, although defended about as well as he has been all season, adding 15 points, eight boards and four steals. Moreover,

Oklahoma State, which had drilled us for 54.5 percent shooting in the first half, hit only 32.1 percent once we cranked up our D in the second half. I think maybe we've proven our point.

In the post-game press conference, they're asking about Edney's impossible shot in the first half.

"What shot are you talking about," pipes in George matter-of-factly, setting up his own punch line. "I've seen those shots so many times during the four years I've been on the team, I just chalked it up as nothing unusual."

Somebody asks Ed about how Tyus took over at the end.

"It goes further than the end of this game," Ed says. "It actually goes our whole career."

Somebody asks Tyus if anybody can guard him. An aw-shucks grin starts to cross his face — but before Tyus can answer, Ed leans into a microphone and calls out: "NO!"

That gets a good laugh.

Then somebody asks Tyus about his wrist.

"It's just a little sore," he answers, and he holds up the wrapping on his wrist for everyone to see. "This," he says, "is just preventative."

Glad to hear it. Tyus Edney owns this tournament. In five games he's had 38 assists and only nine turnovers. He saves us against Missouri, destroys Mississippi State early, scores 22 against Connecticut, including that backbreaking buzzer shot at the end of the first half, and now this.

Back in the locker room, he tells me he really had troubles in the second half. "I had no jumper, Coach," he says. "Boy, I was really struggling just to shoot those foul shots down the stretch."

I'm not feeling much concern. Tyus wasn't so much complaining, just observing. He's a tough kid. There's ice on the wrist and the tenderness will ease. We'll just get him treated in the meantime.

*   *   *

CBS has built a small stage courtside, and they invite me to watch the first half of Arkansas-North Carolina from there.

My assistants, meanwhile, went immediately from the locker room to spots on press row to scout the game. At halftime, I'm interviewed with Pat O'Brien, Quinn Buckner and Mike Krzyzewski — a little analysis, a little reflection on our win . . . but I'm already losing the realization of where I am. I'm just zeroed in on preparing for the next game. You get yourself in this tunnel, and any emotion about having made it to the national championship game gets lost in the narrowness of intense concentration.

North Carolina plays a good first half, but Arkansas gets a big lift when one of their big men, Dwight Stewart, puts up a 50-foot prayer at the buzzer and has it answered. Suddenly, Carolina's seven-point lead has been sliced to 38-34. Arkansas begins to assert itself through the final 20 minutes, thanks in no small measure to Corliss Williamson. He'll score 19 of his 21 points in the second half. Looks like Nolan Richardson's team has succeeded in forcing Carolina to play to its game, and it translates into a 75-68 Arkansas win. I've noticed that both teams relied an awful lot on three-point shots. They put up more in one game than we attempt in a month, it seems.

Remember, Jim, you get in these big arenas sometimes and it's harder to shoot those threes. You don't make as many as you usually do. Could prove a plus for us.

It's time to go back to the hotel. The coaching staff won't go out to eat. We order up room service. Lorenzo, Mark, Steve and I huddle over all the notes and pop the first of several videotapes into the VCR. We analyze and theorize. Because we're so quick and can cover so much ground defensively, we decide we should be able to get enough pressure on their outside shooters but still focus on our main objective: Corliss Williamson. We want to cover down on him, not let him own the paint and the baselines with all those power plays and spin moves. We'll have a one-man cover down off Corey Beck so George can have some help on Corliss. We'll let Beck hit some baskets if he's inclined to. We keep watching the tapes, trying to get a bead on Arkansas. We know they're going to open the floor on us and press and trap, all the things they like to do.

Bring it on. Edney loves that kind of thing. Every team that's tried it, Tyus has made them pay.

Finally, I look at my watch. It's 3 a.m. We break up our session. Even though sleep is finally tugging at me, I can feel the remnants of all this excitement and anticipation that's been driving me — all of us in this room, no doubt — through the night. What I don't feel much is any question about Edney's health. They've iced him and they've checked him out. As I collapse onto the bed, Tyus Edney's sore wrist is a very distant memory.

Sunday, April 2, 1995 — Championship eve.

Sometimes, bad news travels last. I'm up early. Got a couple, three hours sleep. There's much to do. Our trainer, Tony Spino, gets hold of me. He doesn't look too happy. Edney's hand is really swollen, he tells me. He's having a terrible time. It swelled up overnight. He's in a lot of pain. "Well, do what you can do," I tell the trainer.

Not that he won't be able to play by tomorrow night. I know it, my players know it: You DON'T get sick or hurt in the tournament.

I don't get a chance to see Tyus myself. They're going to take him over to the University of Washington training room, where they've got X-ray facilities. I've got to get to the King-dome with Ed O'Bannon and his parents. He's won the National Basketball Broadcasters & Writers' Player of the Year award and he's going to accept it on live TV with Billy Packer.

We head back to the hotel, but stay there only briefly. Our interview session with the media — which has grown and grown into this huge organism as the tournament progressed — is scheduled for 1 p.m. We've got to leave by 12:30. Tyus and the trainer? They're still missing. It's time to go back to the Kingdome.

For a half hour we meet with the media en masse. Then things break up, each player going to an assigned table so the reporters can walk up and talk at length to whomever they choose. At the table reserved for Edney, there's a vacant seat. No Tyus. Somebody asks me if I know where he is. I tell them he's having his wrist checked out. I play it down. When the interviews end, I go back to the hotel to change out of my suit. Our trainer comes by.

"Well, it isn't broken," he says. "But it's very, very stiff and very sore. He couldn't play right now."

That's OK. We don't HAVE to play right now. Tyus has more than 24 hours to get over all that stiffness. A lot of things can change from Sunday to Monday. And they WILL. He'll be ready. He's not hurt THAT badly.

And so, I merely nod at the news.

The NCAA sets aside time in the afternoon for closed practice sessions for the two finalists, but we're not going to use it. We did the same thing the day between the West semifinals and final. Some of my assistants thought that was a gutty move, and I'm not so sure they don't have reservations this time as well. I didn't see any problem then and I don't now. Not very many people on the outside will know, but we are not going to step onto the Kingdome court to prepare for Arkansas. Maybe some of them figured we went to some school in the Seattle area to practice, but we didn't. I learned a long time ago from Coach Wooden that when you stay away from the game you're that much hungrier. The more you stay away, the fresher you are — mentally and physically. I mean, what are we talking here — 36 hours without a big workout? That's not gonna make ya or break ya.

So, our only "workout" is here at the hotel. We've reserved the ballroom and designed a makeshift key with some athletic tape. We walk through some of things we want to do. Then we sit down for some videotape — three sessions in all — and we hold one chalkboard session. That's it. They know everything they need to do.

I want fresh legs out there tomorrow night. Our whole idea is to take it to Arkansas, which loves to wear people down. We want to attack them like they've never been attacked before. Relentless. Having these guys rested and ready to turn it on is what's important. They already know what we want. We've spent a season perfecting it. We're going to roll in tomorrow night like the worst storm you can imagine, and right now it's important to maintain the calm before. Maybe four years ago, I'm a little more tentative. Maybe back then I'm not confident enough to go with this plan. I am now. Fresh legs. Could make the difference. And fresh meat. Get them hungry to get out there again. I feel very strongly about it.

Monday, April 3, 1995 — The NCAA Championship Game: UCLA vs. Arkansas.

Every two hours or so, Tony Spino has been calling me with updates on Tyus. Mostly, of course, it's just a waiting game. They keep working on him, trying to coax the soreness out of the wrist, but we're not really going to know much until we get to the Kingdome.

And when it goes from waiting game to championship game, he'll be ready. C'mon now, Jim, have you ever seen him NOT rise to a challenge?

(Oregon, last year. His back goes out like a rifle going off. He goes one-for-13 from the floor, misses a game-winner and we lose the game and the Pac-10 championship. Don't you remember THAT one, Jim?)

The reminder sends a little shudder of fear through me, but I dismiss it. We paid our dues with that one, didn't we? I let the moment pass.

The day goes fairly fast — aided, I guess, by the fact it's a 5:40 p.m. tipoff, Pacific time. Someone confirms that Coach Wooden has flown up. *(Great. He should be here.)* We're over to the Kingdome by 4:15. Time for the moment of truth. We go out early to put up a few shots. Tyus tries a five-footer. It's about three feet short. We get him back to the locker room. Time to experiment with some different wraps on the wrist. Find something he likes.

What he needs, Jim, is a new wrist. We're in trouble.

I shoo the thought away as quickly as it appears. We go through our drills, without Tyus, and then it's back to the locker room. Get him wrapped right. That'll take care of it. All through this, I've made it a point not to go up to Tyus and ask, "Hey, you gonna be ready to play?" or "How are you doing?" because that always puts a negative in a guy's mind.

They call me back out for a brief interview on CBS. They ask me if Edney can play. I tell them he's going to try to go. But I know. I know. This awful, gloomy feeling starts to wash over me. I head back for the locker room.

Why? Why this? Why now?

We've tried five or so different wraps, including some type of soft cast. This latest one, Tyus says, feels pretty good. I ask the managers to go out and get us a ball. When I get it, I throw it to Tyus. He pulls back, like he doesn't want to catch it. There's a grimace on his face.

Uh-oh.

He tries to dribble it, and the ball just pitty-pats weakly down there close to the floor, where my spirits have dropped as well. I go up to Dollar and I want to say, "Hey, get ready. You're going to have to play." But I just can't say it. My heart is sinking, but it still refuses to believe Tyus can't go. Still, all across this locker room I can sense an ominous feeling. George is sitting in his chair by his locker, head drooped, lightly pounding his right fist into his open left hand. He's psyching. But is he also feeling the frustration of seeing Edney so lame?

Can't let that happen. You've got to rally these guys. You can NOT let on that your worst fear looks like it's going to materialize.

So we go into our last chalk talk. Mark Gottfried focuses on Williamson for a minute. "You've gotta keep him out of the paint, George. Get him outta there, get him outta there, get him outta there." We want to meet him at the foul line and try to make him play one step off the block. We don't want him to power us back in. George is going to use his bulk, but also use some technique. Out from the basket on defense, you normally play one arm-length off a guy's chest to create a gap, because if I'm too close you can go around me and if I'm too far away, I'm just not effective guarding you. But down low in the post, we play half-arm length off the rear end of any guy posting up, and that's what George will do on Williamson. You do it that way, because if you get your rear end planted into me, you've dominated me. I can't move my feet, can't do much of anything. You make that kind of contact with your body, you've beat me. So we teach half-arm length down low. But any time Corliss actually gets the ball, George will chest him and plant high up on him. If he tries to go down low with a spin move, well . . . by then we hope our cover-down help will be there to take the move away. That, and George working hard. Corliss really spun on Rasheed Wallace in the semifinal. Kind of embarrassed him. George will need all his strength, and quick feet, to avoid the same fate.

Meanwhile, Steve Lavin is pointing out that Arkansas has a penchant for stealing the ball after you've received a pass and think you're in the clear. Their people like to rush up from behind in the press and slap it out of your hands. "Keep coming 'til you have the ball in your hands, and then firm up!" Steve tells them. "You get the pass, then rip it through [he clutches an imaginary ball and brings it in strong toward his chest]. Don't get it and drift away to make a lead pass [he takes the ball out from his body like a pitcher reaching back for a high, hard one]. Those guys are on the fly and they'll slap it out of your hand. So, come to meet every pass. Grab it and firm up. Then go and attack."

We've been preaching it over and over. Receive the ball and attack the basket. We want to take it to Arkansas from every angle, matching their relentlessness with our own. "Goin' to the glass and attacking, going to the glass and attack," I call out.

Right. And doing it without our guidance system, fellas.

I find myself pausing, hands in my pockets, head down, silent.

Can't tell 'em Tyus isn't gonna go. But they KNOW. And you know what that means, Jim — what you're asking of these men. You just might be down to six able bodies to throw against all that Arkansas depth — depth, and talent. You're asking these guys to give it their all despite having to look at that little man over there with the wrap on his hand and the pain in his eyes.

For a moment or so longer, I don't say a word. Then I raise my head. The words come out soft and quiet. Sometimes, those are the kind that ring loudest.

"Fellas, you've got to go out there and play the greatest

game you've ever played in your lives. That's all it is. The greatest effort you've ever given. Leave nothing to come back in here with. You're gonna spend it all out there. The greatest victory is the one where you just play your guts out, to come back in here and say, hey, I played the best I could, the hardest I could."

I pause again.

"All right, here we go."

The guys get into their huddle, arms skyward and hands together, but this time, unlike all the other times, the battle cry — if it can be called that — is subdued.

"bruins."

That's all. No capital letters to this call. Meek. Weak. "Concentrate and have some fun, fellas," somebody says. "Top of the world, baby," says another. But it sounds more like it comes from the bottom of the world.

I feel it, too. But now I begin to feel a little pinpoint of anger. I don't ever swear in front of my players. And I don't allow them to. I don't and my assistants don't. But we're waiting there, just a second before I send them out that door, and that tremor of frustration and anger begins to swell into this wave of emotion, stirring to get out. I look at them, and from deep inside I hear a voice, and it's thick with anger and resolve, and I hear it rising in volume. "HEY!" I hear it calling, and every head turns. "F—— Arkansas!" And that's the wave they ride onto the Kingdome court.

Back here, however, inside the locker room and alone with my assistants, I begin to agonize. I think I've fooled the players. I don't think they saw how despondent I was feeling. Four years ago I probably couldn't have fooled 'em. If they all did an about-face and charged back in here now, I don't think I could fake it again. *Why-why-why-why-why?* I am sitting under a ton of bricks. I am nine parts despair and one part hope. It's that little part I try to grab onto as I rise, finally, from my chair and walk through the door. "The hell with it! Let's just go play." I pass through the door, hoping for Edney, my heart knowing it's a futile exercise. But I head toward the bench, clinging to the idea that adrenaline can do what logic says it can't. I start Tyus Edney.

It starts out good. The tip goes to Tyus, he dribbles (left-handed) and sees Ed on the baseline. Hits him with a pass. From 22 feet, Ed goes up. Bingo! We're ahead 3-0 in only six seconds. *(All right now, let's get after 'em.)* What's this? Not good. George is whistled for holding Williamson. *(Silly call!)* Corliss follows up with a 14-footer, but we're breaking their press and there goes Toby Bailey into the paint, banking one in from eight feet. We're up, 5-2. Williamson gets it inside again but — *OH YES!* — Charles O'Bannon comes flying from the weakside and stuffs it back in his face. Huge, huge play.

Attaboy! Make a statement early. Attack!

They get the ball out of bounds, but we get a steal. Then Toby loses control of the ball. Arkansas has it back, and there's Corliss kicking it out to Elmer Martin for a three. Suddenly it's 5-5. It's the press again, but Tyus is breaking through it. He's doing it left-handed, but he's doing it! He goes into a crowd, tries to switch to his right hand to zig-zag dribble through the forest, but — uh-oh — he can't do anything with that right hand and is forced to pull up awkwardly and grab the ball with both hands. He's fouled, but, fact is, if he had a good right hand he'd have blown right by those guys.

Not good, Jim. Tyus is down to one wing, and it's taken away his game.

We fail to score, Arkansas gets it back and they get another three, this one from Clint McDaniel over Edney. We're down, 8-5. Tyus takes the in-bounds pass against the press. He's trying to protect the ball but he's got just one hand. Martin's on him like a wolf smelling blood. He strips Tyus. *(Nobody strips Tyus!)* The ball kicks to Corey Beck, who takes it straight to the hole for a layup. Now it's 10-5.

Maybe a few years earlier in my career at UCLA, I don't take Tyus out so quickly. Maybe back then I try to go with him a little longer, try to ignore what my eyes are telling me, maybe too wary to make that kind of move with this kind of player so early, no matter how wounded he might be — maybe relying on hope instead of facing reality. But not now. Not at this stage of my career. I know what I have to do. I stand up and motion for Dollar to get up. As he heads toward the scorer's table to replace Edney, I stop him.

"Cameron," I say, "you know why you're on scholarship, don't you?"

He gives me a puzzled look.

"To get the ball to Ed O'Bannon," I say.

Cameron nods, flashes a grin and rushes up to the scorer's table. Buzzer sounds and out comes Tyus. I don't drape my arm around him. I just say, "Take a seat, son." I act as if nothing is out of the ordinary, nothing wrong. Over the years, I've found I can do a good job of this.

But out on the court, everything's wrong. In our half-court offense, Cameron is dribbling on the wing, looking for something to open up, and as he studies the situation, bouncing the ball left-handed, McDaniel strikes, like a cobra. Just darts in and slaps the ball away, coming up with it on the dribble and on the run. He sprints downcourt for a layup and we're down 12-5. Arkansas has scored 10 straight.

This could get ugly.

That's what I'm feeling, all right, and the feeling grows darker as George takes a pass inside, gets bottled up, and there's McDaniel again, stripping him. Ball goes to Scotty Thurman and he pulls up for a three. *(This could get REAL ugly!)* Thank God, he misses.

I don't have time to breathe a sigh of relief, because we're pushing it back the other way, hard. Toby whips a pass to Cameron who whips a nice pass to Ed for a layup. Arkansas brings it back, but there's Cameron stepping in to intercept a pass. He pulls up for a jumper on the break, misses it, but there's Charles going high to rebound. *(Attack the glass!)* He comes down and goes back up with a sweeping jump-hook. It's down to 12-9.

Will ya look at that! Cameron gets stripped but comes right back! Shows strong stuff on two straight possessions. Bulldog!

The first TV timeout comes at 15:40 with us trailing 16-12. Tyus gets up to join our huddle. He can't even applaud like the others as our players trot to the bench. When the buzzer comes to life again, the game doesn't. For an eternity, neither of us can score. We fail to do anything on four straight possessions, Arkansas on five. Dollar nearly gets stripped again in that stretch, surviving but throwing a pass out of bounds after dribbling into the paint. Still, he's had far more positives than negatives with the ball, and he's also playing some terrific defense. Finally, at 12:59, Ed breaks the scoring drought with a free throw to make it 16-13. I put J.R. in for Toby.

We're down to six players now. Got to give them a chance to catch their breath, if only a little bit.

Al Dillard misses for them and here we come. Dollar looks like he's going to lose his dribble, but he's hanging on. Gets off a nice pass to George in the transition. Open jumper. Nails it. We've cut it to 16-15, and the crowd's starting to sense something here.

Darned if we're not hanging in!

Arkansas feels the heat, and they're turning to — who else? — Williamson. He gets it down low. He's trying to spin *(Stay with it, George, stay with it!)* and Zidek's got him faced off, one mountain range to another. Corliss tries to pivot to his right, but there's Charles racing in from the weakside and stripping him! Breakout. Charles to Ed to Charles back to Ed and . . . DUNK! *(Attack-attack-attack!)* We've scored seven straight. We're leading, 17-16.

And now it ping-pongs, neither of us able to get much daylight. Leading 21-19, Arkansas gets a steal but — what's this? — there's Ed making a great play, anticipating while on the run where the outlet pass will go and darting into the passing lane at precisely the right moment — *what instincts!* — to intercept. He gets it to Toby, on the run with an open court, and he nails a jumper in the paint. Dwight Stewart shoots an airball from three-point range at the other end and Dollar comes down, narrowly avoiding being stripped, and finds George posted on the baseline. Hook shot. We're up again, 23-21.

What's starting to become obvious is our incredible hustle and determination. We are flat taking it to them. Ed's all over the place, Cameron is applying great pressure defensively and starting to get into a groove handling the ball. George is just brilliant on Williamson, either in his face or on his butt all the time, and we've got guys flying in for cover-down help every time the ball gets to him. Toby's revving up in the open court and Charles, too. J.R. is a bit off, but he's in there fighting.

Dunno how long we can take it to them like this, but we're darn sure letting them know they're in a game, aren't we? These guys have taken it up a notch. A very big notch!

We're ahead, 27-26, and now we really crank it up. On a missed shot, we've got arms everywhere around the rim, slapping the ball again and again to the glass and fighting for it as it finally caroms out of bounds, off an Arkansas hand. Toby gets the ball in the paint and — great pass! — finds Charles under. He's fouled and hits two free throws. Then Dillard misses a three with Dollar right in his eyebrows. We miss, but as they try a long outlet Dollar dashes in to swipe it. We miss again — Ed is hacked; no call — but, just look, Ed recovers from his miss and flies downcourt and gets there in time to get a hand on a pass for Williamson, the ball deflecting off him out of bounds to us. Ed misses a 19-footer at the other end, but we've got the rebound and Toby . . .

YES. Three-pointer. Arkansas looks rattled. Scotty Thurman hits the side of the backboard on a three-point try and, on a give-and-go with J.R., Toby hits a short jumper in the paint. We've scored seven straight. We're leading 34-26. The officials signal for a TV timeout, and a huge roar washes across the Kingdome. There's just 3:53 left in the half. Williamson and Thurman, their big guns, have just four points between them. Beck has three fouls.

Nothing's going to come this easy, of course. With our lead still decent — 36-29 with 2:49 to go — Arkansas gets eight points on three straight possessions, all by McDaniel who drops a pair of three-pointers in the flurry, and suddenly we're down 37-36. Ed hangs in the air and adjusts his shot to put us up 38-37, but Lee Wilson counters to put us down 39-38. They press. We're shaky, but we get through it and, once so, Charles zips a pass to

J.R. for a layup with 10 seconds left. We're ahead 40-39, and that's how the half ends.

We're controlling this game except for McDaniel. McDaniel's killing us!

In the corridor with my assistants, we study the halftime box as the players get their five minutes to cool down and relax. Our defense looks excellent. McDaniel has hit three of four threes and has 16 points. But Thurman is 0-for-3 and Williamson is 2-for-6. They have five points between them, Thurman with a goose-egg. Just as telling, we have 21 rebounds, 12 of them offensively, to their total of 14. We've outscored them on second-chance points, 12-0.

Warrior hearts. These guys are playing with warrior hearts.

But can it hold up? I have no idea, and entertain no fantasy that we can win this thing. Arkansas has worn down too many people. Arkansas has come back from too many deficits in this tournament. Arkansas knows it's in a battle now, but they've been in a bunch of them these last two seasons. They've won all the marbles once, and they know how to win it all this time.

But you can be proud of these guys, no matter what happens from here on out, Jim. This is the kind of effort, the kind of performance, you dream about.

Ed, who's played the full 20 minutes, has 15 points. Charles has five assists. Cameron has four assists and three steals! Toby, who got a whole minute to rest on the bench, has 12 points — this after scoring only two against Oklahoma State. And George is just rock solid defensively. He's also outscored Corliss 6-5 and hit three of five shots.

Nothing much to tell them, nothing more we need to do but just basically play. Look at them. They're looking to Ed. He's like their security blanket. Not a bad choice. Listen to him, walking around telling them "Let's go back out and get it done!" What was it they said Ed told the players right after I sent them out of the locker room before the game? Oh yeah. Ed says: "This is just a pickup game!" I've rarely seen a player with such command. It's such an overwhelming presence, and he's exuded it all season, this feeling that he's not going to let this team lose — so real and vibrant you could almost squeeze it. How often do you get two like Tyus and Ed — two who can take everyone to a whole different level? Well, we're down to one of them now. Is that gonna be enough? Not worth considering at this point. Time to get back court-side. Twenty minutes to go. Might as well be 20 days.

The second half opens with George going strong to the basket for a rebound and putback. Next trip down, Dollar finds him with a no-look pass and George hits again. We're up 44-40. After Wilson hits a 15-footer, Arkansas has a chance to tie but misses. Open court again, and here we come, Charles hitting a fastbreak layup. They go inside to Corliss, but he's bottled up in the paint again, losing another sumo battle with George. He forces one anyway. Doesn't drop. We're out running and there's Toby driving the left side and banking it too hard, but he goes way, way up to rebound his miss. He goes up, has it smacked back in his face by Lee Wilson. Goes up again! Got it!

Man, Toby is really thriving at this pace!

We're up 46-42. We lose a point in a tradeoff between Thurman's three and Dollar's two free throws. Arkansas is going to its bread-and-butter, trying to cut it to three. The pass goes into Corliss, but George just won't budge and Corliss can't make a move on him. He whips the ball back out, makes a cut back into the paint and the ball comes whipping back for him, but George has a hip on him, perfect block out, and Corliss has to cut short his move, what with Ed also converging. Now he has to stretch an arm to try and get to the pass, but he can get no closer than having it deflect off his hand. Meanwhile, Toby's darted in from the top of the key and he picks up the ball.

We're off at warp factor six again! The ball kicks out to Dollar, back to Toby and now into Ed, posted 10 feet from the basket just outside the paint. Ed whips it to Dollar in the left corner. Cameron drives the baseline, shuffles a quick pass inside to Charles. Up with the shot, it dips in and out, but here comes Ed, like a freight train, flying up for the rebound. He tries to put it back up but the ball is smacked back down his throat — huge force! big foul! — and Ed is coming down quicker than he went up. But as the whistle blows, with Ed almost back on the ground, he launches this mighty heave. As his feet hit the ground, backpedaling to keep his balance, the ball hits the backboard and drops through the rim. Ed hits the free throw for a three-point play. We're ahead 53-45.

Man, oh man! Almost wish I was in the stands just watching this one! What a sequence. Says it all. Great defense, pinball passing, huge rebound by Ed and unbelievable shot. A lesser man wouldn't have gotten the ball back on an upward flight after getting hammered so hard. That was as much force of will as it was physical effort. Attack the basket? We're annihilating it!

And it's not stopping. Corliss posts up again. George bodies him again. Corliss gets the ball, tries to spin to his right. But Ed has covered down like a blanket, forcing Williamson to cut short his move. So he pulls up and tries a five-footer, but George is right there, face-to-face, arms straight up. Czech-mate. Corliss forces one over him, but it's not close. And there's Ed, strong with the rebound, coming down, under duress with arms all around him, but he short-cocks his arm and whips this bullet, absolute bullet, three-quarter lengths of the floor to Toby. Toby has it on the fly and — WHOOOMP! — sails up with a half-reverse dunk, his knees somewhere near the rim. We've scored seven straight points. We are up by 10! It is 55-45 only five minutes into the second half.

Savor this one, Jim. These guys are playing their hearts out.

After a timeout, Arkansas gets some life. Stewart hits a long jumper and follows with a three. Counting his free throw before the TV timeout, he's scored the game's last six points and our lead is down to 55-51. Worse, we didn't even get off a shot on our first possession after the break, confused by a switch in Arkansas' defensive setup.

Crank it back up, fellas.

We start to do just that. George comes up with a huge offensive rebound and is fouled trying to put it back. He hits both free throws. Now we get a fast break off an Arkansas miss, and Cameron hits Charles on a runout for an easy layin. We get another rebound. Dollar brings it up, Stewart right in his sneakers as he crosses the midstripe. Dollar tries a spin move on the dribble, just what Stewart was trying to lull him into, and Stewart lunges for the ball, but Cameron's too quick with the move and is free, penetrating into the lane. He goes up, but big Corliss is going up with him, when . . . oh my! . . . he scoops a pass around Williamson's body to George, who goes up and is fouled. George hits both free throws. Six straight points, and the lead is back to 10.

Arkansas scores and now they're turning up the heat with their press. But we beat it with long passes — crisp, quick, beautiful passes — Ed inbounding to J.R., who dribbles twice before being double-teamed. But he doesn't panic, kicking it across to the side to an open Ed, who whips a two-handed pass through the middle to a streaking Toby, who's off to the races, pulling up in the paint, 12 feet out, swish. A couple more scoreless tradeoffs, and we're back and running again. This time Toby steps in to intercept a long outlet pass. He's flying again and puts one up way too hard — *third time he's done that but, hey, Jim, let it be: the kid's on afterburners* — and there he goes, flying up to rebound his miss, putting it back in. Thunder rolls around the Kingdome again. My oh my: a 10-2 run and a 65-53 lead.

No need to get too excited. There's still 11:20 to play. And that's still Arkansas — Comeback All the Time Arkansas — out there.

During a TV timeout at 10:58, I decide to switch to a 2-3 zone. Over the next three minutes, we miss four shots and turn the ball over once on four consecutive possessions. Arkansas gets only four points in the exchange, but after Ed gives us a rebound scoop shot for a 67-58 lead, Arkansas comes back with five straight points on a shot by Stewart and a three by Beck. Then we throw two straight shaky passes against the press, the last one sailing out of bounds, Arkansas' ball. We've been outscored 9-2 in the last four minutes. Our lead is only 67-63. The buzzer sounds as the ball flies out of bounds. Another TV timeout. And not a second too soon. Clock shows 6:59.

Boy, we're really struggling. We've lost our legs a little. OK, maybe a lot. This game has been too much of a rocket sled, too emotional and aggressive a pace, for it not to take something out of them. If TV hadn't called time, I sure would have. Look at them, Jim. They look like they might have given everything they've got. Sit 'em down. Stir 'em

up. There's no more season after these seven minutes. Light a fire, even
if they look like they're out of kindling.

"Hey!" I call out. "You're going to get four [TV] timeouts
this half, and we've got three ourselves, so call them if you need
to. Don't you *dare* get tired on me now! THERE IS NO GETTING
TIRED IN THIS GAME!"

I look at Ed, and in his face I see resolve that matches my
words. No, not just resolve. I see audacity, exuberant and confident. "Yeah!" he yells. "We'll play *another* one if they want to!"
Good ol' Ed. The match that lights the fuse.

Buzzer sounds, and Nolan Richardson has his guys ready
for the kill. This is the time. They need to pounce now. And they
do, Beck getting a steal, Dollar then missing a layup under pressure on one possession and the front end of the bonus on the
next — but while we're having trouble at our end, we're still
scrambling and harassing everywhere on defense. They fail to
score all three times — Williamson again forcing one over Zidek,
Thurman watching an open three in the transition rim out on
him and Corliss missing again, this time with Ed applying pressure. At 5:22 Williamson finally gets behind George and is
fouled, hitting one of two to cut our lead to 67-64. But Ed's back
on it, with a nice turnaround jump-hook. It's 69-64. Williamson
again is fouled, again hits one. 69-65.

And then it happens.

Ed gets the ball and puts up a 15-footer that begins to
bounce off the iron. It's a big bounce, almost straight up, and
as I watch it I see an outstretched arm, pointed skyward, rising
and . . .

Will you look at that!

. . . it's Toby Bailey, going up. And up. And up. He looks
like a space shuttle, his ascent as straight and true as any rocket
off the pad, his hand getting a grip on the ball even as it continues upward, and then, finally at the apex somewhere among the
Kingdome pigeons, he brings it down with huge force, slam-
ming the ball hard through the rim. Electric moment. Noise fills
the arena, the crowd a blaring exclamation point to Toby's dunk.
Huge, huge play.

Jim . . . Jim! We can win this game!

It is the first time I've allowed myself the thought, the first time I sense we can really pull this thing off. On the scoreboard, 4:31 — UCLA 71, Arkansas 65. As Arkansas tries to recover and goes inside to Williamson, this time it's Dollar who rushes in and blocks the shot from behind, before Corliss can go up very high with it. The ball kicks out to them, but they miss again and now Dollar has it and now he's fouled. He sinks both. It's 73-65, 4:06 left. Thurman's still an iceberg, missing another, and Stewart fouls trying to go over Ed for the rebound. Ed hits them both. TV timeout. We have a 10-point lead, 75-65. It is now, officially, crunch time.

In the huddle we talk about eating up some clock, but not so much that we forget what we're about. We came into this game stressing attack and it would be a mistake not to look to do the same now. We can't afford to lose aggressiveness. Arkansas has the ball, and a whole lot riding on this next possession. What they don't have, fortunately, is Ed O'Bannon.

("We'll play another one if they want to!")

You know, I think Ed actually meant it. He hasn't let up one bit, but now he shows that he's as crafty as he is intense. Arkansas is in its half-court offense and Ed follows Landis Williams as he comes out to take a pass, high to the right of the key, maybe 25 feet from the basket. Ed's right up under his chin, giving him no room for a quick-step dribble, and Williams is standing there, standing and standing, maybe hoping Ed gets overanxious and jumps into him or gets off-balance enough to make a move around him. Finally, with an Arkansas teammate rushing up to pick him, Ed backs off. One step.

He's fishing!

That's what it is. Williams starts to dribble, lulled by Ed's step backward and the fact he's standing more upright — but that was just bait, and the dribble is the nibble Ed's been casting for. He lurches forward and downward, right smack into the ball, stealing it and leaving Williams with nothing but air to pat.

Beee-yooooo-tiful!

No more time to appreciate it. "Run some clock!" I yell. And we do, but when the seam presents itself we pounce on it as Toby, left of the key, 14 feet out and wide open, drains the shot. It's 77-65. Arkansas has gone without a field goal for more than four minutes. Beck gets them a free throw at 2:59 and when George, a 74 percent foul shooter, misses a pair of free throws and Williamson hits a bucket — his first since the 16-minute mark of the half — our lead is down to 77-68 with 2:25 left.

And I remember what Cameron Dollar said to me just a few moments earlier. He was standing nearby, looking at me before the ball was to be put in play. "Coach, don't worry," he said. "He'll touch it every time." And I had to chuckle. I knew exactly what Cameron meant, exactly who he was referring to. *("Cameron, do you know why you're on scholarship?")* Cameron Dollar, the Radar O'Reilly of the Final Four. Here he was, reassuring me before I'd even thought to remind him. He's going to get it to Ed. I give Cameron a little grin. No words required.

It makes you wonder if he couldn't play this game in a three-piece suit. He's acting just like he did back as a high school recruit, stepping off that plane and into the unknown, full of command.

Well, sure enough, Dollar spends most of the final four or five minutes looking, and finding, O'Bannon. At the 2:03 mark, Ed gets the ball and is fouled. He hits both and our lead is back to 11, 79-68. Dillard throws up a prayer from three-point range and it's answered, on a bank-in of all things, and suddenly it's 79-71, but Cameron breaks through a two-man trap and kicks it out to Toby, and from near the midstripe with open sailing he just keeps coming, all the way in and scoring. It's 81-71. Stewart misses a three, we get the board and call timeout. Only 1:25 remains.

As we start to huddle, Coach Wooden rises from his chair to leave the building. He's smiling.

We're going to win this thing.

The last 85 seconds are like a painting to me. I want to frame it. After the huddle break, with Arkansas lined up to press, Charles goes streaking behind the defense and Ed, from out of bounds, Troy Aikman's it to him for a rousing dunk — his pass having caught Charles dead on the fly. Touchdown! It's 83-

71. Beck gets a three, but Ed is fouled again and makes two free throws. Then Cameron steals a pass and hits a layup. It's 87-74. Williamson's free throws make it 87-76.

And then, a play that defines this team.

A pass in to J.R., who takes three dribbles, pulls up against the press and rifles a pass to Charles, who's just beyond midstripe and in the middle of the court. And, quick as that, Charles lets loose of it with a pass to Bailey on the right wing and Toby, just like Charles, immediately rockets one across the lane because there's Ed, streaking in like the Roadrunner from the left side, and he takes the ball and goes up without a dribble, flying now, dunking.

A championship play by a championship team. There are 35.3 seconds to go. We are ahead, 89-76 — on a length-of-the-court play that requires only three dribbles, utilizes four passes and takes only 7.5 seconds. It epitomizes our season. All five hands touch the ball, and the ball went from quarter-court all the way to the other basket without ever hitting the ground.

Art.

In those last seconds — the last basket a driving layup by Arkansas' Davor Rimac at 0:29 that will make the final score 89-78 — I am pointing here, calling out there, feeling the arms of my assistants start to envelop me and hearing the yelps of joy rising as the final ticks begin. Suddenly, it is over.

Even in this wonderful, incredible moment, I feel the need to maintain some dignity and not rub it in the other team's face. I walk down to shake Nolan's hand (he will be extremely gracious and complimentary in the post-game press conference), and as I turn to my assistants, happiness on their faces, I can feel it cross mine. Lorenzo huddles with our players, kneeling on the court, and leads a short prayer, thanking the Lord for what we have. I look for Sally.

She is crying.

On the inside, maybe I am a little, too.

*   *   *

You know, in the first three months after Seattle I watched CBS' coverage of the game on videotape twice, I think, from start to finish. You can't indulge your emotions much on the bench, and that's what made it so fun watching it from this perspective. I was thrilled at the sheer force of will my players demonstrated. It was a gritty and fierce performance.

Ed O'Bannon had 30 points, 17 rebounds, three blocks, three assists and not a single second of bench rest. He covered down on Corliss Williamson at all times and yet always recovered to his man. He handled the ball 30 to 40 percent of the time in the backcourt against the press. He ushered fans to their seats, did all the announcing on the PA system and rewrote the tax code to make it intelligible. (Well, he might as well have. He was doing it all that night.) Toby Bailey, meanwhile, scored 26 and had nine rebounds. Together, Ed and Toby took 41 of our 68 floor shots, scored 56 of our 89 points and grabbed 26 of our 50 rebounds. (And we beat Arkansas on the boards, 50-31!)

Charles O'Bannon? Rock solid. He had 11 points, nine rebounds, six assists, two blocks and two steals. Cameron Dollar had eight assists and four steals. George Zidek had 14 points, six rebounds and Corliss (3-for-16 from the field) shaking his head. J.R. Henderson, though off in this game, nevertheless didn't rattle like a freshman might be expected to do with so much on the line. And Tyus Edney, rightly so, had Ed calling out his name at the end, proclaiming him the MVP.

I showed no emotion when I yanked Edney, but three or four minutes after that I walked down to his seat on the bench, hugged him and patted him on the head. You know, your coach-point guard relationship is . . . well, he's an extension of me on the court. We'd spent a lot of time talking, so he knew how I felt about him. It's funny, I started him even though I knew he couldn't play. As a coach, I knew that. But I just couldn't NOT let him have a chance. Tyus is a brilliant, splendid person, and he's going to be a terrific pro. I'm going to miss him.

George? I said earlier how I thought he was the unsung hero of the season. A lot of people have asked what the difference was between this team and the '92 team that had MacLean and Murray, and my answer is George Zidek. Size, strength and presence in the middle, we didn't have back then. A lot of people don't realize that George plugged a lot of holes for us all season. He could get in there and make himself a huge presence with his hands up, where they'd have to stop and pass the ball back out. They'd bump into him and he wouldn't budge. I firmly believe you've got to have that kind of strength to win a national championship. Other teams have done it without great strength, but it's not that common, and having a guy like George really, really helps you.

Remember Cameron's shaky start? He certainly did, but, typically, he didn't let getting stripped of the ball early rattle him. In fact, McDaniel's steal produced just the opposite effect. "It was the greatest thing that could have happened to me at that point," Dollar said in an interview later. "Because at that moment, when I lost the ball, I looked at him laying it up and all the anxiety and tension I had just left. I knew right then it was just a game and I was just going to have some fun. I was going to play like I always do, when Tyus was there with me. I told myself, 'It's just a game. Have fun out here.' " I remember Cameron in the locker room afterward, stretched out on his stomach on the carpet, exhausted but grinning.

Six men played 197 of the 200 minutes our team logged. Six men who never stopped pushing themselves. We beat Arkansas 27-8 in second-chance points. Fifteen of our second-half field goals were layups or dunks. And it was Arkansas that looked more weary than us, even though their depth, and their intent, is designed to always inflict that malady on the other team. "They did wear down some," said Scotty Thurman of my team, "but I think we did also. The game was fast-paced for both of us. I was surprised at times at how they kept attacking the press and finishing. It wasn't the fact they attacked our press, but how they kept finishing. Most teams will get by a couple of times on us, but not every team can capitalize on it when they break it like they did." And while I'm sure Arkansas missed some shots they feel they should have made, we did guard them awfully well.

Near the end of the tape, I heard Billy Packer's words, and I felt them to my bones. In the final seconds, Billy made a reference to John Wooden's Pyramid of Success. "At the top of the pyramid," Packer said, "is 'competitive greatness.' And what we're seeing tonight is a team that entered this floor without their leader, without the guy we thought would be so critical to this game. Without him, no chance. Competitive greatness, at the top of that Pyramid of Success . . . is what's brought this team on."

I almost felt chills when I heard that, because its implication justified all the struggle. I had coached UCLA to its first national championship since Coach Wooden's incredible string of titles, and here my team was being likened to the very quality that Coach himself so treasures. Are these things accidental? I wonder. I like to think it was just a natural consequence of absorbing Coach's wisdom through the years. I like to think it demonstrated that trying to run from John Wooden's accomplishments never was the answer at UCLA. I like to think it showed that if you welcome the kind of excellence he preaches, appreciate not the myth but the man, accept his legacy as a challenge and not as an albatross . . .

. . . well, maybe you discover that the real triumph is having helped instill competitiveness and character in your players, and yourself. Maybe the title itself is just a physical manifestation of something greater. Maybe by embracing the legend, you walk away with qualities far more significant than any trophy.

DAY OF THE DINOSAUR

11

Not long after we won the NCAA championship, someone joked that I had gone from a moron to a genius in three weeks. Sad thing is, there are probably people out there who really believe it, and they were going to believe the moron part until we won the national title. They didn't think I could do anything right — couldn't coach, or recruit, or win big games, or discipline my players. I'd be less than candid if I didn't say that such criticism frustrated and angered me from time to time — and that I think it was patently unfair.

I think reasonable people understand why. I'd been a winner everywhere I'd coached. I'd won 20-plus games every season at UCLA. I'd won seven conference championships in my years at Pepperdine and UCLA. I have 11 former players in the NBA, I've seen the majority of my players earn a degree, and I've never had the NCAA sniffing at my door.

To me, all those things should be what a coach is measured by — but I know that among that certain group of doubters, the only absolution comes from winning the NCAA Tournament. It's that microwave world thing again. To them, I guess they think that all of a sudden I can coach. Well, sorry, but I'm the same coach whether Tyus Edney makes that shot or not. Does that mean I haven't had to grow in the job? Of course not. Have I made my share of mistakes? Certainly. Are there some things I wish I'd done differently? You bet. But all in all, I think my record speaks for itself. I'm a better coach now than I was a year ago, and I hope to be a better coach a year from now than I am today. But I've been a coach, and a pretty good one, for quite some time.

There's a sickness in the perception that if you go to the Final Four, you can coach, but if you fail to make it, you're a bum. How sad is that? Yet that seems to be the case in too many instances. There are coaches who have won 500 or more games who haven't made it to the Final Four. Does that mean they couldn't coach? You gotta be kidding. Funny, one of the items people used against me were a pair of first-round NCAA losses. I wonder if they're aware that Bobby Knight has been knocked out in the first round three times in his career? I wonder if they understand just how tough the tournament can be.

Remember the commentator who was complaining that Dean Smith had won the NCAA Tournament *only* twice? As I've noted, in the history of college basketball, only three men — John Wooden, Adolph Rupp and Bobby Knight — have won more than two NCAA championships. What's more, a total of only 36 coaches have ever won the title at all — and there are only six schools that have won it with two different coaches: Forrest "Phog" Allen and Larry Brown at Kansas, Branch McCracken and Bobby Knight at Indiana, Frank McGuire and Dean Smith at North Carolina, Norm Sloan and Jim Valvano at North Carolina State, Adolph Rupp and Joe Hall at Kentucky, and John Wooden and Jim Harrick at UCLA.

That's why I cringed, after we won the championship, when I saw headlines saying things like "FINALLY!" and "AT LAST!" and "MONKEY OFF HIS BACK." It underscores the sickness of this all-or-nothing attitude that makes a national championship the only worthwhile thing. Measured that way, failure takes in a whole lot of territory. Me? I think anyone who gets his team into the NCAA Tournament is a success. The tournament is your reward for having had a good season. Remember, there's no manifest destiny at work here. They don't let everybody in. You have to earn your ticket to the Big Dance.

Of course, all of us involved in college sports share in the blame for creating an atmosphere where such sickness exists. Money needs to be generated in order to fund athletic programs, arenas have seats that must be filled and, whether we like to admit it or not, the alumni, a primary source for grants and donations, has to be placated. The only way to meet those demands is by winning.

Coaches, I feel, are the ones who suffer the most from these demands. They catch the heat, feel the pressure, get fired. That's why it doesn't bother me that coaches make good money. Our gig can come to an end any time. And we live or die by circumstances that are oftentimes beyond our control. Injuries, academic problems, drugs, aggressive and unscrupulous agents, unprincipled alumni . . . those are but a sample of areas that can lead to a coach's downfall. And no matter how diligent we are from a preventative standpoint, we simply can't always control what happens. All it takes is an injury here or there, a missed shot at a critical stage of a big game, or a bad season, and we're out on the street. Coaches don't have the security of tenure. We're only as good as our last game. *What have you done for me lately?* That question haunts us like a ghost.

Unfortunately, the athletes get lost in the money-versus-education tug of war. We all hide behind education, but the truth is, generating dollars — big dollars — is at the heart of what we do. And we use our athletes to do it. Don't get me wrong, education is really what it's all about, and I truly believe that the majority of coaches see their players as students first and athletes second. Contrary to what many like to believe, we care about our athletes, on the court and off. However, it would be naive on anyone's part not to think of college athletics as big business.

The need for money is great, and everyone from the president on down is under pressure to meet the need. Green is the color of the lifeblood that keeps us going. College athletics have evolved into a monster. Maybe that's good, maybe not. I don't know. But that's how it is.

Take UCLA. Our athletic budget is close to $25 million, and it's sure to grow in the future. We get no state money, which means we're under the gun to come up with it ourselves, through gate receipts, television revenue, donations and fund raising. It used to be that schools didn't have to rely on things like fundraisers, but now we all do. That's been a big change in recent years.

Also, the issue of gender equity has intensified the need for more revenue. For example, women's athletics at UCLA cost $3 million a year. All of a sudden, you've got $3 million more to come up with. Where's that coming from? One of the ways, unfortunately, is to drop some sports. We've cut men's swimming and men's gymnastics. And they were both world-class programs. I really feel bad about that. Then, in turn, we've added women's soccer and women's water polo. We now have a women's swimming team, but not a men's. So there are some real problems that have to be faced in the next few years, serious issues that will hit at the heart of what we're all about. I don't envy the men and women who have the responsibilty of dealing with those problems. That's why I would never want to be an athletics director.

One big goal at UCLA is to expand Pauley Pavilion, hopefully within the next five years. We'd like to add a few thousand seats and perhaps add some offices and update some of the facilities. But I don't know how we're going to get all those things done, given the financial crunch we're under. It's going to require a Herculean effort from everyone.

If I sound like I'm complaining or singing the blues, I'm not. But being involved in these situations is part of the deal, and a coach has to look into them. Today's coaches are like the C.E.O. at a major corporation. The pressures and responsibilities are much greater now than they were, say, even just a decade ago. But I knew that, going in. No one forced me into this profession, and no one is holding a gun to my head telling me I have to stay in it. I can walk away any time. But I don't. I choose to stay. I choose to deal with the job and all that goes with it. And I do so because I enjoy it. It's my life.

But it is damn hard.

*   *   *

After all the heat I took over the years, one of the first questions I was asked after we beat Arkansas was, did I feel any sense of vindication? No, I didn't. I'm not a vindictive person. That's not my nature. Those who offered constructive criticism, I listened to; those who criticized just for the sake of doing so, I didn't. Most of the time I tuned out all the criticism, and most of the time I made it a point not to let it bother me. But I know that it did hurt my wife and sons a great deal. From that standpoint, I guess it did bother me.

Also, to feel vindicated would mean I had somehow bought into the absurd notion that I had to win a national championship in order to prove my worth. I couldn't do that. I *know* I can coach. My fellow coaches know I can coach. So if there's any vindication, it's really in the eyes of the doubters. I don't feel it at all.

Something else I disagree with is this notion of my sudden "growth" as a coach. What does that mean, anyway? That after 35 years of ineptitude, I just woke up one morning and all of a sudden I can coach this game? Stuff like that is overrated by the fans and overplayed in the press. It makes for good reading, but it's more fiction than fact. Jack McCallum, a fine writer for *Sports Illustrated*, wrote an excellent piece on me for the special collector's edition of that magazine after we won the championship. He began the article by saying, "Three decades ago Jim Harrick left his native West Virginia in a 1960 stick-shift Chevy with no radio, no heater and no air conditioner, bound for Los Angeles. On April 3, 1995, he arrived." Now, I understand that Jack was making a dramatic point about the nature of my odyssey, and the significance of the title, and he was doing it in a clever way. I certainly had no great qualms about it

— it was a very favorable story, in fact — but a comment like that does perpetuate the myth that it takes a national championship to validate a coach. Yes, in a very real way, it did take me 35 years to reach that goal. Every step along the way was part of the growth process. Winning the national title is the end result of years of hard work. But it didn't spring up out of nowhere, and it didn't have to happen for my coaching abilities to be legitimate.

Hey, I'm not downplaying the importance of winning a national championship. I'm not a fool — I know what it means. And I know how difficult it is to do. Winning it all puts you in a different category. It changes everything. You join a select club. People view you differently, whether it's in the sports world or the business community. So it is a big deal, professionally, financially and emotionally.

I once sat next to Dean Smith at a banquet and he told me there's all the difference in the world between being first and being second. Dean's been on both sides of the fence, so he knows what he's talking about. Nobody remembers who comes in second. My team won, so I became a hot item. "The Tonight Show" with Jay Leno, the White House, Disneyland, the Masters Golf Tournament, the Academy Awards . . . I was all over the place. Speeches, dinners, banquets — everybody wanted to talk to me. I've said that, before coming to UCLA, five people wanted 200 minutes of my time; but that afterward, it was more like 200 people wanting five minutes. Well, after we won it all, it seemed more like 600 wanting five minutes, every day. And yet, this popularity is all so fragile. If Tyus Edney misses that shot, or if he dribbles the ball off his knee, then I come home and get raked over the coals. It would have been 10 times worse than before.

There is no way I can adequately describe the feelings of joy, excitement, happiness and accomplishment that ran through me when the final horn sounded. It was — and still is — overwhelming. And I'm sure that if we had lost that game, my feelings of sadness and disappointment would have been equally powerful.

The line between hero and zero is a fine one, indeed. Believe me, I know that better than anyone.

*   *   *

I don't believe I've worked any great miracle during my years at UCLA. What I have done is bring stability. Five coaches in 13 years . . . that's nuts. During one stretch, several UCLA players played for three coaches in four years. You can't have anything but chaos in an environment like that.

When I was being interviewed for the UCLA job, I was asked what I thought I could bring to the table. My answer was the same one I gave when I interviewed for the job at Pepperdine. I said, "We're going to come in and be consistent. Year after year, we're going to do well. We're going to win basketball games, we're going to graduate our players, and we're going to do it in the framework of a high moral value system. Are we going to the Final Four and win a national championship? I don't know, that's too hard to predict. But we will be consistent, sound, solid, and strong morally and fundamentally."

Consistency, tenacity and integrity are three of my strongest personal characteristics, and by exploiting those strengths to the maximum level, I've been able to restore some order to the UCLA program. I'm a very consistent guy. I get up at the same time every day, I work out at the same time, I go to bed at the same time — I'm such a consistent guy that it drives my wife and sons crazy. But that's just the way I am. And I brought that consistency to UCLA. These days, high school recruits know what the situation is at UCLA. They know who the coach is now, and who the coach will be next year and the year after that. There is no confusion or lack of clarity.

It certainly wasn't that way when I first took over. Back then, virtually every player I talked to was gun-shy. The first thing I had to do was convince them I was here to stay, that I *wanted* to be at UCLA, that I wasn't going to bring them in, then leave them hanging out to dry two years down the road when I took off for some other place. That wasn't an easy sell, either.

Not after what they'd seen. Remember, these players had come of age during the years when all these coaching changes were taking place. They were too young to remember what it was like when Coach Wooden was here.

Thank heavens, those days of instability are long gone. I'm a career guy, and once the players realized I was going to be here for the long haul, they started looking at UCLA in a different light. Recruiting is never going to be easy — like all schools, we'll lose more players than we get — but it is much easier now than when I first got to UCLA. At least now when I lose a player, it's not because of any dark cloud of mystery that hangs over the coach's chair.

Much of the credit for what's happened goes to Don MacLean and Darrick Martin. They were the first two players I signed, and that kind of broke the ice. Both were highly recruited, and both were leaning toward other schools when I got the job, yet they had the guts to give us a chance. They were the cement we poured to help build our foundation. The next year we got Tracy Murray and Mitchell Butler. That made the foundation that much stronger. Talk about four guys I love and appreciate. What they did for this basketball program — and for me — can't be measured. I'll always have a special place in my heart for them.

*   *   *

In some ways, the real challenge is just beginning. The main thing now is to remain focused and not allow myself to embrace success. If I relax and start remembering the past rather than zeroing in on the future, I'm dead. One of the ironies in sports is that we really can't enjoy the fruits of our successes until long after they've happened. Once a new season begins, what you did last year doesn't count for a thing. Except, maybe, to make your opponents come at you just a little harder than they did before. That's why there is no time to relax and let down my guard. Now, more than ever, I have to stay on top of my game. I have to be hungrier next year than I was last year.

I look at what Coach Wooden did and I say to myself, "How did he do that? How was he able to stay focused all those years?" I've won it once, so I have a pretty good grasp on the situation. I know what the pitfalls and dangers are, and how easy it is to fall victim to them. I know there's a great temptation to sit back in your chair, cross your legs and just ride out the rest of your career. Coach didn't allow that to happen. He won it 10 times and never so much as slipped an inch. That's incredible. The same holds true for people like Magic Johnson, Larry Bird, Michael Jordan and Pat Riley. Those men have an unbelievable hunger burning inside them, and that's why they were able to come back and win championships year after year.

Coach Wooden is an amazing man, and without a doubt the greatest coach in the history of college basketball. That's not even open to debate. The records are testament to his greatness. He's also something else — one of the last dinosaurs. That group of men who coached at one school for decades, men like Adolph Rupp, Hank Iba, Ray Meyer, Ed Diddle, Don Haskins and Guy Lewis, just to name a few. They were fixtures in this business, many of them remaining at the same school throughout their entire coaching careers. While there remain a few coaches like that today — Dean Smith, Bobby Knight and Denny Crum come most quickly to mind — the day of the dinosaur is fast becoming a thing of the past.

More and more you see coaches getting out of the business, many while they are still quite young. There are probably several reasons for this exodus, but I suspect the main ones are the incredible pressures and demands placed upon them, professionally, emotionally and time-wise. Another factor is money. That may sound crazy, but it's not. The perception is that all coaches are getting rich, but in truth, only a small percentage of coaches make the really big bucks. The rest don't, yet they have many of the same demands and pressures on them that the highly paid coaches have. When they look at the overall picture, I guess they feel it's just not worth it, that there are easier, less-stressful ways to make a living.

In the old days, when those dinosaurs were around, coaching was a much simpler profession. Basically, all those men had to do was win games and stay out of trouble with the NCAA. Do that, and all was well in their small universe. Many of them had no relationship at all with their players from the time the season ended until the next October 15, when practice began. They had little or no involvement with the players' educational needs, they left the disciplining of players in the hands of others, and they had no interest in the social life of their players. They were coaches, *only* coaches, and their hands-on time with the players was from October 15 until that final game. After that, coaches and players parted company and went their separate ways. I'm not saying all coaches were like this, but the majority of them were. That's just the way things were back then.

It's not that way anymore. We coaches today aren't just expected to win, fill arenas, graduate players and keep our noses clean with the NCAA, we're also expected to be priest, policeman, psychologist, tutor and opinion guy. That's a lot of hats for one person to wear. It dumps an enormous amount of responsibility into your lap, and not everyone is willing — or cut out — to deal with it. It takes a special kind of person to do it.

The only way to do it is by staying grounded. Keeping it all in perspective: understanding that one person can only do *so* much; realizing that, as Coach Wooden always says, your value as a human being shouldn't be based on whether or not your team scores more points than another man's team; constantly listening to family and close friends; remaining true to your religious and spiritual faith — following those guidelines is the only way to remain sane in this crazy profession. Even then, it doesn't always work.

Mike Krzyzewski is a perfect example of how impossible the coaching profession has become. Mike is the most successful college coach of the past decade. By far. His Duke teams have been unbelievably successful: two NCAA championships, regular trips to the Final Four, ACC titles . . . you name it, Mike's teams have done it. And he runs a class program from top to bottom, 24 hours a day. Problem is, 24-hour days can make you vulnerable to the pressures and demands of this business. It happened to Mike.

What's so scary is that the dangers are insidious. They can sneak up on you, slowly engulfing you while you're unaware that it's happening. And once you're in trouble, you still tend to want to work right through things—exhaustion, physical pain, whatever. The result, of course, can just make things worse. That's what happened with Mike. The summer before the 1994-95 season, Mike began to experience lower back pains from a bulging disk. Finally, on October 22, he underwent back surgery. Most doctors will tell you that to recover, you need a month of inactivity followed by two months of limited activity. Not Mike. He was back studying game film a few days after the surgery, and back at practice after just a week and a half.

Well, things kept getting worse. Mike kept pushing. He'd be lying on the floor at practice sometimes, just trying to stop the pain. He just kept going and going. His wife Mickie had been watching all this with growing alarm, apparently unable to convince him just how dangerous the condition was to his health. It wasn't just the back. Mike was pushing himself in every area, just the way so many of us coaches do.

So, in early January, as Mike was leaving for work, Mickie told him she had scheduled a doctor's appointment for him that afternoon. Mike said, "I got practice! What are you talking about!" And Mickie said something like, "If you don't meet me at that doctor's office, I'm leaving." So Mike got in his car and started driving and suddenly what Mickie had said hit him like a sledgehammer. So he says something to himself like, "Wait a minute now, there's a reason she'd say something like that." And he decided to meet her at the doctor's office. What the doctor and his wife said finally convinced him. He was flirting with even more serious, and possibly lasting, problems—not only with his back but maybe with his psyche as well.

His Duke team, 8-3 at the time, was about to board a bus to the airport for a game at Georgia Tech when Mike told them he wouldn't be going. He went back into the hospital. He turned the team over to his assistant, Pete Gaudet. As badly as his back needed rest, so did the rest of him. Mike was basically ex-hausted. After the hospital, for three weeks he was in virtual seclusion at home. Mickie wouldn't even let old friends like P. J. Carlesimo get through to him on the phone. He wound up not returning to coaching the rest of the season. Duke finished with a losing record, but may have saved its coach in the process. The school administration was understanding and supportive, and you have to admire them for valuing a man like Mike and giving him the time needed to heal and re-energize.

I'm beginning to fully understand how that can happen to someone, because, since the national championship, I haven't come up for air too often. During the Final Four I talked to Mike a couple of times and Sally talked to Mickie. After it was over, they called and congratulated us and we got to talking a little about his situation. Then, one day Mike called when I wasn't there, and Sally told him I was going about 800 miles an hour.

Not long after that, I got a call from Mike. He told me to make sure I didn't do as he did. He said I needed to be careful not to do more than I'm capable of, because you can forget to allow enough time for your family, not to mention yourself. You can get so out of touch with yourself that you forget what's good for you. "We all think we're invincible, Jim," he said, "but we're not."

Mike never thought he was a candidate for burnout. Obviously, anyone can be. For me, that's the scary thing, because I don't really know the symptoms. I've been an awfully busy man since I won the title, and for awhile there I couldn't say "no" to any request. I was flying from one end of the country to the other on an average of at least once a week. But I've also tried to take some time off. Sally and I took a vacation to Europe, and later we spent another week at the beach. And I always get in a round of golf whenever possible. But I realize it can happen. When I find myself going a little too fast now, I remember Mike's advice and pull back off the throttle a bit. At least I hope I do. I don't think it could hit me out of the blue, but it is a concern. I've made it a point to listen up if Sally says things are getting out of hand—

and I thank Mike Krzyzewski for being concerned enough to warn me of the danger signs.

*   *   *

Why has the coaching profession changed so dramatically? That's a good question, and one that has no simple or clear-cut answer. A host of reasons, I guess. Societal changes (that microwave world), more involvement by college presidents, the media . . . I suspect all those things have played a role. However, it's my firm belief that the two biggest reasons are money and television. And, of course, more often than not, those two walk hand in hand.

Television's impact on college basketball has been so profound that in some ways it has become the dominant force in the sport. From a purely financial standpoint, that's certainly true. A huge portion of NCAA basketball revenue is generated by television. Through television, the NCAA Tournament has joined the World Series and the Super Bowl as one of the three biggest, most popular and most lucrative sporting events in this country. The month of March belongs to college basketball. Everything else is put on the back burner. Even people who aren't everyday followers of college hoops suddenly become fans when March Madness rolls around. The biggest reason is television.

So, in one respect, television has been a savior by providing much-needed monies for college athletic programs, the majority of which are still operating in the red. TV has also been a blessing because of the interest it has created in our sport. No question about that. So many games are televised these days that people on one coast are familiar with teams and players on the other coast. Increased TV exposure has probably helped make recruiting easier for coaches at certain schools, especially those smaller ones not everyone is familiar with.

What's happening is a natural by-product of the college situation. Players come and go after two, three or four years, but the coaches can remain the same. As a result, fans identify certain schools by the coach. Mention Indiana and who do you think of? Bobby Knight, of course. Same with Dean Smith at North Carolina, Mike Krzyzewski at Duke, Denny Crum at Louisville, Rick Pitino at Kentucky. Only die-hard Indiana fans can tell you who that school's last All-American was, but even casual fans know that Knight is the coach. So, in a sense, coaches have become celebrities.

Coach Wooden abhors many things about today's game, and most of what he dislikes is a result of television's impact. He hates all the hot-dogging that goes on. All sports, not just basketball. He detests all that high-five, chest-thumping, ostrich-strutting stuff you see. Just play the game, that's his philosophy. That other garbage is unnecessary and only serves to detract from what is, if played properly, a beautiful and eloquent game. Baggy shorts, increasingly physical play, more emphasis on the individual than the team — these are additional sins Coach lays at television's doorstep. Everybody's prime-timin' it.

Coach also says that television has had a negative impact on some of the coaches. He thinks many of them are perhaps a little too cute for their own good, and that they have a tendency to over-coach their teams. And he thinks maybe they're playing to the cameras, which are more than happy to oblige. Flamboyance and showmanship in any form are not John Wooden's style. He was the model of restraint and self-control, so it's no surprise that he finds much of what he sees in today's game distasteful.

Another matter that troubles Coach is shoe contracts for coaches. He never had one during all his years at UCLA. His feeling is that it's wrong for a coach to take money from a particular shoe company and then force his players to wear that company's brand. He says coaches, if they do take the money, ought to give it to the university, endow a scholarship, or give it to the athletic department.

Coach isn't alone in his thinking when it comes to this controversial subject. There are a lot of people who agree with him, including Chuck Young and Pete Dalis. They feel very, very strongly that everything should go through the university. My deal with Reebok is set up that way. My compensation is then figured into my contract. That's a different setup from my days at Pepperdine, where I got direct payment from the shoe company. I certainly don't see anything wrong with it. It's not unethical or against the rules in any way, shape or form.

I seldom disagree with anything Coach says, but when it comes to the matter of shoe contracts, I respectfully have to disagree. I think a coach, like anyone else in this country, has a perfectly legitimate right to make as much money as he can. This is, after all, a capitalistic society. Personally, I've always respected people who went out and made a lot of money, so long as they came by it honestly and without hurting others. There are many, many people all over the country who have their own gig, their own shtick, where they make an excellent living. Why shouldn't coaches make every penny they can get? What's wrong with that? How are we any different?

Our teams bring in big bucks for the university. I know UCLA made a lot of money from our winning the national championship. Through ticket sales, television revenue and sports paraphernalia, the basketball program brought in money that goes to support non-revenue programs at the school. And it goes far beyond that, extending out to the community. The restaurants and sports bars in Westwood Village got fat during our tournament run. I was walking in Westwood Village a week or so after we won it, and the guy who runs Maloney's came out and said, "Boy, you have really helped us. It's been great." College basketball is big business. Why shouldn't coaches get whatever they can? You'll never convince me that when UCLA and USC play in the Rose Bowl, with 100,000 people there and the game on national television, that the coaches earn too much money.

Critics like to point out that while coaches are raking in hundreds of thousands of dollars, college professors are struggling to get by on much smaller salaries. They say there's a basic unfairness at play in a situation where a basketball coach makes more money than an English professor. Well, that's a nice-sounding theory, but it's not as cut and dried as those critics want you to believe. They're leaving out some pretty important facts.

First, those English professors have tenure; coaches don't. We can have a two- or three- or four-year contract jerked out from under us at any moment. Coaches don't have any real job security. We can be out of a job in a heartbeat.

Second, college professors have outside means for making additional income. Their "shoe contracts" come in the form of writing books, consulting and grading standardized exams. The same people who criticize a coach for signing a shoe deal will praise a professor for signing a book contract. Seems to me there's a double standard in that kind of thinking.

Third, and this is the biggest misconception of all, only a small percentage of college coaches make the huge salaries. It's really a very small minority. Most are making a decent living, but they're a long way from being financially well off. And there are some coaches whose income isn't anywhere close to that of a college professor. Of course, you never hear about them. No one writes or comments on them.

Most coaches, like most college professors, didn't get into the business to make a lot of money. I know I certainly didn't. Hey, I worked 19 years before I made $25,000 a year, so I can't be accused of being a greedy guy who got into coaching to get wealthy. And, you know, if I had stayed at the high school level as a coach and an English teacher, that would have been OK with me. But I didn't. I became a college coach, and it just so happens that in this crazy sports-oriented country, the marketplace pays coaches more money than it pays professors. Maybe that doesn't make any sense, maybe the priorities are topsy-turvy — I don't know. But that's the reality. And I'm not about to apologize.

*   *   *

I've worked 35 years and never missed a paycheck. Not one. Throughout my adult life, getting that paycheck on time has been the thing that drove me. *Not* getting one has been my biggest fear. It doesn't take a great psychiatrist to figure out why such fear has always been inside me. My father, of course. Here was a man who never drew one paycheck in his life. Sometimes he had a few dollars in his pocket, sometimes he didn't. Since there was never any consistency, we didn't know from week to week whether we would get by with a little breathing room or just barely struggle by. That caused a lot of hardships for my family, especially my mother. My father's rather indifferent attitude toward money (and hard work) meant that extra burdens were placed on my mother's shoulders. She had to carry far too much of the load by herself. It wasn't a 50-50 deal like it should have been. You see things like that when you're young and they stay with you for a lifetime. It creates a fear — a kind of perpetual panic — that gnaws in your gut like a buzzsaw. It's not a good feeling. I'm a driven man for several reasons — the need to achieve, the desire to prove myself, competitiveness and the desire to excel. But more than anything else, I'm a driven man because my father wasn't. Simple as that.

For most of my professional life, I've had to struggle to get by. It's only been in recent years that I've made enough money that I could provide my wife and sons with a few of life's luxuries. There has been no opulence in the Harrick household. Over the years, with the salary I made as a teacher and coach, we've had beans and potatoes a lot more than we've had steak and shrimp. There were times when I wondered if maybe I shouldn't get out of coaching and find something a little more lucrative, times when I wondered whether or not I was doing the best I could for my family. Like any concerned provider, I wanted them to have more. I especially didn't want our three boys to feel the way I did when I was a kid. More than anything else, I wanted them to feel a security I never had.

I remained in coaching because I love doing it and because I had the complete support of my family. Without their backing, especially Sally's, I probably would have gotten out and done something else a long time ago. But we made it, and even though there were difficult times, we've never been close to being down and out. We *always* had a paycheck on the way.

Sally has been the glue that held our family together. In some ways, she practically raised our three sons by herself. I was always on the go, recruiting, hauling players to games, scouting, working on my master's, playing industrial league ball, officiating, camps, clinics, taking care of administrative duties — you name it, I did it. My absence from home shifted a great deal of the responsibility for raising our sons onto Sally. That Glenn, Monte and Jim have turned out to be fine, decent, fair and honorable men is a credit to her. She's the real hero in our family.

You can never accurately put a value on your marriage, but Sally and I have been together for 35 years and I'd say we've had as good a marriage as I've ever seen. There is tremendous love and respect for each other. We've always done everything together, as a team, and that's the only way to do it. If you don't, the marriage won't work.

Sally has allowed me to pursue my dream of becoming a successful college coach. She's made personal and professional sacrifices so that I could follow my rainbow. As a result, I've been able to achieve some success. I'm one lucky man, and a day doesn't go by that I don't give thanks for having had Sally at my side. Anything I've accomplished is as much hers as it is mine.

What would I have done if I had chosen to leave the coaching profession? Tell you the truth, I don't know. Not working on an assembly line, I can promise you that. After my Mattel experience, I knew mass production wasn't my calling. Henry Ford never would have recruited me. I've always been interested in stocks and bonds, although given my track record with investments, I don't know how that would have worked out, either. Every investment I've ever made has gone belly-up. We've never made a nickel, not one nickel. Nothing.

Once upon a time, I trusted everybody. That's not the case anymore. Over the years, I've been burned enough times to learn my lesson. A few years back, when everybody in Southern California was making a fortune in real estate, a guy who was building some condos came to me and said, "Give me $25,000 and I'll give you back $40,000." He even wrote me a note, saying "I will repay you $40,000." What do I do? I take $25,000 out of my retirement fund, 13 years worth of work, and just hand it over to this guy, thinking that he was going to make me a wealthy man. The guy goes broke and I never hear from him again. I lost it all.

As you might expect, Sally wasn't too thrilled with my get-rich-quick schemes. Finally, after enough hard-earned dollars had gone down the tubes, she said, "That's it. No more investments." So now we just don't do it. Sally keeps a closer watch on our money.

*   *   *

I used to look at coaches who were highly successful and marvel at how they could remain so humble. Well, now that I've been to the mountaintop, I understand how easy it is to keep an ego under control.

My wife and three sons keep me humble. No way they're ever going to let me get a swollen head and become someone I'm not. I don't care how many NCAA championships I win, or how many Coach of the Year honors come my way, it'll still be my job to take out the garbage. That won't change.

Something else that humbles you is recruiting. Getting back on the road, scrambling, fighting, scratching and clawing for every guy you can get — that'll knock you down off cloud nine and bring you face to face with the real world in no time at all. You can smile until October 15, then you'd better wipe that grin off your face and get serious again.

Coaching *is* a humbling experience. It's like a ride on the ferris wheel — you never stay at the top very long. There is great joy one minute and great despair the next. Sometimes it's not even a minute. Sometimes it only takes 4.8 seconds to experience the full range of emotions.

Why does any sane man want to stay in this business? Another good question. Because we're competitors, because the thrills outweigh the agonies, because we love challenges, because we enjoy working with young people, because it keeps us young, because . . .

. . . it gets in the blood. That's the best answer I can come up with, the only one that helps explain why we are willing to put up with all the frustrations and problems and pressures and demands. Simply put, we love it, warts and all.

Many of the greatest joys a coach can experience come away from the court — ones that have nothing at all to do with wins and losses or numbers on a scoreboard. I know that's true for me. There's nothing I enjoy more than having a former player, one who maybe had some personal or social problem when he was younger, walk up to me, shake my hand and thank me for putting him on the right path. Or maybe it's that player's father or mother who thanks me. We don't reach them all, but when we do, it gives you a tremendous feeling. Some of our biggest victories come from the smallest situations.

I have enormous respect and affection for the vast majority of coaches. And I'm not just talking about college coaches. I'm including coaches at all levels, for all sports. There are thousands of them across this country doing a wonderful job who never get any recognition or fame and glory. All they get is the satisfaction of knowing they are having a positive impact on the lives of young people. To my way of thinking, that's far more important and far more lasting than having your name in the newspapers or being on television.

College coaches are a brotherhood, a fraternity, and even though we're constantly competing against each other, there's a lot of empathy within the ranks. That's why the convention at the Final Four is so popular. We'll discuss problems, talk about sportswriters, trade coaching philosophies . . . everything. Certainly we don't all like each other, but we do understand the problems common to us all. That's why when a fellow coach is down, or is going through hard times, we try to help him all we can.

*   *   *

College basketball is a great game played by some of the most gifted athletes in the world. More than any other sport, it's a fans' game. Exciting, thrilling, fast-paced, high energy — college basketball has it all. And it keeps getting more popular each year. The growth our sport has made over the past two decades has been unbelievable — in this country and around the world.

That's why I'm keeping my fingers crossed that the powers that be don't tinker with the game too much. We've got a good thing going, and I'm afraid that if too many changes are made, it will have a negative effect. It goes back to that old watch analogy: If it isn't broken, don't fix it. I agree with that 100 percent. I like the game the way it is.

Oh, sure, there are a few slight alterations I would like to see. I certainly wouldn't mind going to a 30-second shot clock. Women already use it and I don't see any reason why the men can't. I like the fact that the clock stops after every basket during the last minute of a game. Without that change we don't beat Missouri, so I *love* that rule. I like the removal of the five-second call. It was unnecessary. The less an official has to worry about, the better. We need to take as many things out of the officials' hands as possible.

I don't want us to go to a wider lane, like some people are proposing. In my mind, that would be a mistake. It would discourage a player from playing with his back to the basket, which is a big part of the game. Well-rounded players can play with their back to the basket or facing the basket. Think of a guy like Larry Bird, how he could back a defender into the lane and hit the turnaround jumper, or take the defender away from the bucket and hit a three-pointer. Widen the lane and you'll lose players who bring a rare and special versatility to the game. That would be a great loss.

Those who are in favor of widening the lane say it needs to be done in order to negate the physical play going on down low in the paint. There's no doubt that the game has become much more physical, but I'm not sure widening the lane is going to solve that problem. Not as long as players keep getting bigger, stronger and quicker, and coaches keep putting more and more emphasis on defense. Maybe the only answer to the problem is to widen the whole court.

Things run in cycles, and right now we're in a period where the big, strong centers dominate the game. Look at the

NBA. A few years back, the marquee players were point guards. Magic, Isiah Thomas, those guys. Now it's the giants. Shaq, David Robinson, Hakeem Olajuwon, Patrick Ewing. But who knows? Maybe in a few years, with players like Damon Stoudamire, Tyus Edney and Travis Best entering the league, it'll be the point guards again. Things are forever changing, and that's why I don't want to see a knee-jerk reaction that will end up hurting what is a great sport.

One big change I would like to see involves the officials. I've had my share of run-ins and disagreements with the zebras over the years, but for the most part I think they do a terrific job. Basketball is just a hard game to officiate. Sometimes I think it's an impossible game to officiate. I've done some officiating, so I know. The guys who do it have my respect (and sympathy).

But I would like to see the label taken off the officials, so that a guy wouldn't be designated a Pac-10 official or an SEC official or a Big-Ten official. That label announces what a guy is, and I think that puts too much pressure on them. I feel that it's wrong for an official to come to our place and the fans know his name. Some officials have become stars, when what they should be is anonymous. If you notice an official, chances are he's not doing a very good job.

My suggestion would be to have four federations — West, Midwest, Southeast and East — out of which the officials would be assigned. That way we wouldn't see the same guys all the time. And I think that would be better for everyone.

One major change that some folks advocate is to pay the players. They contend that since the colleges are using the student athletes to generate money, the athletes ought to reap some of the profits. I'm absolutely against that. To my way of thinking, the athletes are already getting paid. A college education doesn't come cheap, and an athletic scholarship is the only way many of today's athletes can get to college. Athletes get free housing and free food. They get to travel all over the world. Take a guy like Ed O'Bannon, who was at UCLA for five years. Yes, the school made quite a bit of money in those five years, but think how much Ed has gotten from his college experience. And at no cost to him.

I would have no problem with giving athletes a monthly stipend to help them buy some of the incidentals a college student requires. That seems fair to me, especially since athletes, unlike many of their fellow students, don't have the time to take on a part-time job. I would give them a small monthly allowance for things like laundry, school supplies, snacks and a movie now and then, but I wouldn't give them a salary like some people advocate doing.

*   *   *

You have to give up something to get something. In basketball, we may have to give up a little bit of our offense to make our defense better. Or, if we're having trouble putting points on the board, we may be forced to give up a little on the defensive side in order to get our offense going. There are always tradeoffs that have to be made.

It's that way in life, too. For me to live this dream of mine — and to be successful at it — I've had to spend a lot of time away from my family. Far more than I wanted to, I know that. I'm sure every C.E.O. in every company has to deal with the same situation. So do doctors, who are always on call. Women in the work force, those trying to balance career and motherhood, are perhaps most affected by this dilemma. They get hit from all sides, which is really unfair.

The question that runs through your mind is, am I being selfish? The answer is, yes, I probably am being selfish. The only way for a relationship to work, then, is to have a supportive and understanding spouse. And a very strong one. If you're lucky to have one like I do, then your relationship has a good chance to survive. Without Sally's ability to offer support, not to mention making me listen when it was necessary, our relationship and our family life might have fallen victim to my selfish desire to become a successful coach. Thanks to her strength, it hasn't.

I do have one major regret, one thing I wish I could change. It troubles me greatly that I didn't spend more personal time with our youngest son, Glenn. I was OK with Monte and Jim, because when they were younger I was still coaching at the high school level. I had plenty of time to be around them, to be actively involved in their growing up. Especially in the summer, when school was out. But by the time Glenn reached the age when my presence was really needed, I had moved up to the college ranks, first as an assistant. And when I got the job at Pepperdine, I really put my heart and soul into my work. As a result, Glenn didn't get the attention from me that he should have gotten. He missed out on some important things in his life, and through no fault of his own. If I could turn back the clock and make one crucial change, I would have spent more time with Glenn and less time recruiting, speaking and going to coaching clinics.

My single greatest pleasure is playing a foursome of golf — my three sons and me. That's as much joy as I could ever get in life. Forget coaching or winning basketball games. Forget awards and personal glory. That's nice, but a distant second behind playing a round of golf with Monte, Jim and Glenn. That's as good as it gets for me, being around those three. They're not only my sons, they're my three best friends.

Coach Wooden once said that his priorities were family, religion and coaching — in that order. "I think the Lord will understand," he said. "At least, I hope so."

That's my lineup, too. And I do think God will understand.

*   *   *

I'm a lifer in this business, and if all goes well, I'll finish my coaching career at UCLA. How many more years will it be? I can't say for sure. My new contract takes me through the year 2000. After that, we'll see what happens. Personally, I'd like to stay in it another nine years, which would give me 16 at UCLA. That would make me 65 when I retire. If I can make it that long.

Since we won the NCAA Tournament, I've been asked on

several occasions if I have any interest in moving up to the NBA. No, I don't. You can never say never, but I can't envision myself coaching in the pros. It just doesn't interest me. Too many problems away from the game that I don't care to deal with. Agents, labor negotiations, strikes . . . who needs that mess?

It doesn't surprise me to see the NBA owners and general managers showing an ever-increasing interest in college coaches. That's because there are some outstanding coaches in the college ranks. The talent pool is very rich. It's a smart move on the part of the owners and GMs to try and dip into that pool. They'd be crazy not to. If something good is right in front of your nose, you'd be a fool to ignore it. And the guys who run pro teams aren't fools. I predict that in the future, more and more college coaches will take a stab at the NBA. Certainly, a lot more of them will have the opportunity.

Rick Pitino's already been an NBA coach, so he could jump back into the pros anytime he wants to. Cincinnati coach Bob Huggins was seriously courted by the Miami Heat, and I know that Mike Krzyzewski could go to the NBA if he chose to do so. P.J. Carlesimo already has, jumping from Seton Hall to Portland. And there are plenty more coaches who will face that possibility in the future.

I enjoy the college game too much to harbor any dream of coaching in the pros. At this level, I can still affect the lives of young people in a positive way. That's the primary reason I became a teacher and coach in the first place. And in my heart of hearts, I'm still a teacher. Always have been, always will be. Ever since I stood in front of those seventh-grade students in Smith River all those years ago, there is nothing that brings me more satisfaction than knowing I'm helping young people learn. I don't think I would get the same fulfillment from coaching professional players.

What will I do when I retire? Maybe do some consulting or work for one of the shoe companies. Work a few clinics here and abroad, but only on a limited basis. Mainly, I'd spend most of my time with my family. And I'd play a *lot* of golf. A *lot* of golf. I'd try to make up for all the rounds I've had to pass on because

I was so busy trying to succeed as a coach. Maybe if I work on my game hard enough, I can get to the point where I can beat my sons. That sure would be a nice change.

                        *   *   *

No one can predict the future, but all of us can comment on the past. I've been about as lucky as one person can be, sometimes so much so that I feel a little guilty. I've got the greatest wife in the world, and my sons are healthy, intelligent, kind and gentle people. I've worked for and with some of the finest people anywhere, and I've come into contact with thousands of young people who have enriched my life in ways I probably haven't begun to fully understand or comprehend. More often than not, they were the teacher and I was the student.

Here's another quotation. It's from Sir Isaac Newton. Referring to Copernicus, Galileo and Kepler, he said, "If I have seen farther than other men, perhaps it is because I have stood on the shoulders of giants." Well, I feel the same way. Whatever I've managed to accomplish, it's because I've been surrounded by loving, talented and giving people. I'd say that makes me a mighty lucky guy.

WHY NOT?

12

There's another quotation I've held onto, this one from a fellow coach, Jack Ramsay. It's helped me keep my focus when all the peripheral stuff intrudes, when I've needed to remind myself what this crazy profession is *really* about. It's what a coach must follow if he's true to his mission, and to himself. Here's what Jack wrote:

> Coaching is a means of self-expression. Successful coaches, like artists, have a characteristic style. No coach lacking a firm sense of what he wants to accomplish through his team can succeed. A coach's philosophy will guide him in selecting the kind of game he wants to play, the expectations he has of his players, and the manner in which he will teach his game.
>
> A coach's personality, and hence the character of his team, is reflected in his philosophy of the game. This is not a matter of innovation or of creating some formidable new defense or a new offense. There are no original ideas left in basketball, given the fixed nature of the game. You can field five players at a time, who, within the established limits of a 94 by 50 foot court, try to put a ball slightly more than nine inches in diameter through an 18-inch hoop placed exactly 10 feet above the floor, while simultaneously preventing the other team from doing the same thing.

It is within this fixed form that a coach must express himself. Determining his philosophy is, therefore, a coach's primary task; he must decide, before anything else, what it is he wants to say of himself through the game. As with any artist, a coach's style will evolve. He borrows freely from his playing experience, if any, and from predecessors and colleagues refining his game. But the game he plays must be his own.

*   *   *

He must decide, before anything else, what it is he wants to say of himself through the game.

I guess it's no surprise if I tell you that basketball is the greatest game in the world. I've always felt that way. It takes a minimum amount of equipment. One rim, one ball and just one person, for that matter, is all that's needed for a great workout. But it's more than that. Remember the movie, *Hoosiers,* and those scenes of a kid shooting a ball against the backdrop of an Indiana countryside? I'll tell you, it sure took me back to my youth, and if you've ever played the game, I'll bet it did for you, too — all those days and evenings outside, just putting up shot after shot, even in the middle of summer when the heat was so brutal, even late into the year when you needed a jacket to keep out the chill. Didn't matter, did it? You were out there, alone, shooting that ball — over and over again, for hours at a time. It was so much fun. Maybe you imagined taking that last-second shot in the Final Four, or maybe you imagined going one-on-one with your favorite pro. Or maybe taking that imaginary pass from your hero. Playing all those games in your mind. Time didn't matter, did it? Time stood still.

For a coach, the beauty of basketball is fascinating. Five players moving all the time, either with the ball or without it, passing, cutting, screening . . . there's just such constant movement, with such finesse involved. The way the game unfolds, it just never fails to intrigue me.

So many people's lives have been touched by the game.

Millions, really. The college game in particular has so much inherent excitement. People spend all winter bantering over who's number one, and the emotions run so high once the tournament begins. I think that's the big reason the game has become so popular, because there's such passion and excitement that you can feel — even through the TV screen. It just builds and builds, all those upsets and players jumping up and down in victory, or collapsing in defeat. All of it builds to Final Four Saturday, when those four teams who've survived this fine madness square off to get to the title game. It's tough to top that kind of drama.

The values young people pick up are right there in the center of the buzz, values like leadership and cooperation and unselfishness, facing up to defeat and learning to handle victory in a proper fashion. I think the best lessons are the ones you receive under fire. I think maybe that's why this game means so much to me. Your philosophy isn't a passive one. It's always being put to the test.

What is it I want to say of myself through this great game? Mainly, that I have never felt more alive than I have around the game of basketball, because it encompasses so much. Because it's that kid shooting in the backyard, but it's also the man having his ability and his beliefs challenged to the hilt. It's like an art form through which I can express my emotions, channel my energies and communicate with others. It gives me the chance to be a leader, but also to learn.

*   *   *

Here's another favorite of mine. It's from Abraham Lincoln:
"If I were to read, much less answer, all the attacks made on me, this shop might as well be closed for any other business. I do the very best I know how, the very best I can, and I mean to keep doing so until the end. If the end brings me out all right, what is said against me won't amount to anything. If the end brings me out wrong, then angels swearing I was right would make no difference."

Sorta makes you wonder if Honest Abe didn't coach at UCLA at some point. Seriously, though, we were lucky to have Abraham Lincoln at a time when our nation was going through one of its worst periods. His words remind me how important it is to have that attitude, to make the tough decisions and hold to a vision in the face of criticism. Ultimately, Lincoln paid for his resolve with his life. That sort of puts the UCLA situation in proper perspective, doesn't it?

The point is — whether you are an Abraham Lincoln operating in a higher arena or just a coach in a basketball arena — wherever you are, you've got to remain true to what you believe is the correct course. Like I've said, you don't ignore constructive criticism — you'd darn well better pay attention to opinions, because nobody's infallible — but you simply can't afford to get caught up in attacks aimed at you, the ones that are unfair, or based on emotion, or poorly thought out — or the ones that are mean spirited for the sake of being mean spirited. In the '90s, that attitude seems to sell. That, at least, is what this dinosaur believes.

* * *

Lastly, there's this passage, its author unknown to me. It's titled "Who But a Coach Would Want to Be a Coach?" Part of it goes like this:

> Who but a coach has the opportunity to see a gangling youngster, who can hardly walk without tripping over his own feet, mature by hard work and the sweat of his brow into a graceful athlete?
>
> Who but a coach would let the agony of defeat affect him to the point he spends a sleepless night tossing and turning in bed? He repeatedly contemplates his decisions: should he have used a different play; why didn't he take out the boy with four fouls; why did he let the pitcher stay in; why . . . why . . . why?
>
> Who but a coach has a greater feeling of loneliness, igno-

rance of his profession and insecurity because he has suffered through a long, losing season?

Who but a coach would have a lump in his throat when a young man who, only minutes after graduating from high school, strides over and extends a firm right hand and says with tears running down his cheeks, "Coach, it was great playing for you"?

Thank God, I am a coach!

*   *   *

Who but a coach has a greater feeling of loneliness . . .
Why . . . why . . . why?

I guess we've pretty much come full circle. I began this book in that Kingdome locker room, when that very same question — "Why?" — kept running through my mind. I think by now you can understand all the weight that was behind the dejection and depression I was feeling — when I'd worked so hard for so long, had travelled to this spot every coach dreams of reaching, only to see all the struggle about to be wiped out by fate, or so it seemed, in the form of Tyus Edney's useless wrist.

Why?

Well, why not?

That's the lesson I learned. Asking why might be a natural response, but in the end it doesn't do you much good if you only use it as an exercise in self-pity. If it helps you to reach a greater understanding of things, fine. If it only serves as a means to feel sorry for yourself and not persevere, then it assures your defeat. And I don't mean defeat on a scoreboard. I mean a defeat of your spirit — of the will to go on, to do your best, regardless.

Saying "why not?" is a way to acknowledge that there are things beyond your control. Always have been, always will be. It's a way to accept those curveballs life can throw you. Once you accept that, you can go on with the idea that it's important to do your best even if the outcome isn't guaranteed, even if your doubters will have more fuel for the fire, even if only you appreciate the effort and sincerity behind your struggle. Win or lose against Arkansas, I saw in that game a tremendous spirit and sense of resolve in my players — and that fact wouldn't have changed even if we'd lost. Warrior hearts, regardless.

Remember when I got on my team hard after the near-loss to Missouri in the tournament? I didn't see it then, but one of the things I told my players held the very answer to the question "why?" that I was asking myself a couple of weeks later. I told them of an incident I'd seen, not as a coach, but as a father sitting in the stands when one of my sons was playing in high school.

It came during a state tournament game. There was one kid on my son's team who drank and smoked and ran around. He was undisciplined, but he also was one of the two best players on the team. So now they're in the state playoffs and the game is a cliffhanger and, boom, he — of all players — gets fouled. My son's team is down one point and this guy's got two free throws to win the game. And I'm sitting there in the stands and everybody's cheering for this kid to make 'em, and it's the team that my son is captain of, but the only thing I'm doing is thinking that this guy doesn't deserve it. Because he really doesn't care about the team. He doesn't care about anything. So there I sit, everybody cheering for him to make the shots, and that's my son out there with his fate in this kid's hands — and believe me, it's harder to watch your son play than it is to coach, because you want it so badly for him. But here I am, and all I'm thinking is that this guy isn't worthy of winning. Lo and behold, he misses both shots.

Why did he miss those shots? Because he didn't deserve to make them.

Now, I know what you're thinking. People who don't deserve things get them all the time. Fate sometimes doesn't have a thing to do with justice. But, see, those are things that are beyond your control — whether it's happening to you or somebody else. I'd been upset because I thought one of the reasons Missouri nearly beat us was that we'd been a little too lax, a little too full of ourselves, before the game. And that's why I hammered home the message to my players that if we went to Oakland and got beat in the regional finals, we were at least going to lose right. That's the same as winning right. In other words, we were going to at least put ourselves in the best possible position to win. By preparing well. By giving ourselves our best. It's that thing about being able to look in the mirror afterward.

I may not win, but it's important that I know I deserved to win. To me, that's where your sense of worth and your sense of integrity come from. No one can take that away from you. And that, I think, is probably the thing that's sustained me at UCLA. Coaches deal with reality — or at least like to think they do — while most "fans" want their fantasies fulfilled. That's all the more reason to have your ducks lined up in a row. You have to know, in your heart, that you deserved to win. And you have to let go of any idea that you always will. That's just another form of addiction, always looking for something outside of yourself to make you feel good about yourself. If you know inside that you've done everything possible to do it the right way, to win or lose on terms you can live with, you don't have to rely on newspaper headlines or fan applause to measure yourself.

Or championship trophies, for that matter.

I'm not saying that recognition isn't nice. In the months since Seattle, I haven't grown one bit tired of people walking up and saying "Congratulations!" What I am saying is that you can't rely on those things — either applause or boos — to define you. That's what John Wooden always taught. And that's what I've tried to embrace. You don't just learn from victory. Sometimes defeat teaches you more. If you've given your best, you shouldn't need anything else. That's hard to accept sometimes, but what counts is what you put into the effort. That's the only thing you can really control.

Why not keep going?

Why not give it your best shot?

Why not?

INDEX